WIMBLEDON, MERTON AND MORDEN

AT WAR 1939–45

WIMBLEDON, MERTON AND MORDEN

AT WAR 1939–45

RUTH MANSERGH

Pen & Sword
MILITARY

First published in Great Britain in 2018 by
PEN & SWORD MILITARY
An imprint of
Pen & Sword Books Ltd
Yorkshire – Philadelphia

Copyright © Ruth Mansergh, 2018

ISBN 978 1 47389 454 9

The right of Ruth Mansergh to be identified as Author of this work has been
asserted by her in accordance with the Copyright, Designs and Patents Act
1988.

A CIP catalogue record for this book is
available from the British Library.

Printed and bound in England by CPI Group (UK) Ltd, Croydon, CR0 4YY

Pen & Sword Books Limited incorporates the imprints of Atlas,
Archaeology, Aviation, Discovery, Family History, Fiction, History,
Maritime, Military, Military Classics, Politics, Select, Transport, True
Crime, Air World, Frontline Publishing, Leo Cooper, Remember When,
Seaforth Publishing, The Praetorian Press, Wharncliffe Local History,
Wharncliffe Transport, Wharncliffe True Crime and White Owl.

For a complete list of Pen & Sword titles please contact

PEN & SWORD BOOKS LIMITED
47 Church Street, Barnsley, South Yorkshire, S70 2AS, England
E-mail: enquiries@pen-and-sword.co.uk
Website: www.pen-and-sword.co.uk

Or

PEN AND SWORD BOOKS
1950 Lawrence Rd, Havertown, PA 19083, USA
E-mail: Uspen-and-sword@casematepublishers.com
Website: www.penandswordbooks.com

Contents

Dedication

To my grandparents (late) Peter and Rita Weightman – 'the Goshes'. Grandad lived at 100 Calabria Road, Highbury Corner and Gran at Gallia Road, Highbury Corner during the war. They moved to Seascale, west Cumbria in the late 1940s. Grandad, a nuclear scientist, worked at Sellafield (it was then Calder Hall and Windscale).

Introduction

Reports suggest that during the First World War, only one enemy bomb fell on Wimbledon. It reputedly was dropped from a Zeppelin on the King's College School, Wimbledon Common playing field during the summer of 1917 where it failed to explode (*merton.gov.uk*). In the Second World War, more than 350 bombs fell, killing 150 residents and injuring a further 1,071. Around 12,000 houses were damaged and 810 destroyed (*Museum of Wimbledon*, 2016).

Wimbledon – ranked in May 2017 as one of the top three places for young professionals to live (Lloyds Bank report) – has been inhabited since at least the Iron Age. The original medieval village – now known as Wimbledon Village – developed with a stable rural population coexisting alongside nobility and wealthy merchants from the city. Wimbledon Village/Wimbledon Park has seen many fine houses, none more so than Elizabethan Manor House (1588–1720), the Janssen House (1721–1900), the Marlborough House (1734–1785), and the Spencer House (1801–1949). The Old Rectory, a ten-bedroom house just north of St Mary's Church, is Wimbledon's oldest house, built around 1500 by the lord of the manor, the Archbishop of Canterbury, and used by Henry VIII. (It was on the market for £26 million in 2012).

Wimbledon railway station opened on 21 May 1838, south of the current station. Until 1851, fresh water was only available from wells or springs. There were also a few deep artesian wells, such as the one that was dug for Wimbledon Park House in 1798. Under an Act of 1852, water was to be filtered and drawn from above Teddington Lock only. The Lambeth Water Company had already, in 1850, built ten miles of four 30in pipes taking water from Thames Ditton to Brixton. Water could therefore be supplied to Wimbledon in 1851, although it could not be pumped higher than half way up the hill. The Southwark and Vauxhall Company followed with a substantial waterworks at Hampton in 1854, supplying northern Wimbledon in 1857. Local historian Kirk Bannister, who won the Richard Milward Prize for Local History in 2014, said that clean water and local land companies were the real driving forces behind the development of Wimbledon town in the 1860s, rather than just the arrival of the railways.

Wimbledon Common acted as a barrier to the advance of London. In 1864, Earl Spencer, Lord of the Manor of Wimbledon, attempted to pass a private parliamentary bill to enclose Wimbledon Common for the creation of a new park with a manor house and gardens and to sell part of it for building. In a landmark decision for English common land, permission was refused and a board of conservators was established in 1871 to take ownership of the common and preserve it in its natural condition. Today, it is a 1,100-acre public green space. The Wimbledon branch of the District Underground Line opened on 3 June 1889.

On 4 July 1891, the Emperor of Germany, Kaiser Wilhelm II, made his first official visit to England and was honoured with a grand military display staged on Wimbledon Common: 22,000 British soldiers were lined up for the Kaiser to inspect. When the First World War started, many local people wanted to erase this event from Wimbledon's history.

The Tooting–Wimbledon–Hampton Court electric tram got under way on 2 May 1907 (the *Wimbledon Society*, 2012). In the early 1930s, Wimbledon was the final stop on the Tooting line. In 1950, the London Transport Executive announced 'Operation Tramaway' and the service disappeared from Wimbledon in January 1951. (Today's Tramlink between Wimbledon and Elmers End, via East Croydon, Mitcham Junction, Morden Road and Merton Park, opened on 29 May 2000).

South Wimbledon Underground station, between Colliers Wood and Morden on the Northern Line, opened in September 1926. It is on the corner of Merton ('Mere tun' – town on the marsh) High Street and Morden Road. Large areas of Wimbledon town centre including Centre Court Shopping Centre and the Everyday Church may be demolished to make way for Crossrail 2, a proposed rail route running from nine stations in Surrey to three in Hertfordshire (*Wimbledon Guardian*, 23 November 2015).

Wimbledon Park is the name of an urban park in Wimbledon, an Underground station between Southfields and Wimbledon stations, and also of the suburb south and east of the park in the London Boroughs of Merton and Wandsworth. *The Times* described Wimbledon Park in 1865 as 'covered in stately villas'. Parts of Wimbledon Park that had previously escaped being built on saw local authority estates constructed by the borough council to house some of those who had lost their homes in the Second World War.

Merton Park had not only been the dream of the estate developer John Innes in 1867 but it also became his joy while living the life of the country gentleman and farmer as the owner of the Manor House. He and his brother James decided that the many fields around St Mary's Church, Merton should be transformed into a semi-rural suburb for City businessmen.

By the 1930s, the new focus for local growth had moved to neighbouring Morden, a rural parish throughout the nineteenth century. Morden Cinema, where the main feature film was always a Western, opened on Thursday 8 December 1932. The first major development of Lower Morden was the establishment in 1891 of Battersea New Cemetery.

In the inter-war years, the stretch of London beyond Tooting into South Wimbledon, Morden, Mitcham and out into Beddington was one of the areas of greatest growth of light industry. The housing needs of this locality were met by the construction of the St Helier estate, which stretched from Morden Underground station to the River Wandle (which flows into the Thames at Wandsworth). The St Helier 'a home in the country' estate to provide good homes for the poorest Londoners housed 40,000 people by 1936.

The London Borough of Merton was created on 1 April 1965 by uniting three local authorities. The Wimbledon and Mitcham Boroughs had long and quite heated debates about which of their names should dignify the new London Borough, with Merton eventually being chosen as a compromise, while Wimbledon (in Surrey from 1866–1965) ceased to be an independent borough in the county. Five new residential areas, with their own shopping centres, emerged to form the 'Surrey-in-London' Merton we know today: Colliers Wood, Mitcham, Morden, Raynes Park and Wimbledon. The original village of Mitcham lies to the west of Mitcham. Morden Hall, in the grounds of Morden Hall Park, is in the London Borough of Merton. In the 1870s it was sold by Sir Richard Garth to tobacco merchant Gilliat Edward Hatfeild (1864–1941), and was a military hospital during the First World War; after the war, Hatfeild made his home a cottage on the estate. He died in February 1941 and by his will, the estate was bequeathed to the National Trust. The Baitul Futuh Mosque in Morden, which describes itself as the largest mosque in Western Europe, was completed in 2003.

CHAPTER ONE

Be Prepared, Germany is Arming

'All the while, across the North Sea, a terrible process is astir. Germany is arming,' Winston Churchill, July 1934.

The 1934 Wimbledon Championships took place at the All England Tennis Club (Church Road, Wimbledon) from 25 June until 6 July. By August 1934 Adolf Hitler, a wounded, decorated soldier of the First World War, had declared himself Fuhrer – the leader of Germany. In British history, rearmament covers the period between 1934 and 1939. Churchill's demands for rearmament were not intended towards war (*RAF Museum*). He felt that the carnage of the First World War was terrible and should not be repeated.

On 1 August 1936, Hitler opened the 11th Summer Olympic Games, held in Berlin; the *Hindenburg*, a large German commercial-carrying rigid airship, flew over the opening carrying the Olympic flag behind her. According to the International Olympic Committee, the Berlin Games are best remembered for Hitler's failed attempt to use them to prove his theories of Aryan racial superiority. As it turned out, African-American sprinter and long jumper Jesse Owens (1913–1980) won four gold medals. There were 208 participants for Great Britain: 171 men and 37 women. Barbara Burke (1917–1998), Kathleen Margaret Tiffen (1912–1986), born in Croydon, and Dorothy Odam-Tyler were affiliated to Mitcham Ladies' Athletic Club. James Ginty (1908–1999) was affiliated to Belgrave Harriers athletics club, Wimbledon. Burke won the silver medal in the 4x100 metres with her team mates Eileen Hiscock (1909–1958), Violet Olney (1911–1999), and Audrey Brown MBE (1913–2005). Tiffen qualified for the hurdles semi-finals but finished fifth out of six. Tyler won silver medals in the 1936 and 1948 Olympic Games high jump. Ginty competed in the men's 3,000 metres steeplechase in the 1936 Olympics.

The first Air Raid Precautions (ARP) Act came into force in January 1938, compelling local authorities to appoint ARP Wardens, set up emergency ambulance services, first aid posts, rescue, repair and demolition services, and expand their local fire services by forming and equipping an Auxiliary Fire Service (AFS). The AFS's role was to supplement the work of brigades at local level.

Two Wimbledon ARP Wardens delivering gas masks in September 1938 use a pram to speed up their work. (Merton Archives)

An ARP Warden's helmet, armband, whistle, badge and torch with hood to prevent light being seen from the air. (Wimbledon Museum, 2017)

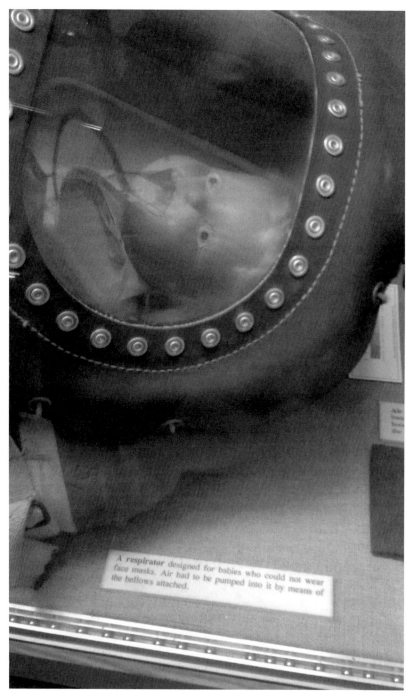

A gas mask designed for babies who could not wear face masks. Air had to be pumped into it by means of the bellows attached. (Wimbledon Museum, 2017)

A small percentage of ARP Wardens were full-time and were paid a salary, but most were part-time volunteers who carried out their ARP duties as well as full-time jobs. One in six were women, and among the men there was a significant number of veterans of the First World War. At the beginning of the war, ARP Wardens had no uniform. They wore their own clothes, with the addition of a steel helmet, wellington boots and an armband. In May 1941, full-time and regular part-time wardens were issued with blue serge uniforms.

The ARP Wardens were responsible for the handing out of gas masks, including gas masks for babies, and pre-fabricated air raid shelters such as Anderson shelters. The Controller of the ARP/Civil Defence (in 1941, the use of Civil Defence replaced the existing ARP) was normally the Town Clerk. At the beginning of the war, the Clerk to the Town Council of Wimbledon was Herbert Emerson Smith, born in 1897, appointed in 1919, a lawyer and dairyman's son of Worple Road, Wimbledon, but he was forced to retire due to ill health. Until his successor Edwin Marrat Neave (1894–1978) of Birmingham was appointed, the task of organising Civil Defence fell to the Deputy Town Clerk, Arthur Rolt (1893–1972), who, in 1939, lived in Coombe Lane.

Rolt was assisted by the Borough Engineer and Surveyor, Thomas Webster, who was also responsible for the Rescue Service and Communications throughout the war. F.H. Neville was ARP Shelter Superintendent (*Merton and Morden News*, 8 January 1943). Neave was later awarded an OBE for his work as Controller.

Webster established a system of observation posts on the roofs of both the Town Hall and seventeenth-century property Eagle House on High Street, Wimbledon Village, from which almost every part of Wimbledon could be seen. Later, when the bombing started, compass bearings could be taken from these posts, which enabled the location of an incident to be established within a few minutes. (Eagle House has been converted into eight apartments, ready for occupation from Autumn 2017).

The Council's ARP Control Centre was established in the basement of the Town Hall (now the Old Town Hall and next to Centre Court Shopping Centre) at the Queens Road end of the building. More than 2,000 men and women staffed the ARP Control Centre, the thirty-eight ARP Wardens Posts, the First Aid Posts, the Auxiliary Fire Stations, and the Mobile Services Depots (*mertonhistoricalsociety.org.uk*). Wimbledon Air Cadets helped to take messages between different ARP Posts. And young people worked as fire watchers, warning the ARP Wardens if they saw fires started by enemy bombing.

A frequent visitor to the Control Centre in the basement of the Town Hall was Alderman Augustus William Hickmott (1877–1972), Mayor of Wimbledon from 1926 to 1928, who retired from the Council in 1960 after

A watercolour sketch (1810) of Eagle House. Credit Museum of Wimbledon

forty years unbroken service. Whenever reports of damage or casualties came in, he would go out on foot to offer aid and advice to those who had suffered in any part of the borough. Hickmott, born in Kent, was a grocer who lived at 52 Merton Road with his wife, Marion Elizabeth Hickmott.

I have found references to the following ARP Posts in what is now the London Borough of Merton:

- Corner of Adela Avenue and Douglas Avenue KT3
- All England Tennis Club SW19
- Old Raynes Park library building in Aston Road SW20. Open-air billiards provided a popular pastime for Aston Road ARP workers (Raynes Park library has been housed in four different buildings all on the same site in Aston Road)
- Corporation Depot, Queens Road, near Queen's Road School SW19. This ARP post had been proposed on 6 December 1938 by Regional Inspector Captain Toyne of the Home Office in correspondence to the chief inspector. (This chief inspector may have been Colonel Pickering). On 3 July 1939, 161 personnel were proposed at this depot.
- Fort Bailey, 56 Mitcham Park CR4. An image, taken on 31 January 1940, can be found on *merton.gov.uk*

Wimbledon Air Cadets serving as cycle messengers.

- Lingfield Road Village Hall SW19. Captain Toyne proposed to adapt the village hall into an ARP depot, but this had been earmarked by the military.
- London Road, Morden, an ARP training centre.
- Sewage Works, Durnsford Road SW19. This ARP post had been proposed on 6 December 1938 by Regional Inspector Captain Toyne in correspondence to the chief inspector. On 3 July 1939, forty-nine personnel were proposed at this depot.
- Hall attached to Raynes Park Methodist Church, 195-205 Worple Road SW20. On 3 September 1939, eighty-three personnel were proposed at the Worple Road depot.

The ARP Mobile Services comprised the Stretcher Parties with fifteen ambulances and ten cars, the sixteen Light and three Heavy Rescue Teams, and the Decontamination Parties. The Heavy Rescue Teams were based at the Council Highways Depot in Garth Road, Lower Morden, and the Decontamination Parties at the Control Centre (with some of their equipment stored behind the fire station next door). The Stretcher Parties were at the pavilion in Morden Recreation Ground, at Morden Farm school in Aragon Road and at the old Library building in Aston Road, Raynes Park. The Light Rescue Parties were based at these three and also at Garth Road. (*Merton Historical Society, Bulletin No 167*, September 2008). The Garth Road site was a Merton and Morden Urban District Depot, and not used by Wimbledon Borough.

Medics and stretcher-bearers at an ARP post in Worple Road, 1942. (Museum of Wimbledon)

The Merton and Morden Urban District Auxiliary Fire Service (AFS) station was based in the grounds of Joseph Hood School in Whatley Avenue, Raynes Park. The swimming pool at Wimbledon College, Edge Hill was a valuable source of water for the local fire brigade. The long-established District Fire Service, based at its station on Kingston Road, was integrated with ARP emergency procedures, but was still expected to deal with 'civilian' fires as well. This AFS brigade tackled the fires during the Blitz in central London.

Dr Harold Ellis, Medical Officer of Health (MOH) for Wimbledon, headed First Aid and was assisted by Dr Patrick Doody, later to be MOH for the London Borough of Merton. Dr Doody was called to the armed forces in November 1940; his duties were taken over by Dr Cecil Stedman Cloake, who, in 1939, lived in Queen's Road, Wimbledon. His son John Cecil Cloake (1924–2014), born in Wimbledon, where he attended King's College School, served in the Royal Engineers in India and Japan during and after World War Two. After the war, he read History at Cambridge University. In 1948, he commenced a career in the UK's Diplomatic Service, within the Foreign Office. He was appointed Third Secretary in Baghdad in 1949. His final post was in Sofia as Ambassador of the UK to Bulgaria where he was in charge of the UK's diplomatic mission between 1976 and 1980.

First Aid Posts were established at the following locations:

- All England Tennis Club SW19, which also served as a mortuary, under Sister Rutter.
- Blakesley House by the Nelson Hospital SW20. In 1944, Blakesley House was converted to accommodate night nurses and a physiotherapy department.
- Cottenham Park SW20, under the direction of Margaret Roney (a Margaret Roney was Mayoress of Wimbledon from 1941 to 1943).
- Lindisfarne Road SW20, under Sister Wadey.
- Council Highways depot in Garth Road.
- Oberon Sports Pavillion SW2O.
- Pelham School SW19. This was under Sister Rosie.
- Queen's Road depot SW19.
- Southey Road SW19.
- Beside South Wimbledon (Merton) tube station, on the corner of Merton High Street and Morden Road SW19.
- Wimbledon College, Edge Hill SW19.

The main ambulance stations were at Cottenham Park, where one of their first ambulances was adapted from a newsagent's delivery van, and at Queens Road School (currently The Priory C of E primary school). At the beginning of the war, there were a number of men in the ambulance service, but most of these were called up and the service became staffed almost entirely by women.

Wimbledon Borough was also responsible for the provision of ARP Rest Centres, organised by the Women's Voluntary Service (WVS), places of temporary refuge for people who were bombed out or evacuated from their homes. These were at the Catherine Gladstone Home, in Bishopsford Road SM4, the Salvation Army Hall, Kingston Road SW19, and the Church Hall adjoining the Baptist Church, both in Crown Lane, the Farm Road Mission, and the Parochial Hall of St Saviour's in Grand Drive (*Merton Historical Society, Bulletin No 167*, September 2008). Their first test was imposed on them by the first significant raid on Greater London on Friday, 16 August 1940. The YMCA Rest Centre in Kingston Road, Merton Park was run by YMCA and Women's Voluntary service personnel, and helped more than 200 people on the Friday. The Village Club, Lingfield Road, Wimbledon Village, was requisitioned in 1940 as a Rest Centre for families bombed out of their homes. Five families were still there at the end of the war; the last one moved out in 1949. The WVS also took upon itself the duty of finding homes for pets because no animals were allowed at the Rest Centres.

Rations, clothing and furniture had to be provided for those who had lost all their possessions. A large clothing depot was set up in Raymond Road, Wimbledon Village where the WVS cleaned, sorted and repaired second-hand clothing for distribution to the victims of bombing.

Air raid shelter in our garden in Wimbledon

John Clark, born in 1930, contributed to the BBC's *WW2 People's War* archive in 2003. He said:

> My memories of the war itself are very vivid. However, I do clearly remember my father making a crude air raid shelter in our garden in Wimbledon in 1938.
>
> The shelter consisted of a deep trench – I can still see the yellow clay my father had to dig out to get sufficient depth – lined with wooden planks and covered with corrugated iron and a pile of earth on top. He made a smaller ladder for access. We were all issued with gas masks in cardboard boxes with a string loop on them so that they could be hung round our necks. My first real war memory was being piled into our 1927 Austin 7 on the evening of September 1 1939 and driven to my grandparents at Didlington in Norfolk where my grandfather was the butler at the Hall and the car had no luggage rack so the back seat was removed to make space for the luggage, and my brother and I sat on a suitcase together with our dog. On the day war was declared, there was an air raid warning at Didlington and I can remember standing on the front step with my grandfather looking for aircraft and brandishing my toy pistol. For a few days, it was just like being on our usual summer holiday. But after a short time, an elementary school from the east end of London arrived and was billeted in the villages and farms around Didlington. I made my first contribution to the war effort that winter. I think it was the Women's Institute in the area which encouraged people to knit mittens for the North Sea trawlermen.

Despite the fall of France and the real prospect of German invasion, Mr Clark returned to Wimbledon in late June 1940. During the Second World War, Didlington Hall, a seventeenth-century mansion visited on several occasions by Royalty, was requisitioned by the army and was the headquarters for General Sir Miles Christopher Dempsey (1896–1969), commander of the British Second Army during the D-Day landings. It was demolished in 1950/52. Reason: Wartime neglect (*lostheritage.org.uk*). A new house has been built on the site of the original.

According to *Semi-Detached London* by Alan A Jackson (1991), in 1937 and 1938, as international tensions grew, a number of London builders started to advertise concrete shelters, supplied as an extra to the house, at around £25. In March 1938, a booklet had been issued entitled 'The Protection of your Home against Air Raids'. It gave advice on how to form a refuge-room within each house. Advice was also given on blacking out windows, precautions to be taken against fire, and notes on basic first aid. A number of ARP Wardens had now been trained and their first duty was to establish a personal relationship with the householders in their area and to explain to them the need for these precautions and preparations.

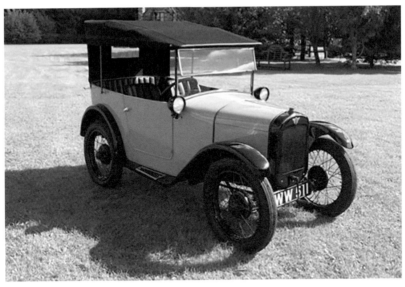

The Austin 7 was built in England from 1922–39.

David Webb, in an interview for the Museum of Wimbledon on 27 March 2012, recalled that his father built a concrete air raid shelter in the garden in 1939 at the family home in Burstow Road, West Wimbledon. He said: 'When we were bombed every night, we used to sleep in there all night on bunks. You could feel the ground shaking all around because they were bombing the main line to Portsmouth which was about 60 yards from our house.'

The family were evacuated to the Blackpool area and Grange-over-Sands, south Cumbria (then Lancashire) for a few months in 1941. 'We came back at the end of 1941 and we didn't get bombed much until the *V1*s [flying bombs] started in 1944,' he said. He was sent away to Loughborough, a town in Leicestershire, to a family for a few months until the end of September 1944. He came back to Wimbledon College.

On 1 January 1939, women sandbagged Wimbledon Power Station (now Wimbledon Substation, owned and operated by National Grid), Durnsford Road, Wimbledon Park as a precaution against attack. Meanwhile, the recreation ground adjacent to Wimbledon Park Primary School was dug up with tunnels underground to provide air raid shelters for the school. (The school itself was never hit). The Wimbledon College and Donhead school buildings both had cellars which, with minor adjustments, were approved by local ARP Wardens. Sandbags were brought in and timber frames used to reinforce the ceilings. Early in 1939, a dugout was built at the Merton Park Garage. This was taken over and completed by the Council as part of its ARP scheme to provide accommodation for the transport officers' stuff and first aid personnel, twenty people in all, according to *Long Lodge at Merton Rush*, a booklet available at Merton Archives, Morden.

London Firms Moved

In 1939, Chester House, West Side Common, Wimbledon Village – built during the 1690s and the home of the radical politician and reformer John Horne Tooke (1736–1812) from 1792 until 1812 – was in danger of being pulled down. But as soon as war became likely, London firms looked for large mansions in the suburbs to which they could transfer their employees. Barclays Bank headquarters, 54 Lombard Street, City of London took over Chester House, which became Barclays' first centre for learning counter transactions and mechanised accounting (Barclays' HQ moved to Canary Wharf in 2005, where it has a Second World War Roll of Honour to 128 staff members; Barclays left Chester House in the early 1990s and it has been transformed into a luxury private home).

The sixty-eight staff of Liverpool & Martins Bank, Lombard Street were transferred to Ricards Lodge, Lake Road, Wimbledon. (After the war, Ricards Lodge was chosen for the relocation of the Wimbledon Day Commercial School for girls, now Ricards Lodge High School). Liverpool & Martins Bank was acquired by Barclays Bank in 1968 (the Martins Bank London District Second World War memorial is at Barclays Bank Group Headquarters, Canary Wharf; there are twenty-four names on the memorial).

> We older ones do sometimes find it hard to realise that about 40% of our present staff were either not born or were very small children when the Second World War broke out. Comparatively few of the older ones remaining were involved in the evacuation of Head Office and District Office departments which was an essential feature of the security arrangements carried out in order to keep the organisation of the Bank functioning despite disruption which might be caused by air raids. The accompanying photographs, therefore, should go on the record not only for their curiosity value, but as a reminder of those far-off days during which civilians as well as soldiers were in the front line. The home is Ricards Lodge, Wimbledon, which was the evacuation centre of London District Office during the war.
>
> (*Martins Bank Magazine*, Spring 1959)

Further research

A manuscript relating to Barclays Bank's Chester House can be found at Wimbledon Museum: LDWIM011171

At the table in Ricards Lodge are (from left to right) J. B. Furniss, C. J. Carpenter, D. M. P. Hulbert, D. McNair, F. R. Ravenshear, and H. Francis. Image © Barclays, courtesy of Martins Bank Archive www.martinsbank.co.uk

Ricards Lodge. (martinsbank.co.uk) Image © Barclays, courtesy of Martins Bank Archive www.martinsbank.co.uk

Territorial Army increased

On 29 March 1939, Secretary of State for War Isaac Leslie Hore-Belisha (1893–1957), who bought part of Old Warren Farm, Wimbledon Common in 1938 (he was the last resident of Old Warren Farm to stock dairy cattle), announced that the Territorial Army (TA), a volunteer reserve force, was to be increased. On 27 April 1939, he persuaded the cabinet of Conservative prime minister Neville Chamberlain to introduce the Military Training Act 1939, a limited form of conscription due to the deteriorating international situation and the rise of Nazi Germany.

The Act was superseded by the National Service (Armed Forces) Act 1939, enacted on 3 September 1939. It enforced full conscription on all males between the ages of 18 and 41 who were residents in the UK. Senior Conservatives believed Hore-Belisha, a Jew, was more concerned about the fate of Jewish people abroad than of Britain itself. Hore-Belisha was forced by Chamberlain, prime minister from May 1937 to May 1940, to resign in January 1940. His resignation was a sensation at the time and has remained a mystery ever since.

Former company director Kenneth Young (1914–2016), who lived in Dorset Road, Merton Park for about ten years and then moved to Murray Road, Wimbledon Village, joined the TA in 1938 and was called up on 24 August 1939 as Sapper Young. In an interview (9 June 2011) with the Museum of Wimbledon, he said:

Hore-Belisha entered public school in Clifton, Bristol in 1907. After Clifton, he was educated at Oxford

I was called up on 24 August 1939. I was on searchlights with the 26th Battalion Royal Engineers. Strangely enough the headquarters was a big drill hall at Merton Road and it is still there today. It was a new building in those days. Although I had been called up, my only previous practice camp had been in June 1938 at Enfield (north London) where there was a searchlight. I had gone over there in great state in a lorry. During the fortnight we were there we had a night run. We were all in our tents at night and then a plane came over at maximum speed of 95 mph, painted white so that we could pick it up easily with the searchlight. We followed it with the searchlight across the sky until it went out of sight. Then it came back again on the way to Southend (Essex). That happened twice in two weeks and it was all the training we had in two weeks.

On the 24th August, a week before the war broke out, I got a phone call at work to join immediately. I went to the Duke of York's headquarters at Chelsea, wanting to get with my old detachment. I was dispatched to Kennington Oval (south London) and had the distinction of digging the first hole in the middle of the Oval pitch for a Lewis gun position. I was then moved to a searchlight site at Rotherhithe (south London), near to New Cross dog track and was there until Christmas 1939. After a spell at headquarters in Merton Road, SW19, in June 1940 I was sent to the Officers Training Unit at Llandrindod Wells in central Wales. Here I was transferred to the Royal Artillery and in November 1940 I 'passed out' as 2nd Lieutenant Young RA. I joined the City of London Yeomanry RA (the Rough Riders) with Bofors AA guns and was with the same regiment for the rest of the war.

I spent some time with my regiment in the UK in various training operations until 1942 when we embarked with the 1st Army for North Africa, landing at Algiers in November. I was with the 1st Army at the fall of Tunis and subsequently crossing to Italy, worked our way up the Adriatic coast all the way to Florence, Venice and into Austria. I was de-mobbed in December 1945, by that time with the rank of Major. I got married four days after de-mobilisation.

I remember the part of the Common around the Windmill during the war. There were big anti-aircraft guns there. There was a laundry at West Place with an open air drying area. The Italian prisoner of war camp on the Common was gone by the time I returned to Wimbledon.

Laetitia moved

The golden statue of Laetitia, the Roman Goddess of Gaiety, on the roof of the New Wimbledon Theatre on the Broadway, Wimbledon, was an original feature back in 1910. It was moved in 1939 as it was thought to be a direction finding device for German bombers. The New Wimbledon Theatre was described in January 1943 as 'still going strong'. Apparently, it offered a diet almost exclusively of revivals of musical comedy. Richard Tauber (1891–1948), an Austrian tenor who remained in the UK for the entire war, came in person several times. Dame Myra Hess (1890–1965), famous for her lunchtime concerts at the National Gallery, London throughout the dark days of war, performed several times at Wimbledon Town Hall.

Laetitia was buried for safekeeping, but its true resting place was forgotten. The rooftop remained bare until a modern 'angel' was added in 1991.

New Wimbledon Theatre, which has around 1,670 seats across three levels, opened in 1910. It closed in 2003 and re-opened in February 2004.

Wartime preparations in full swing at the All England Tennis Club

On 31 August 1939, the 'crowd' moved in to the All England Tennis Club – Nursing Sisters, Red Cross and St John Ambulance personnel, ARP squads, doctors and the 'whole grim paraphernalia of the Civil Defence', according

A First Aid post in the Gentleman's Dressing Room, 1940. (Lawn Tennis Museum)

to Norah Gordon Cleather (1902–1969), who attended the Roman Catholic Our Lady of Sion Convent in Kensington. She was one of only four staff who kept the Club going during wartime, according to the *Lawn Tennis Museum*. The Members' team room became a canteen. The reading room became a dormitory. Dr Sweetman, Nurse Rutter and Nurse Douglas ran the First Aid Station in the Clubhouse.

The other side of the Centre Court building was devoted to preparations for the decontamination of food. All the space around No 2 Court and the rooms and spaces under the big stands on No 1 Court were used by the National Fire Service (NFS). The big buffet was turned into a garage. 'But the NFS also brought a welcome and familiar flavour of tennis to Wimbledon, for we agreed that they should use two of the outside courts for play. They held matches there and in return for the use of the courts they helped to keep them in playing condition', said Norah Gordon Cleather.

Wimbledon in the Blackout

Blackout regulations were imposed on 1 September 1939 before the declaration of war. These required that all windows and doors should be covered at night with suitable material such as heavy curtains, cardboard or paint, to prevent the escape of any glimmer of light that might aid enemy aircraft. It was often too difficult or too expensive to black out churches properly. At the Sacred Heart, Edge Hill, Wimbledon Village, the solution was a 'dim out'. On the altar, there was a small hooded reading-lamp for the priest to see the missal and in the nave long flexes hung down from the main lights and to these were fixed small black lanterns with a blue bulb.

Two nurses on the court at Wimbledon, while the court was used as a First Aid headquarters. (Lawn Tennis Museum)

Wimbledon Windmill on Wimbledon Common, built in 1817, operated until 1864. During the Second World War, it was camouflaged with a drab green scheme to reduce its visibility, as it was in close proximity to army camps set up on the Common. The Windmill was repainted after the war ended. (It was turned into a museum in 1975).

Postcard of 1906 showing Wimbledon Windmill and the London Scottish Golf Club (the third oldest golf club in England). (Wimbledon Windmill Museum)

Signpost on the A219 at the junction with Windmill Road. (Wimbledon Windmill Museum)

Since no significant German air raids followed the outbreak of war, the main duties of the ARP Wardens in the early months were to register everyone in their sector and enforce the blackout. Many blackout offenders were fined. The *Fulham Chronicle* of 26 April 1940 reported that a man from Kenley Road, Merton Park was summoned for permitting an unobscured light to be displayed during the blackout on 16 March at North End Road, Fulham. Light shone through an open door of an outhouse at the rear of the premises, and the defendant was fined £1. (The *Wimbledon Boro' News* reported eighteen cases at Wimbledon Police Court on Wednesday, 15 January 1941).

Further research

The film of the Morden and Merton Auxiliary Fire Service during World War Two follows a Percy Porker cartoon *The Fireman Goes on Duty*. The amateur film records the activities of members of the local AFS, from the phoney war period until the Blitz, taking part in various exercises and drills before a re-enacted episode records the support provided by this brigade in tackling the fires during the Blitz in central London. Visit *londonscreenarchives.org.uk*

CHAPTER TWO

Evacuation

At 11.07am on Thursday, 31 August 1939, the government ordered the evacuation from towns and cities in danger from enemy bombers. Under 'Operation Pied Piper', the code name for the evacuation scheme, children set out for mainline train stations carrying a suitcase or pillowcase containing items of clothing which had been prescribed in letters sent out from their schools. They also carried food for the journey, their gas mask in its regulation cardboard box, maybe clutching a favourite toy, and had a label attached to their coat giving their name, number and school. At the stations, they were herded on to trains by station staff and willing Women's Voluntary Service members to destinations unknown. (*War on the Home Front*, Juliet Gardiner, 2010.)

In every district throughout Surrey, evacuation plans were coordinated by the Women's Voluntary Service for Air Raid Precautions Services – founded in 1938 by Stella Isaacs (1894–1971), Marchioness of Reading, Baroness Swanborough GBE, as a British women's organisation to recruit women into the ARP services to help in the event of war. It later was referred to simply as the Women's Voluntary Service – WVS. The WVS recruited women across the country – one million by 1942.

The WVS had two evacuation officers in Surrey: Lady Phyllis Greig (1885–1972), nee Scrimgeour, of Thatched Lodge, Richmond Park, and Helen Lloyd of Weston Lodge, Albury, Guildford. Secretaries were chosen from each area. The WVS laid on trains, coaches, arranged clearing stations, set up canteens and dealt with all billeting arrangements. (Source *Surrey Mirror*, 14 October 1938.) Issues of welfare to manage included adequate footwear for children. Lady Phyllis married Group Captain Sir Louis Leisler Greig (1880–1953) in 1916.

Herbert Aubrey Crowe (1890–1967), Mayor of Wimbledon from 1938 to 1941, wrote to the Mayor of Bournemouth, Alderman Isaac William Dickinson (1871–1961), in September 1939 thanking Bournemouth citizens for the welcome given to evacuated mothers and children from Wimbledon. Crowe, who worked as a solicitor and lived in Cavendish Avenue, New Malden in 1940, was succeeded by Anthony Anstruther Drake, Mayor between 1941

Stella Isacs, née Stella Charnaud, in a WVS wartime poster. She became the first woman to take a seat in the House of Lords in her own right.

Children from Merton Infants School, 'merrily on their way bound for a temporary home in the sunny south', wait to be evacuated from Wimbledon station in September 1939. (Wimbledon Boro' News)

and 1943. Wimbledon's Mayor from 1943 to 1945 was T. Reid Daniel, who was succeeded by Cyril Wilson Black (1902–1991).

Dorothy Weyers was interviewed as part of *Wartime Memories, Fifty Years On, members of Holy Cross remember World War II*, Holy Cross, Motspur Park (1995). She said:

> In September 1939, my sister Jean and I, who were nine and five years old, were evacuated to Guildford with other children from our school. We caught a train from Wimbledon station. On arrival, we were taken to a school and given a few items of food to take with us. Then we waited until an elderly couple, Mr and Mrs Greaves, took my sister and I into their home. Jean and I went to school there and I remember sitting around a fire at school and having roast chestnuts. When we came back to Mr and Mrs Greaves' home, we used to sleep in an air raid shelter in the garden. While we were with Mr and Mrs Greaves, my parents would come to see us when they could and would take us to the Castle grounds where my sister and I enjoyed playing.

Cathy Scofield was also interviewed. She said:

> When my sister and I were evacuated, we were lucky-because my mum
> and gran came with us, my dad staying behind to look after our home and
> continue working. First of all, we went to Exmouth in Devon, but Hitler
> hated Exmouth almost as much as he hated London, and soon we moved
> on to Burley-in-Wharfedale near Leeds. At first, we were billeted in the
> servants' quarters of a large house belonging to an actress, and I soon
> remember the big double doors that divided 'them' from 'us'. But soon
> we moved into a house that we shared with another family of evacuees.
> We were made to feel very welcome, particularly by the WVS, and
> I remember going to the village hall on weekdays for our dinner which
> was organised by them. After a couple of years, my father packed up and
> joined us in Burley. He had enough of the war, having experienced some
> very harrowing scenes as an ARP Warden in the Elephant and Castle (On
> 10 May 1941, a giant fire at Elephant and Castle, caused by bombers,
> killed more than 1,400 people and left 155,000 families without gas,
> electricity or water). We stayed in Burley until the war was over.

Girls from Mayfield Girls' School in Wimbledon were evacuated to Knaphill, a
village in Surrey west of Woking. Pupils of Pelham Road School, Wimbledon
were evacuated to Bosham, a village in West Sussex. A warm welcome was
extended from the teachers at Chichester, West Sussex to a second party of
Wimbledon evacuees, reported the *Wimbledon Boro' News* on 5 January 1940
(the name of the school was not given). Children from Queen's Road and
Central Schools, Wimbledon went to Chichester. More than 250 children
were sent to Barnstaple, Devon and Ilfracombe, Devon. Text in the *North
Devon Journal* of 24 December 1940 read: 'To the Mayor and Inhabitants
of Barnstaple. The Mayor and Mayoress of Wimbledon (Councillor and
Mrs HA Crowe) trust that you may find comfort and joy in the Message of
Christmas and that the New Year will bring peace and happiness to all mankind.'
    Early in the war, the first group of schoolchildren from Rutlish School
– then a grammar school located on Rutlish Road, Merton Park – went to
Woking to join with the secondary school there. At different times during the
war, other locations were used by different groups of Rutlish boys, including
Weston-super-Mare, North Wales and Heanor, in Derbyshire. In July 1940,
children of St Mary's Roman Catholic School, Wimbledon were evacuated to
Ilfracombe. (Rutlish School, which former UK PM John Major attended, is
now on Watery Lane).
    'Don't bring them back from the evacuation areas,' appealed chairman
of Wimbledon Council G.E. Baker to the parents of Merton and Morden
children in the *Wimbledon Boro' News* of 12 January 1940. He said: 'The
children are safer in the country. Although the Nazis have not bombed as yet,
the danger still exists, and if it came it would come suddenly.' Shortly after the

outbreak of war, the Spencer Guild was formed in Wimbledon to supply the children of Wimbledon who had been evacuated with warm clothing. By May 1940, the Spencer Guild had distributed more than 2,500 garments.

A second, much less official, wave of evacuation began with the start of the Blitz (7 September 1940), when the Luftwaffe now concentrated on night raids, though some people delayed until early 1941. Peter Ramsey lived in Hillcross Avenue, Morden. One night, a landmine dropped on the Morden Park Golf Club (which had disappeared by 1951), flattening the houses opposite and removing the tops of the houses on his side of the road. 'Our house was declared uninhabitable, so we moved... My two sisters and I went to stay with an aunt in Guildford, and mother and father stayed with another aunt in Godalming.' Desmond Langley (11) lived in Templecombe Way, Morden. He recalled standing with his twin and their elder brother (12) on top of an Anderson air raid shelter in the back garden watching dogfights over Croydon in 1940. 'In 1941, because of the Blitz, we were evacuated to Didcot, Berkshire, to live with our Granddad. It was deemed safe enough for us to return home in Spring 1944. Then came the doodle bugs (*V1*s) ... a frightening time.' Ronald Portway of Merton had just left school and was working in a factory when his mother and sister were evacuated because of the bombing. 'So there I was, all on my own, aged 14, and I soon learned to be self-reliant,' he said.

A letter by Heather Bell printed in the *Wimbledon Boro' News* in August 1941 reported on the bright side of evacuation. She wrote:

> The result of a recent visit to the West of England convinces me that you hit the nail plump on the head in your leader of last Friday when you urged parents to allow their children to remain in the reception zones till better days dawn.
>
> The children I saw looked supremely happy and contented, and are apparently leading an open-air life in the best of surroundings. In one case I was informed that children had sat for a Wimbledon scholarship examination in the distant area in which they were living, and having satisfied the examiners, were taking up the scholarships in the local school, which will receive the grants from Wimbledon.

Dick Jessett from Morden, then aged 9, was evacuated to Bury in Lancashire in 1942. His mother brought him back to Morden two years later. In February 1945, Wimbledon was adopted by Leicester, to which many children were evacuated. Leicester did not suffer bombing in the same way as many other cities. However, it was on the direct flight path from the German bombers targeting Coventry (an important engineering and manufacturing city before the Second World War) and the Black Country. The result was that the residents woke most night to the wail of the sirens and heard the aircraft flying overhead. Later in the war, gifts of furniture came to Wimbledon from Leicester.

Victor Spink's (b1938) evacuee memoir is at the University of Reading. He was born in south-east London and the firm his father worked for, Kiers, was moved to Wimbledon in 1940 to get away from the East End, vulnerable because it was the docklands centre of London. He was evacuated from Wimbledon three times during the war, twice with his mother and once with his elder brother Grahame, on 17 July 1944, to Keighley in West Yorkshire, which, in 1939, had a population of 56,631. From 1952 to 1957, he went to Wimbledon Art School. He is now Honorary Vice Chairman of the Friends of Chertsey Museum, Surrey.

The Kiers he refers to is the Kier Construction group. The company had been formed by two Danish emigrants, and assisted in building the Mulberry Harbours and in rebuilding Rotterdam Harbour after the war. I contacted Victor Spink and he replied with the following information:

> My father Leslie Cecil Spink worked for the concrete magnate Keir(s) at London docklands as a wages clerk. Mr Keir moved to Wimbledon in 1940 to get away from the bombing. My parents (and the lodger) followed suit. Mr Keir bought a house on Wimbledon Hill which suffered bomb damage, so moved not far away near Gap Road, where I once went firewatching.
>
> Trinity Infants School in Effra Road Wimbledon was where I went to school and it was damaged by a V1 flying bomb which took out ten houses in Faraday Road. The gap is still there if you look online on Street View.

Refugees arrive in Wimbledon

Large numbers of refugees from Poland, Belgium, Holland and France arrived in Wimbledon during 1940, including seamen. The WVS was ready and waiting to receive and feed them at Wimbledon Stadium, where they were billeted until accommodation could be found. Among the earliest of the refugees from Holland and Belgium to reach Wimbledon was Jack (John) Joseph, a well-known ex-footballer, and his Dutch wife, as reported by the *Wimbledon Boro' News* on 31 May 1940. At the time of their hurried departure from near Amsterdam, their two daughters, aged 14 and 16, were in another part of Holland. The *Wimbledon Boro' News* reported on 26 July 1940 that 'of the 130 Belgian, Dutch and Polish refugees originally received in Wimbledon, twenty-two have now left. Seventy-six are billeted with board and lodgings, twenty-nine in reception houses, and three billeted free with relations or friends'.

Lincoln House, opposite Wimbledon Common, was a refugee hostel and closed in Easter 1940. During the Second World War, the Wimbledon Guild in Worple Road, Wimbledon – which since 1907 has provided a range of services to support local people – became a focus for community services.

These included the billeting of refugees and searching and caring for the victims of air raids and their subsequent care. The Guild premises were themselves damaged eight times as a result of the bombing.

Margaret Sargeant organised a Housewives Service throughout the borough, according to *Safe as Houses* by Norman Plastow. In almost every street, groups of housewives were formed who, with basic training in first aid, could assist at incidents in their area.

Further research

Doris Thomas was evacuated from Wimbledon to Keighley. Peter Staples was evacuated from Worcester Park to Chesterfield, Derbyshire. Marilyn and Michael Bartlett were evacuated from Morden to Oxford. Their evacuee memoirs are at the University of Reading.

C.H. Lee's evacuation diary of Wimbledon Central Schools to the Chichester (West Sussex) area in 1939–40 is at the Imperial War Museum (Document 4557).

Jozef Massart left Mechelen, Belgium on 13 May 1940, together with his British wife, Lilian May, his two young children Loline and Raymond and their neighbours Jan and Francis. They arrived in Folkestone, Kent on 20 May 1940. The Massart family lived in Brixton and then moved to Morden at Lynmouth Avenue. Jozef Massart's war diary can be found on *bbc.co.uk*

CHAPTER THREE

Early Stages of the Second World War

On 3 September 1939, BBC radio announcer Alvar Lidell (1908–1981), born in Wimbledon Park on 11 September 1908, introduced Chamberlain from 10 Downing Street as he told Britain that the deadline of the British ultimatum for the withdrawal of German troops from Poland had expired at 11am and that 'consequently this country is at war with Germany'. Lidell attended King's College School, Wimbledon and Exeter College, Oxford. During the Second World War, in the days when radio was the only form of broadcasting, his calm and controlled voice became synonymous with the reading of news. It was only during the war itself that the BBC allowed its announcers to identify themselves so that listeners could distinguish them from enemy agents such as William Brooke Joyce (1906–1946) ('Lord Haw Haw'), who briefly attended King's College School on a foreign exchange. (See Chapter Twenty-one, Military Deception).

By 3 September 1939, most of the population had their gas mask and those who had missed out acquired them during the rest of that month. Police and ARP Wardens had a special mask because they had to be on duty outside during air raids. Many children were given bright red or blue 'Mickey Mouse gas masks'. When worn, they made a funny noise as the children breathed. This was a way of making the masks seem less scary. *When the sirens sounded, a wartime childhood (AAPPL,* 2012) by Kathleen M. Peyton, the children's author, recounted an incident at Wimbledon High School when the first practice for 'filing in an orderly manner to the air raid shelters while wearing gas-masks' dissolved into rude noises, misted-up eye-pieces, hilarity and chaos, and hence became the last such practice.

Early closing of shops and business houses was agreed by the Chamber of Commerce to allow workers home before dark. Cinemas shut for a few weeks on the outbreak of war but they soon re-opened. The cinema was one of the few entertainments still open in the early days of war. Three hundred enumerators were employed to make a War census, and identity cards were issued under the National Registration Act 1939: each person had a number.

Alvar Lidell was born in Wimbledon Park and attended King's College School. (Wimbledon Society)

The head of the household was indicated by the final digit being one, the next by two, and so on. Identification was necessary if families got separated from one another or their house was bombed, and if people were injured or killed.

Ronald Read wrote *Memories of a Morden Lad 1932–1957* for the *Merton Historical Society* (published in 2010). He said:

> In the early stages of the war, we would have gas mask drill at school, where we would all assemble outside in the playground, and when commandeered we would don masks. However, the habit of carrying gas masks soon fizzled out. By the end of 1939, just three months into war, no one carried them.
>
> We children had a lot of fun in the blackout during the winter when it got dark early. It gave a great advantage to those who were hiding over those who were seeking. I didn't mean 'Hide and Seek' as such, but games such as what we called 'One Chase Over Two Chase', where one boy was in pursuit of the rest and each one caught helped to catch the others. But the blackout brought no enjoyment to the public at large. Road accidents had almost doubled, and there were many accidents caused by people falling into rivers and walking into lamp-posts and trees, toppling from railway platforms, and so on.

The Phoney War was an eight-month period at the start of the war, during which there were no major military land operations in the Western Front. War raged at sea instead; on the day that war was declared, the *Athenia*, a passenger liner sailing from Glasgow to Montreal, Canada, was torpedoed. Of the 1,418 aboard, 98 passengers and 19 crewmembers were killed. John Baines of Wimbledon had made plans to send his daughter, Audrey, to Vancouver, Canada if war should break out (*A Passion for the Past: The Odyssey of a Transatlantic Archaeologist*, 2010). But when the liner was torpedoed, he changed his mind. Regardless of the *Athenia*'s fate, a small but steady stream of British children were shipped to Canada and the US.

By early 1940, many children had returned home, and some sports activities were resumed (though not Wimbledon tennis). The public's growing confidence in Wimbledon being a safe place kept estate agents busy, according to the *Wimbledon Boro' News* on 12 January 1940. There was a demand for houses of all types to purchase or rent and also houses for investment purposes. Sales (since the outbreak of war) reported in this issue included a newly-erected house in Albert Drive, Wimbledon Common; a modern detached house in Raymond Road, Wimbledon Village; 31 Alwyne Road; a modern detached house in Woodside; a house in Tabor Grove, Nos 5 and 7 Leopold Road and 9 Chatsworth Avenue.

Rationing

A headline in the *Wimbledon Boro' News* of 5 January 1940 read: 'Borough is Now All Ready for Food Rationing'. In a report in the same edition, Labour Councillor Augustus Frederick Herbert Lindner, born in 1894, a solicitor who, in 1944, lived in Grove Road, Cranleigh, Surrey, said queues provided admirable food for propaganda, for the enemy.

Food rationing began on 8 January 1940 with the first things being bacon, butter and sugar. The Wimbledon Food Committee (Lady Emily Roney, Mayor of Wimbledon 1933–1935, was chairman and Councillor William Ernest Hamlin vice-chairman) efficiently directed the distribution of Ration Books from Wimbledon Food Office in Worple Road, Wimbledon. Each man woman and child was issued with a food ration book, which lasted one year and was then replaced with another. Everyone was encouraged to 'Dig For Victory' and grow their own. Young people grew vegetables, did household chores and ran errands to help their families. Alderman Edwin James Mullins, born in 1863, of Gladstone Road, Wimbledon, Mayor of Wimbledon from 1937 to 1938 and a railway signalman for fifty-two years, was chairman of the Wimbledon Allotment Committee (March 1940).

The *Wimbledon Boro' News* reported on 19 January 1940 that the 'systematic pilfering of produce from allotment store huts has been causing much loss and annoyance at Cottenham Park' (West Wimbledon). The newspaper said that the offenders could be traced to young people getting out of hand in the absence of the head of the family. Several thefts were also reported from Dunsford Road (Wimbledon Park) allotments, the newspaper said. The then occupiers of land at the rear of Garth Road Cemetery, Lower Morden (now Morden Cemetery) formed an allotment association in January 1940.

Edwin James Mullins, Mayor of Wimbledon, 1937-8. (Merton Archives)

In January 1940, F. H. Lawrence, Secretary of the *National Honey Show* (founded by the *Kent and Surrey Beekeepers' Association*), which – but for the war – would have been held in Wimbledon Public Baths, Latimer Road (now Wimbledon Leisure Centre) on October 1939, said it was the duty of every British subject to help reduce the shipping of sugar to this country to a minimum. 'One way to help is to have a beehive in your garden,' he said. There were no shows during the period of the war. (The show continues to be held each year in October and 2016 was the 85th). Under the steps of Wimbledon Town Hall, a notice read: 'Due to current Ministry of Food regulations, the throwing of rice is forbidden'. Owing to paper restrictions, it was illegal to manufacture confetti during wartime.

In March 1940, a Wimbledon man was fined £5 with the alternative of a month's imprisonment for the theft of margarine from Tower Creameries, Mitcham. (He pleaded guilty). The boys of King's College dug for victory on the Royal Wimbledon Golf Course, the *Wimbledon Boro' News* reported on 21 June 1940, and on 2 August 1940 it reported that there were 745 allotment holders under the jurisdiction of Wimbledon Borough Council and a waiting list of 180, and that applications were coming in every day.

Grass lawns of Ricards Lodge, Wimbledon were converted into allotments by Wimbledon Police. Allotments were opened on Robertsbridge Road, St Helier, to help with the dig for victory scheme. These allotments were closed after the war to make room for post-war prefabs (a flying bomb wiped out houses in Robertsbridge Road). Before 1939, there were five cricket pitches in Morden – including Morden Cricket Club (established 1891) in Lower Morden Lane – but most of this space was cultivated as temporary allotments during the war. The pastures facing the Cricket Green, Mitcham, called The Canons, were turned into allotments.

The All England Tennis Club car parks were ploughed up for vegetables and a farmyard established. There were pigs, rabbits, chickens, ducks and geese – even a donkey. The pigs were housed in one of the car parks. Pieces of guttering and bits of scrap from the Centre Court, bombed on 11 October 1940, were used in the building of their sties. Mitcham Common returned to its agricultural roots; it was farmed to help the war effort.

> With no competitive lawn tennis to handle, officials of the All-England Tennis Club at Wimbledon intend rearing pigs on a more ambitious scale than last year. Miss Nora Cleather, the secretary, stated yesterday that the "Holy Land" – the famous centre court – was being carefully nursed, and that play was allowed only on the outside courts. She said: "We have just received a consignment of two-month-old Berkshire and Hampshire pigs and these will be fattened for next Christmas. We may try farming yet. (*Aberdeen Press and Journal*, 25 July 1941)

A letter to the editor of the *Newcastle Journal* printed in the newspaper on 17 March 1941 criticised Newcastle as 'not yet war conscious', and said both Corporations and citizens of Newcastle should take note of work in Wimbledon. The writer said:

> In Wimbledon, apart from individual effort in the past (which was considerable), many additional tons of vegetables will be grown as a

Marie Bompas, a member of Club staff who died in 2008, feeds one of the pigs. (Lawn Tennis Museum)

result of the lead given by the Town Council itself. All public recreation grounds have been scheduled for cultivation, including the famous Wimbledon Common. In the adjacent suburb of Merton and Morden, the Council has encouraged the allotment movement to such an extent that the number of wartime allotments under cultivation is over six times the strength of pre-war allotments. Can Newcastle show such an increase?

In both these districts, there is nightly bombing and, almost every day, there is rescue demolition rebuilding and allied work to be carried out to repair the ravages of the previous night. How much more could be done in Newcastle, by both Corporation and citizens?

One way of supplementing meat rations was to join a pig club that invested in a small pig farm. The pigs were fed mostly with scraps from homes. Pig clubs originated in Wimbledon during the First World War, according to the *Wimbledon Boro' News* of 18 October 1940. Merton & Morden ARP started a pig club in August 1940 with a membership of ninety. Trafalgar Pig Club was established at a disused shop, formerly a butcher's, on Merton High Street next to the Dark House pub (No 131), now the Kilkenny Tavern. The pig pens were built in the yard behind the shop. Bins were placed by the entrance to the club for people to put food in for the pigs, such as potato peelings or cabbage leaves (*mertonhistoricalsociety.org.uk*, March 2012). There were still two farms on Lower Morden Lane during the war, one with a dairy herd, horses, pigs and a hay barn that stood opposite the entrance to Cardinal Avenue. From this farm, twice a day, cows would make their way down Lower Morden Lane at a leisurely pace, go around the roundabout at the Beverly and were pastured in the field opposite the shops and Co-op in Grand Drive (*Boyhood Memories of the Blitz*, Ralph Swift, 2002). Today, Pig Farm Alley, Lower Morden, is a footpath that runs from Green Lane, past the back of the Hamptons and to Trafalgar Avenue, Worcester Park.

> My father belonged to a Pig Club that was just near Rosehill (between Sutton and Morden), the top end by that big Community Centre. When the war started, a group a men could join together and form a Pig Club. You got special dispensation that if you kept so many pigs, about eight or nine, then at Christmas time you could have one of the pigs between

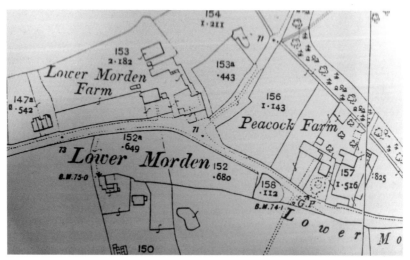

A map showing Lower Morden's farms, 1913. (Morden Park, Notes on Local History)

the nine people. That was extra off the ration, you see, and that was allowable. All the pigsties were along Rosehill, just the other side from here looking towards Sutton.

*(Mrs Q, Reminscences of St Helier Estate,
St Helier Estate Reminscence Group*, 1999).

Clothing became scarce

In January 1940, a depot was opened at Merton Park for knitted garments for the Royal Navy, merchant service and wreck survivors. 'Knitters will be welcomed who undertake to make sea-boot stockings, balaclava helmets, pullovers, circular scarves, steering gloves and wristlets. The depot will be open from 3 to 6pm on Thursdays for the collection of subscriptions and garments and the distribution of wool and patterns,' the *Wimbledon Boro' News* reported on 19 January 1940.

This article (pictured), *Women's Gossip* by Myra, in the *Mitcham and Colliers Wood Gazette* of Saturday, 13 January 1940, included advice for women on wartime gardening, a reversible coat, housecoats, rough weather wear, and 'sensible umbrellas'. A housecoat is a woman's long, loose, lightweight robe for informal wear around the house. According to the article, a reversible coat, one side indigo blue, the other raspberry, made in soft Angora wool, is as cheery as it is cosy. While housecoats in chiffon velvet in all the new rich shades – grape purple, ruby and myrtile – are really possible for any evening out.

Clothes rationing began on 1 June 1941, and ended on 15 March 1949. The wartime diaries of Wimbledon shopkeeper Leonard Syrett Greenaway for 1941, 1944 and 1945 can be found at the Museum of Wimbledon (LDWIM000710). He said: 'Clothing rationing announced. Not too good for us from a business point of view.' He kept the shop on the corner of the High Street and Ridgway, which he sold to Frank Lewin and his brothers early in the 1960s.

Weddings

Many couples married in a hurry before the man was called up. In October 1939, the *Surrey Comet* reported that on one Saturday alone, twenty-four marriages took place in Kingston Register Office.

Lieutenant William Frank 'Bill' Tudhope served in the RAF and was engaged to Mollie Christopher of Springfield Avenue, Merton. They had agreed to go and live in Canada after the war, but Bill was killed on the Homberg Operation on the night of 10/11 August 1940, while piloting a Hampden which crashed into the Ijsselmeer, an inland bay in the central

Women's Gossip
By Myra

e long black-out nights create con-
s highly favourable for the activities
he criminal classes. and, as might
expected, housebreakers are busy in
ated residential areas. Thousands of
s and flats have been vacated by
occupants and left shut up during
war. In most cases, no doubt,
bles have been removed, but, al-
the expert burglar may pass them
empty houses and flats offer tempt-
opportunities to the less professional
of housebreakers. Householders
have vacated their homes rely, as
on insurance compensation for
damage caused by burglars, but
ordinary "Comprehensive" policy
is an "unoccupancy" clause which
the burglary insurance if the
s are left unoccupied for more
specified number of days in
r period covered by the policy.
edition is a matter of importance
y holders who have left their
in vulnerable areas to reside else-
while the war goes on.

TIME GARDENING

p to householders in Britain who
garden to see what it can be
contribute if anything, to home-
d supplies. Intensified economic
makes individual help in this
an urgent matter ,whether by
ing of live stock or raising
arden produce. Nothing much
one in the winter about grow-
bles beyond the preparation of
, which, if not hitherto used
purpose, will usually serve for
without the application of
Kitchen waste will provide
s or poultry, or for rabbits,
er cannot be objected to as a
near neighbours. A four
old rabbit should weigh at

For example, a reversible coat, one side
indigo blue, the other raspberry, made
in soft Angora wool, is as cheery as
it is cosy, while houscoats in chiffon
velvet in all the new rich shades—
grape purple, ruby and mauve—are really
possible for any evening out. But, un-
doubtedly, frocks in fine wool materials,
satins, dull silk crepes, and velvets, em-
broidered with gold or silver cog-wheel
sequins, crystal drops, and coloured stones,
are smarter for the evening, and so are
dresses for daytime, wear in wool or crepe,
trimmed with sequins that match in tone.
For the evening designers favour necklines
square in front and high at the back,
sleeves long and close fitting, and skirts
of ankle length. Skirts for day wear are
short, many only just cover the knee,
and a ll swing.

ROUGH WEATHER WEAR

Greatcoats made from thick woollens,
untrimmed save for epaulettes aslant
shoulders, welted seams, or single, un-
pressed box-pleats, throng-faced a little
below the neck at the back, are found
in all collections. Pockets abound—one
model shows six—and storm collars, or
hoods that look equally attractive when
covering the head, or dropped to drape
the shoulder line, are the usual "neck
finishes." A few buttons, spaced apart,
fasten fronts, and the colours mostly
favoured include Air Force blue, bright
though dark green, beige, and ginger
brown. Higher than ankle boots to be
worn with these coats are of ginger
brown reverse suede, lined with white
sheepskin. They have thick crepe rubber
soles and plain leather trimmer tops.

UMBRELLAS

Myra's advice. (Mitcham and Colliers Wood Gazette)

Netherlands. Although his aircraft has never been found, his body was buried at Kampen General Cemetery, Netherlands. Mollie moved to Canada after the war, just as she had once agreed to do with Bill.

Frank Ewins (1908–1940) of Tooting Junction was killed in an air raid in Mitcham two days before the date arranged for his wedding at Mitcham, on 14 September 1940.

CHAPTER FOUR

Air Raid Precautions

On Friday, 2 February 1940, Admiral Sir Edward Evans (1880–1957), naval officer, Antarctic explorer and London Regional Commissioner for Civil Defence, visited Wimbledon. He noted in files kept by the *National Archives*:

> As in many other boroughs, very little has been done by those who are required to provide shelters for themselves, and the latter presents a problem if bombing begins. There is probably prepared protection for not more than 30 per cent of the total inhabitants, and the inevitable result will be that the public shelters which provide for about 10 per cent will be very much overcrowded, leading to all kinds of difficult problems of public control. In conclusion, I think the borough is reasonably well organised so far as Air Raid Precautions parties are concerned.

An air raid shelter at Avenue Preparatory School, Richmond Road, West Wimbledon was referred to in the January and February 1940 editions of the *Wimbledon Boro' News*. An air raid shelter at William Morris Hall, the Wimbledon Labour Hall, was ready for use by March 1940, with the proviso that occupants of the Labour Hall buildings would have first use of it during air raids. One of these occupants was the Workers' Education Association, founded in 1903, an education movement committed to widening participation in learning and education with a social purpose. By April 1942, it was used as a reception centre for people who had been made homeless by the bombing. For a few months in 1944, the whole of the original building was placed at the disposal of Rutlish School, after the school was partially bombed out. Several other organisations were still able to use the building in the evenings and at weekends. One such group was a youth club established by the Education Committee of the Royal Arsenal Co-operative Society.

On 2 May 1940, there was a combined Southern Railway (Southern Railway was a British railway company established in 1923) and Wimbledon ARP air raid display in Wimbledon. Civilians disappeared into an air raid shelter, in front of a heavily sandbagged building, as the ARP Wardens looked on. The wardens then entered the shelter, before they re-emerged to tackle a fire. Equipped with gas masks and hoses, they successfully extinguished the fire, under guidance from an instructor. Mock casualties were carried on stretchers, before being attended to. A fire engine arrived (identification plate 'LIGHT – R LONDON – WIMBLEDON), along with a motorcar towing a water pump. An ambulance and its female staff also arrived. A man with a 'CAUGHT LOOTING' sign was escorted away by a policeman and an ARP Warden.

Rutlish School had to be closed for three months in 1940 for the construction of air raid shelters. At Rutlish School, these were brick constructions with thick concrete roofs set in the year yards. For older boys with important exams looming, some masters conducted classes in their own homes. John Uppington, a pupil at Rutlish School for the duration of the war, recalled in an interview for *memoriesofwar.org.uk*:

Admiral Sir Edward Evans

> We were told in the event of a sudden attack to enter any shelter, but to try to enter the correct one to enable the register to be checked. As the shelters were unlit pupils had difficulty in entering them until someone produced a match to light the only candle there. Some shelters had a hurricane lamp to be lit, but they usually produced black smoke as well as light!

According to the *Wimbledon Boro' News* of 31 April 1940, Merton and Morden Council reported that 5,515 Anderson shelters had been erected, or were in the course of being erected by householders, and 1,896 by the council. In September 1940, Wimbledon Mayor Herbert Aubrey Crowe made the following comment about public shelters:

> I myself have seen wives coming early to the shelter, reserving seats for their husbands, and telephone messages have been received at the Town Hall asking that a seat may be booked for the night. This sort of thing will not help. It's quite unreasonable to expect one class of community to face the enemy in hand to hand attacks and other portions of the community to think of nothing but their own safety.

Public shelters were always open to the public whether there was an air raid or not, and they were out of wind and rain.

There was an air raid shelter by Beehive Bridge on the grounds of The Boys' County Public School, Mitcham. The sign at the entrance read:

BOROUGH OF MITCHAM

This Public Air Raid shelter is only for
the use of persons caught in the street
during air raids and not for occupiers
of adjoining premises

Many London parks had public trench shelters. Public trench shelters were a relatively economical and quickly produced means of providing air raid shelters for large numbers of people. Unfortunately, the 'ladder design' of intercommunicating trenches meant they were very vulnerable to bombs landing nearby, which could cause whole trenches to collapse, instantly burying their occupants. On the evening of 15 October 1940, 104 were killed when a bomb fell on a public trench-style bomb shelter in Kennington Park, north-east of Wimbledon. Forty-eight bodies were recovered and most of them buried in Lambeth Cemetery; the remainder still lie, unidentified, beneath the park. Known victims are listed on *vauxhallandkennington.org.uk.*

In a letter printed in the *Wimbledon Boro' News* on 8 November 1940, a reader suggested a deep shelter at Wimbledon Park:

> Street and trench shelters are better than nothing; but in case of direct hit, they may cause the annihilation of several families compared with one family in a bombed house.
>
> Some years ago, the borough council did a disservice to the people by selling a part of Wimbledon Park where terrace gardens would have been an attraction to one of greater London's beauty spots. There is now an opportunity to make amends. Let the Council provide large shelter accommodation by tunnelling from the level of the tennis courts, under Home Park-road, into Arthur-road hill. The suggestion has added recommendation besides that of certain safety for a large number of people. After the war the 'galley' could be used for a much-wanted branch library; reading and rest rooms; social service focal points; theatre for hire to amateurs; indoor badminton, tennis and bowling; and perhaps even a swimming bath – and the initial cost of all these things would be largely met by ARP funds.

Public trench shelters were in the following Wimbledon locations (2 January 1942):

A memorial to the victims of the Kennington Park tragedy, funded by Lambeth Special Opportunities Fund, was unveiled on 14 October 2006 by Mayor of Lambeth Liz Atkinson in front of more than 100 people. (vauxhallandkennington. org.uk)

The Kennington Park shelter.

1, Wandle Park, trench, seating capacity 450
3A, Haydons Ground Rec, trench, seating capacity 350
3B, Haydons Ground Rec, trench, seating capacity 350
4A, South Park Gardens, trench, seating capacity 350
4B, South Park Gardens, trench, seating capacity 350
5A, Lucien Road, trench, seating capacity 350
5B, Wellington Road, trench, seating capacity 350
6, Wimbledon Park, trench, seating capacity 350
7A, Dundonald Road Rec, trench, capacity 350
7B, Dundonald Road Rec, trench, capacity 350
9, Holland Gardens, trench, seating capacity 350
10, Cottenham Park Rec, trench, seating capacity 350
11, Queens Road School, trench, seating capacity 350
12A, Garfield Road Rec, trench, seating capacity 350
12B, Garfield Road Rec, trench, seating capacity 350

A photo taken from 16,500ft by an RAF plane on 7 August 1944 shows trenches criss-crossing Wimbledon Common and overhead wires to stop German gliders successfully landing in 1940. In a letter dated 23 November 1940 to Ellen Wilkinson MP, who served in Churchill's wartime coalition as junior minister, Dr Dorothea Fox said the trench shelters in Wimbledon were wet: 'The wet comes up through floors, and down through the roofs.' She further stated that there were no bunks, and the shelterers either slept on the wet floors or the wet benches:

> From one shelter, my partner and I have had two cases of rheumatic fever in the last fortnight. It would not seem unsuperably difficult to persuade the local authority to caulk up the leaking roofs, to put duck boards on the floors, to install bunks, and to put doors over the closets.

A suggestion was made 'to take advantage of the natural contour of Wimbledon Hill and tunnel under it to the Common for an air raid shelter. It would, of course, accommodate hundreds of people, and it is suggested that after the war the tunnel could be made a one-way traffic entrance to Wimbledon, and thus relieve traffic on the Hill.

Underground stations

On 19 September 1940, William Mabane (1895–1969), parliamentary secretary to the Ministry of Home Security and Minister of State for Foreign Affairs from 25 May 1945 to 26 July 1945, urged the public not to leave their Anderson shelters for public shelters, saying it deprived others of shelter. The Ministries of Home Security and Transport jointly issued an 'urgent appeal', telling the public 'to refrain from using Underground stations as air raid shelters except in the case of urgent necessity'.

However, the government was then confronted with an episode of mass disobedience. On the night of 19/20 September, thousands of Londoners were taking matters into their own hands. They had flocked to Underground stations for shelter. Police did not intervene. Some station managers, of their own initiatives, provided additional toilet facilities. The government realised it could not contain this popular revolt and on 21 September, it abruptly changed policy, removing its objections to the use of Underground stations.

Some stations – such as South Wimbledon – put up bunks where people could sleep but families also bedded down on the platforms and even on the stairs and escalators. The WRVS supplied shelterers with tea and snacks. Many people would chat, read or even have singsongs to keep their spirits up. As many as 1,400 people took refuge here during bomb raids, according to *merton.gov.uk*. South Wimbledon was shown as 'South Wimbledon (Merton)' on Tube maps from 1928. From the early 1950s, the '(Merton)' part of the name fell out of use.

However, Tube stations and tunnels were still vulnerable to a direct hit. For example, on 14 October 1940, a bomb penetrated the road and tunnel at Balham, blew up the water mains and sewage pipes, and killed sixty-eight people. The highest death toll was caused during an accident at Bethnal Green, east London, on 8 March 1943, when 1,500 people entered the station. The crowd suddenly panicked on hearing the sound of an unfamiliar explosion (in fact this was a top-secret anti-aircraft rocket being tested in Victoria Park nearby). Someone stumbled on the stairs and a domino effect started; 173 people were crushed to death in the disaster. A list of the victims can be found on *stairwaytoheavenmemorial.org*.

CHAPTER FIVE

Home Guard Operational from May 1940

The Phoney War ended with the German attack on France and the Low Countries on 10 May 1940. Britons – 'at bay' with only the English Channel holding back German forces – rallied together to defend the island against the Nazis. In a broadcast to the nation on 14 May 1940, Anthony Eden, Churchill's foreign secretary, appealed 'to all men between 17 and 65 who had handled any weapon of offence or defence, and were willing to enrol in a citizen army to be called Local Defence Volunteers (LDV)'. This was considered too much of a title and it became, in a speech by Churchill on 31 July 1940, the Home Guard, also fondly known as 'Dad's Army', operational until late 1944 when there was really no risk of a German attack.

'The primary object of the Home Guard is to have available an organised body of men trained to offer stout resistance in every district, and to meet any military emergency until trained troops can be brought up.' (*Home Guard Manual 1941*)

A meeting at Wimbledon Police Station on 16 April 1940 was held to decide the commanders of the Home Guard in the greater London area. Major Charles Micklem (1882–1955) of Long Cross House near Chertsey, awarded the Distinguished Service Order (DSO) in 1919, was appointed Zone Commander for the area. At the same meeting, WPC Tenison (later lieutenant colonel) was given command of the 54th Surrey Battalion of the Home Guard. It comprised men from Wimbledon, Merton and Morden, and within a year formed a Battalion 1,500 strong and had a good armoury of weapons. It was not composed simply of First World War veterans. Among its members were those from the special platoon from King's College School Officers' Training Corps. They had bicycles, so were given a mobile role.

Its headquarters was at the Old Drill Hall in St George's Road (where applications to join were made), backing on to the railway. It was here that it had its officers' mess, storeroom and rifle range. It also used the rifle range at Rutlish School.

There were eight companies in the Battalion. It fell to the lot of 'C' Company, under the command of Major Arnold Frank Stapleton Harris (1890–1959), whose son Captain John Stapleton Harris (1925–2012) was born in Wimbledon, to guard Wimbledon Common. In 1939, Arnold Harris lived in Bernard Gardens. The Company headquarters was at 3 Parkside Gardens. The Common was used for training and there were regular all-night patrols, especially during the period of the Blitz. The Wimbledon Home Guard also helped the police and the Civil Defence Service, standing guard over unexploded bombs and bomb-damaged buildings. There were a lot of motorcyclists in the Battalion; the Motor Cycle Section was headquartered at the Old Drill Hall. The motorcyclists, who were housed in a building opposite St Georges Road, Wimbledon, acted as guides for defence forces travelling southwards through south-western areas of London and into Surrey.

The *Surrey Advertiser* reported on 13 July 1940 that:

> Technical training of Army trainees will now be given at Wimbledon Technical College. [Earlier, the school was known as Wimbledon Technical Institute, and was where munitions classes were held in 1915. Later, it was known as Merton Technical College until the school closed] In response to the government's request, war work is being done in the workshops at Kingston, Wimbledon, Redhill and Guildford Technical Colleges by ex-junior technical school boys, handicraft teachers seconded for the work, and others.

Compulsory Home Guard service was introduced in February 1942. From 1943, the Wimbledon Home Guard also recruited Women Auxiliaries, known first as 'Nominated Women'. Lieutenant Colonel Rowland Feilding (1871–1945), author of *War Letters to a Wife* (1929), fought in the First World War and served in the Home Guard during the Second World War. He died in Wimbledon in September 1945, aged 74.

Billeted on Wimbledon Common

The Prince of Wales Company, 1st Battalion, The Welsh Guards was billeted on Wimbledon Common, in West Side House and in Stamford House. Welsh Guardsman Fred Bowden, born in 1920 in Swansea, trained for battle in Wimbledon before heading off for D-Day. In an interview for the Museum of Wimbledon, he said:

> We all slept on the floor. I spent my war years mostly sleeping on the floor, on a pallet. And there we did our drilling on Wimbledon Common, just outside the house and the battalion parades. We had company parades on the grass outside, battalion parades. We route marched from Wimbledon up to London every week; we did a 25-mile march with

full kit. We practised digging slit trenches when we were on Wimbledon Common in 1940. That's the basic trench. A slit trench.

He met his wife Pansy, a volunteer at a canteen for the troops at Emmanuel church, Wimbledon, and in 1942 they were married. Bowden fought in Normandy (June–July 1944), then the Welsh Guards advanced to Brussels. Bowden's son David was born in 1947. He went to Tiffin Grammar School, before attending Trinity College, Cambridge and becoming a GP.

Spitfire Fund, July 1940

Lord Beaverbrook (1879–1964), whose home was in Leatherhead, Surrey (1940), suggested through the pages of one of his newspapers, the *Daily Express*, that each town and city in Britain should pay for a Spitfire, quoting the sum of £5,000 (the aircraft were priced at an entirely theoretical £5,000). Worcester and Wimbledon were the first to respond, according to *We Can Take It!* by Mark Connelly, and were promised Spitfires named in their honour.

Wimbledon Mayor Herbert Aubrey Crowe launched his Spitfire Fund in July 1940, and stated that the staff of Kennards, Wimbledon (a store that became Debenhams in 1973) had promised a donation of £100 as a kick-off. ARP Wardens raised £150 for the fund, mostly in coinage, from people who visited the shelters. In the following month, it was announced that the fund had reached the £1,000 mark. The *Wimbledon Boro' News* reported on 6 September 1940 that the fund was nearly £2,000:

> Most of the recent donations have been from young people. For instance, some children in Allington Close (Wimbledon) held a fair and raised 5s. Some boys and girls in Darlaston Road (Wimbledon) arranged a fete which realised £6. A German doctor refugee has given his gold wedding ring, which is to be sold on behalf of the fund.

On 27 September 1940, the paper told how a German bomber that had crashed in Merton the previous Friday morning had helped the Spitfire Fund. A parachute and parts of the machine were collected and put on display in an exhibition in a shop near Wimbledon Town Hall and visitors paid a 6d entrance fee. Exhibits included the rear engine gun, which fell in the garden of Woodside House, and the parachute by which one of the airmen escaped from the burning machine. Woodside was the home (1941) of Ethel Donoghue, wife of racehorse trainer Steve Donoghue (1884–1945).

The *Surrey Advertiser* reported on 28 September 1940 that donations to the North-West Surrey Spitfire Fund now amounted to £6,400. In October/November 1940, the Commissioner of the Metropolitan Police permitted a house-to-house collection to aid the fund. Those willing to volunteer to undertake the collections were requested to apply immediately to the Town Hall.

Further research

The Museum of Wimbledon has a loose-leaf notebook that contains, in alphabetical order, the names and addresses of organisations and persons involved in Civil Defence in the Merton and Morden District. Meanwhile, the names of the men who died while serving with the 57th Mitcham can be found on *stheliermemories.org.uk*. JB Pritchard has written about his 1940–42 memories of service with the Home Guard Mitcham. He was posted for a week's attachment to the 1st Battalion Welsh Guards on Wimbledon Common. The Museum of Wimbledon also has three notebooks of W.A. Phelp, Aylward Road, lieutenant commanding Signals for 54th Surrey (Wimbledon) Battalion (LDWIM001013).

Route 127 – between Morden and South Wimbledon via Worcester Park-converted in 1941 from single-deck to low-height double deck (the low bridge at Worcester Park meant that normal double-deckers could not be used). As London Transport initially had no available low-height buses, the route was converted using buses loaned by Manchester Corporation. Ninety buses were loaned by Manchester Corporation to London Passenger Transport Board (LPTD) for the war period. LPTD's area covered 2,000 square miles. In 1940, there were 82 bus garages, 31 tram and trolleybus depots, 181 railway stations, 3 generating stations, and 5 overhaul works to look after. LPTD's Home Guard was organised into localised units in November 1941. The 42nd County of London Battalion was made up of 5 Companies and 21 Platoons. D Company was Merton Garage, Morden Depot, Morden Station, and Kingston Garage. In all, the LPTD's Home Guard built or converted 137 guardrooms and manned 76 strong points during its four-and-a-half year term of service.

The Southern Railway, which linked London with the Channel ports, South West England, South coast resorts and Kent, raised six Home Guard Battalions; D was Wimbledon. *Southern on Guard* magazine, begun by the Southern Railway in May 1940, was free to any employee interested in the Home Guard. It carried a variety of articles giving readers news from all six Battalions. Volunteers for D include (August/September 1941 magazine) A Meager, and (June 1941 magazine) A. Izard, A. Coleman, E.F. Bateup, W.E. Biddecombe, D.W. Newport, and C.J. Bryon. The Southern Railway was nationalised in 1948.

It was not only vehicular methods of communicating that were utilised by the Home Guard. Pigeons were also a favourite, according to *Surrey Home Guard* by Paul Crook. Pigeon racing was suspended.

CHAPTER SIX

When Toys Gave Way to Real Munitions

The Lines family first became involved in the production of toys in 1850. Lines' Tri-ang Works on Morden Road, just beyond South Wimbledon Station, where the Deer Park industrial estate now stands, opened in 1924. The main pre-war products were prams, tricycles and pedal cars, 'Minic' model cars and 'Pedigree' dolls and soft toys. In winter, women would sit with their feet in cardboard boxes with sacking around them as the heating was totally inadequate, according to a contributor to *Factory Life and Labour in Merton and Beddington*.

Lines Bros founded International Model Aircraft (IMA) in 1931, together with Joe Mansour, an expert modeller and an innovator in plastic and paper moulding. IMA made model aircraft, particularly the FROG ('Flies Right Off the Ground') range of flying models. Their works lay immediately to the east of the Tri-ang factory sports field.

At the start of the Second World War, production of toys was deemed non-essential by the government. The Tri-ang Works was required to abandon toys for munitions and the workforce expanded to more than 7,000, many of them female. In January 1940, a statement was made at the Sutton Trades and Labour Council at St Helier by Miss Heggot in connection with Churchill's appeal for women to go into munitions factories. She said women would work for less than men. In a letter to the *Wimbledon Boro' News*, printed on 9 February 1940, Florence Underwood of Crossway, Raynes Park said:

> The country needs the work of both men and women in the present crisis: and the country does not want to see the standards of its workers lowered. Why, then, should not trade unionists agree to put industry on a sound basis by seeing that the union rate for the job shall be paid to the worker, irrespective of the sex of the worker?

Surrey County Council was approached by St Helier Community Centre in May 1940 on the subject of provision being made on the estate for the feeding and care of children whose mothers were engaged on war work. According

30. *In 1924, Tri-ang Toys was registered as a brand name and a new high-tech factory in South Wimbledon was named the Tri-ang Works.*

to the *Merton and Morden News* of 26 March 1943, there was a classroom exodus on the St Helier estate to war factories.

The only Tri-ang links with the past were the Utility prams, which continued in production throughout the war. '(Only) just capable of fulfilling their function' was the sad comment of Walter Lines, one of the three Lines brothers. They were fit for purpose, however, and a good example of the work of the production engineers, who pared their pre-war designs to the bone to produce an item of an acceptable standard, though made with minimum cost and effort. The work was hard and the factory was full of noise, dirt and grease. At peak production periods, compulsory overtime meant an exhausting schedule. There were compensations, however, as young women who previously were lucky to earn a pound a week now earned considerably more. By the middle of the war, the factory had developed a good canteen service and also benefited from a nearby British Restaurant, a public eating centre, and the growth of local fish and chip shops and cafes.

The factory was itself partially bombed in 1940. On 13 December 1940, the *Wimbledon Boro' News* reported that a workman there had been asphyxiated by fumes. He worked on a degreasing machine.

In 1941, a cheap way was needed to train the civilian seamen on Defensively Equipped Merchant Ships (DEMS) to aim their anti-aircraft guns accurately. The wartime Admiralty Department of Miscellaneous Weapons Development (DMWD) proposed that the trainees should fire light guns at model aircraft, the idea being that shooting slow bullets at a slow aircraft would give the gunner a good idea of just how far in front of a fast enemy aircraft he should aim his own 'real' bullets.

The officer in charge of the project, Lieutenant Commander N. S. Norway (alias Nevil Shute the novelist), consulted Mansour, whom he had met previously. The first model was a 3½lb glider of 6ft span, designed by A.A. ('Bert') Judge of IMA and constructed mainly of balsa wood and silk. It was winched up to a height of 200ft by a long cord slipped onto a hook under the nose, and then circled down in free flight. It was used on several DEMS firing ranges, but launching a reasonable number of targets in a short time involved too many people making too many adjustments for wind speed and direction, etc. In addition, the government Controller of Timber forbade further supply of balsa wood for the project. DMWD decided to modify the design and add rocket power.

The new requirement was issued in January 1942. In a very short time (legend says overnight), several IMA designers each produced a sample model, and a single design evolved from these over the next few days. The new model was soon placed in production, now officially as the Rocket Glider Target, and it was issued to DEMS firing ranges 'throughout the British Isles'. (With thanks to research carried out by David Haunton at the National Archives, Kew for the *Merton Historical Society*.)

The duralumin magazines (containers for bullets or shells) for Hurricanes and Spitfires were made at the Tri-ang Works, as well as Bren gun magazines and millions of shell cases for 20mm cannon shells. Eleven million land mine cases were also made. One of its most important products was the Mark III Sten sub-machine gun. Lines had already made parts for the Mark I and

Mark II versions but these were too slow to manufacture in the emergency that followed the retreat from Dunkirk between 27 May and 4 June 1940.

The Mark III was a simplified version in which Walter Lines used his engineering experience to reduce the number of components from sixty-nine to forty-eight. They proved to be so efficient that an order for 500,000 was placed immediately after their first test firing. Altogether, 1.15 million were produced at a rate of 3,000 to 4,000 per day. In South Wimbledon, the sound of machine gun fire could often be heard as samples were tested at the Tri-ang Works. They were not just used by our own troops but many were also dropped into occupied countries for use by the resistance.

Rose Deakin, interviewed for *Women in Industry in South London in World War Two* by Sue Bruley, worked on land mines assembly line at Lines. When asked what that involved, Ms Deakin said:

> Well, it was strips of metal and then you put your rivets in and you put a bracket on and a pound-and-a-half hammer you used. And then when you'd done them you'd put them on another part and it was sheared round and then it went under a hand press and you hand pressed them flat so they were strong and then another, someone else took the other operation on. There was no finished object, it was all parts.

Recognition of the importance of Tri-ang to the war effort can be seen in the number of royal visits made, including that of King George VI (1895–1952) on 10 June 1941. He was shown around the factory by Walter Lines to inspect the munitions production. Princess Marina, Duchess of Kent (1906–1968), visited the factory on 28 May 1943.

Further research by David Haunton (National Archives) includes the following:

> Following up Walter Lines' mention of 'special optical apparatus to enable troops to see in the dark', I found that the only British night vision device used by the Army was the 'Tabby', developed during 1942–43. It came in two forms: Type K, a monocular telescope for spying out the land, and Type E, a special pair of headlamps, plus binoculars for the driver, which enabled soldiers to drive vehicles (including tanks) in convoy at night without using any visible lights. Presumably Lines made components for the main 'Tabby' contractors, CAV, EMI and The Gramophone Company, from 1944 onward. Since the firm had little optical or electrical experience, I suspect their contribution was the kit of parts (metal strips, posts, locking nuts and webbing) with which the driver's binoculars were clamped to dashboard or cab roof and adjusted to a convenient position to suit each driver.

Wood was used in many products – the Sawmill employed 240 people, fifty of them women. One of Lines' final wartime projects was to make detailed

On 10 June 1941, King George VI visited the South Wimbledon toy factory to inspect the munitions production as part of the war effort. (triang.nl)

On 28 May 1943, the Duchess of Kent visited the South Wimbledon factory. (triang.nl)

scale models of the Normandy landing beaches in preparation for D-Day. Manufacture of toys and prams resumed shortly after the war ended. The early years were difficult as fuel and steel shortages sometimes made stoppages unavoidable. Many of the women who joined the firm in wartime had married during the war and wanted to start families in peacetime. Unionisation had occurred during the war, so that by the late 1940s all the major sections had shop stewards and a factory committee existed to hold joint negotiations with management. Lines continued to employ large numbers of women, mainly in routine assembly.

A valued Lines' employee in 1943 was Peter, who worked there despite having no hands. While serving with the Home Guard, he had an accident with a hand grenade which exploded in his hands, inflicting such injuries that he had to have a double amputation. Aged 19, he was fitted with artificial hands. When a gathering of Wimbledon and Croydon engineers visited the factory, he was seen at work carrying out a highly technical process of arc welding in 'a very capable manner'. (*Wimbledon Boro' News*, 3 September 1943). Arc welding is the process of joining metal to metal by using electricity to create enough heat to melt metal; as the metals cool, they bind together.

On 29 October 1946, Tri-ang released this picture with the following text: 'TOYS COME BACK TO ENGLAND – Finished toys, ready for the

Toys ready for 1946 Christmas markets. (triang.nl)

Christmas markets of England and the rest of the world, line the display shelves in the Lines Bros. factory in London. The factory is turning out toys by the millions with use of mass production methods. Dolls, forts, trains, boats, motor cars and scores of other items are made in this manner.'

Lines continued its growth throughout the 1950s and soon even the vast South Wimbledon site was inadequate for its needs, particularly for exports. The company was refused permission to expand on the site, but developed extensively elsewhere. At its peak, Lines had forty companies worldwide, including the Hornby, Meccano and Dinky brands. In 1971, due to failing business overseas and uncertain demand in the UK, Lines collapsed. The South Wimbledon site closed in 1972.

Lines' South Wimbledon site was near Merton Abbey railway station on the Tooting, Merton and Wimbledon Railway. The station was opened in

HOW TO GET
TO OUR WORKS

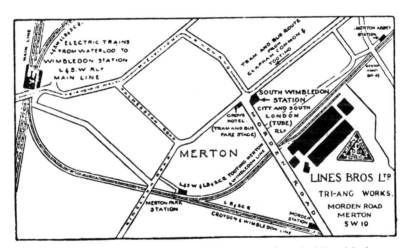

Edgware-Morden Line Underground to South Wimbledon Station (top of Morden Road). By means of this Tube and its connections, it is easy to reach our Works in about half-an-hour from any part of London. From Wimbledon Main Line Station (Southern Railway) i t is five minutes by 'Bus to the entrance of our Works.

This map from 1937 shows details of how to get to Tri-ang Works by public transport.

October 1868, closed to passengers in 1929 and to goods on 1 May 1972, and closed completely in May 1975. The site of Merton Abbey railway station lies under a road, the Merantun Way on the A24. Merantun Way was constructed in the early 1990s to relieve traffic congestion on Merton High Street. Part of the Chapter House of Merton Priory has been preserved under Merantun Way and can be viewed from a subway under the road.

CHAPTER SEVEN

Captain William Schermuly

Buried in St Lawrence Churchyard, Morden is Captain (Augustus) William Louis Schermuly (1857–1929), seaman and inventor of the ship-to-shore line-thrower. St Lawrence Church, built in 1636, is located on London Road, at the highest point of Morden, overlooking Morden Park.

The picture shows a Pains shoulder shotgun, used to fire a line-thrower, held by Schermuly. It is not known whether these shoulder guns were made at Pains Fireworks in Mitcham. Schermuly, who lived at 7 Frederick Road, between Sutton and Lower Morden, in 1911, formed a company in 1897 to manufacture the world's first viable ship's line-throwing rocket apparatus (ship-to-shore line-thrower) to his own design.

He was born in Holborn, London. He was the son of former seaman Augustus Schermuly, a man of Dutch ancestry (the family emigrated from Holland in the mid 1600s). In 1911, William Schermuly lived at 7 Frederick Road with his wife Susan Schermuly (b1864) and their four children: Courad Schermuly (b1895), Alfred Schermuly (b1901), Charles Schermuly (b1903), and Blanche Schermuly (b1905).

William Schermuly experienced to the full the vicissitudes of a sailor's life. Dead calms, with the air like the breath of a furnace and the sea like a molten mirror; winter gales off Cape

Captain William Schermuly testing out his line-thrower – then fired using a shotgun rather than a pistol rocket. Courtesy of Newdigate Local History Society

This type of unwieldly line-throwing apparatus was still being used when Schermuly was born. 1842 drawing.

Horn when the frozen rigging blistered the bare hands that gripped it; the never-forgotten thrill of making port after a long voyage, and the agonising waiting for the final crash as one ship's drifted helplessly on to a lee shore.

The Biography of William Schermuly compiled by C.R. Thompson.

'Lost ships can be replaced – but lives lost are gone for ever', William Schermuly.

He received his first large and encouraging order in 1912, from The Royal Mail Steam Packet Company. Orders from other British shipping companies followed at intervals, while foreign concerns also began to display an interest in the apparatus. One effect of the HMHS *Rohilla* hospital ship disaster was the placing of a large number of orders for line throwers – devices for throwing lines to remote positions – from the Admiralty. *Rohilla* ran aground in October 1914 near Whitby, North Yorkshire, with the loss of 92 lives (*National Archives*). The *Rohilla* had no line throwers of its own.

In 1920, he discarded a gun in favour of a pistol-rocket apparatus. He registered his new Schermuly Pistol Rocket Apparatus (SPRA) Company in 1926. The factory (Spra Works) operated from Haredon House, 810 London Road, North Cheam, south of Morden, and the original ship-to-store rocket was first tested in the fields of a neighbouring farm (1927). An Act of Parliament came into force on 1 January 1929 making compulsory the carrying of line-throwing appliances in British-registered ships of more than 500 tons.

His factory, opposite the Lord Nelson pub, moved from North Cheam to Newdigate, Surrey (Spa Works) in 1937 because North Cheam –

The demonstration at North Cheam on 25 March 1927 of Schermuly's line-throwing pistol. A line was accurately thrown 350 yards, and representatives of the Board of Trade and shipping companies were present. Courtesy of Newdigate Local History Society

Captain William Schermuly. Courtesy of Newdigate Local History Society

countryside 100 years ago – became surrounded by suburban housing developments too close for safety. Greater space was needed, too; the North Cheam district offered little chance of expansion.

Once again, the hurricane of war swept the world, but this time it found the Company established firm as a rock, ready for whatever share they were to be called upon to take in the gigantic task that lay ahead.

The Biography of William Schermuly compiled by C.R. Thompson

Prominent among the wartime products designed and made in the Newdigate factory, which was surrounded by woods and consisted of a very large number of small buildings, were target indicator bombs and illuminating flares. At the peak of wartime production, there were around 1,400 employees. By 1973, SPRA was taken over by the Wilkinson Sword Group and amalgamated with Pains-Wessex. The Newdigate works closed in 1981. Today, the site is Becket Wood, a housing development.

William Schermuly died at Sutton in January 1929. His granddaughter Alice Palmer lived in Garth Road, Lower Morden in 1982, according to an article in the local *News*. On his gravestone is an engraved sailing ship and the inscription 'HOMEWARD Bound'. It also remembers his son Rifleman William Louis Schermuly (1885–1917), London Regiment, who was killed in action at Salonika, Greece on 8 April 1917. He is buried at Karasouli Military Cemetery, Greece. It also remembers William Schermuly's wife Susan, their daughter Rose Sparkes (d1966), and their grand-daughter Rose May Banks (d1972).

Gravestone of Augustus William Louis Schermuly. (Author)

Further research

The Biography of William Schermuly and the History of the Schermuly Pistol Rocket Apparatus, written in 1946, is available on *pyrobin.com*. It includes tributes from Admiral Lord Mountevans KCB, DSO, LLD and Captain HTA Bosanquet CVO RN. Bosanquet, a member of the Committee of the Marine Society and later its secretary, said: 'After the First World War and during the last decade of his strenuous life, he was able to take things more easily when his three highly gifted sons came into the picture, each of them endowed with a large share of their father's inventive genius and dogged pertinacity.'

CHAPTER EIGHT

Calling All Workers

Deans

Before the Second World War, Deans at High Path, close to the Lines'
factory, made rag books and soft toys. It soon converted to war work. Deans
made life jackets and soldiers' stripes and was so overwhelmed with work
that apparently it was quite common for women to take work home. Despite
this, war production was popular with the workforce because the pay was
better than for toys. Although supervision was strict, *Music While You Work*
was introduced and working relations were good. Overtime and basic pay
improved so that the single girls could enjoy quite a good social life in their
hard-earned leisure time.

The BBC instituted *Music While You Work* in 1940, following a
government suggestion that morale in industry would be improved if there
were daily broadcasts of cheerful music piped into the factories. The concept
was for two half-hour programmes each day, one at 10.30am and the other
in mid-afternoon. It was felt that the best programmes were those which
made workers feel inclined to whistle or sing along. The music would have
to broadcast through a tannoy system and to compete with factory noises, so
the BBC insisted on a fairly constant sound level, plenty of familiar tunes,
nothing too slow and nothing very fast. The first programme was on Sunday
23 June 1940. During the war, many factories were in production throughout
the night (particularly munitions), so a third edition of *Music While You Work*
was introduced in 1942, at 10.30pm. This programme of broadcasts lasted for
the duration of the war. BBC executives were quite sure that *Music While You
Work* had helped to win the war – there was apparently a 13 per cent increase in
production during the times of transmission. *Music While You Work* featured a
weekly (sometimes twice-weekly) slot for brass and military bands, including
all the Guards bands, the Royal Artillery, the Royal Engineers and the RAF
Central Band among others. War produced a great revival in interest in band
music throughout Britain.

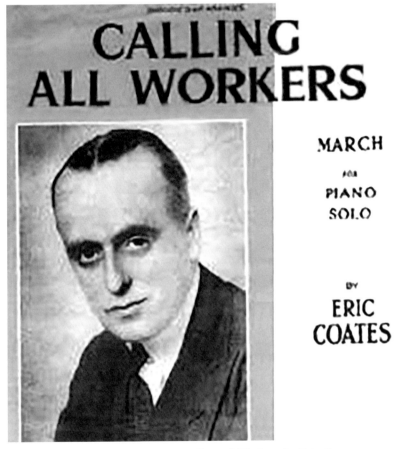

The stirring theme tune was called Calling All Workers *by Eric Coates.*

Decca

The gramophone manufacturer and record producer Decca was sited at Burlington Road, New Malden, in the southwest corner of Merton (closed 1980). During the Second World War, Decca was approached to manufacture the hyperbolic radio navigational aid that became the Decca Navigator System, which allowed ships and aircraft to determine their position by receiving radio signals from fixed navigational beacons. In turn, this led to the creation of the company Decca Navigation, at New Malden in 1946. The system was shut down in Europe in 2000.

Liberty Print Works

Arthur Liberty's works (closed 1970s), Merton Abbey Mills, produced thousands of yards of hand-printed silks. Liberty – a household name in fabric design – continued to print throughout the war, although on a much reduced scale, but it did have an unusual success with a Varuna wool headscarf.

David Luff in *Trouble at Mill*, published in 2002 by the *Merton Historical Society*, said:

> During the war, headscarves had a boost in popularity, due to the cinema newsreels, which were showing our recently-acquired east-European allies, the women of whom all seem to be wearing them. To fulfil the ladies' desires at a time when silk had become a very scarce and expensive commodity, Liberty introduced the woollen one. They became an instant success and, being far cheaper than silk, the ladies could buy more of them.

William John 'Bill' Rudd (1925–2014), who worked for Morden Post Office until September 1985, published a booklet for the *Merton Historical Society* in 1993 entitled *Liberty Print Works, Wartime Remembrances*. Bill started work at Liberty Print Works on 27 December 1939 when he was 14; he worked as a tier-boy/tray-boy, it was a messy job and he started at 7am and finished at 5.30pm each day. With no works canteen, meals were limited to sandwiches from home or fish and chips from Merton High Street. He said:

> I bought tea from Morden Woolworth stores and tins of condensed milk. One day, with tea going on the ration, I went back in the shop for another 2oz packet – and lost my bike. Three days later, I got two weeks' summer holiday pay, 41/6d – and lost a ten shilling note. My mother, worried about my not getting enough to eat, brought hot meals well wrapped up, all the way from home, which I found most embarassing. The problem was solved by the opening of a British Restaurant in a church near South Wimbledon Station serving meals at reasonable cost to local workers.

Liberty's Block Shop was where all the print blocks with their pattern numbers were stacked on shelves. A two-storey building, it later had ground floor extensions at each end. The extension at the north end was built as an air raid shelter. The south end was used, if only in part, as an ARP Wardens' post manned by some of the Liberty workers.

As the war progressed, the staff situation became acute with eligible men being called up for military service. Some printing was done on Saturday mornings. On Saturday, 28 March 1942, Bill had to attend an interview under the Youth Scheme published by the Board of Education on 22 December 1941 under which boys born between 1 February 1925 and 28 February 1926 were required to register. He joined the Civil Defence as a cycle messenger and reported to the Civil Defence Headquarters in Kingston Road, Merton on 1 April 1942. He was issued with a steel helmet and a gas respirator, and received a metal lapel badge and the navy blue uniform with appropriate gold lettered cloth badges on 15 August 1942. He said:

> The worst part came during the night alerts when I had to race on my single-speed roadster with shielded lights from home in Easby Crescent, Morden to the HQ in the blacked-out roads. The anti-aircraft guns were no real comfort as jagged metal fragments would clink and spark all over the place. You were fairly safe if the shell-burst was directly overhead as the fragments fell outwards. Other than that, I never, fortunately, saw active service when the bombs fell.

Bill joined up in November 1943 and served until 1947, when he returned to the St Helier estate. Bill's sister, who left school in December 1940, worked for the British Rototherm thermometer manufacturers in Station Road, Merton Abbey. She later worked for Coxeter & Son, who made anaesthetic apparatus, in Lombard Road. Early in 1943, Bill's father fire-watched with his neighbours; his mother joined the WVS, headquartered in Crown Lane, Morden, and regularly donated blood; and his sister joined the Girl's Training Corps.

Merton Abbey Works

In 1881, William Morris (1834–1896), born in Walthamstowe, best known in his lifetime as a designer (this is how he is described in Fiona MacCarthy's book about him), took over an existing factory at Merton Abbey, on the banks of the River Wandle, on what was practically open country (nearest tram stop Phipps Bridge Station). The complex included several buildings and a dyeworks, and the various buildings were soon adapted for stained-glass making, textile printing, and fabric, tapestry and carpet-weaving. His works should not be confused with those of what is now Merton Abbey Mills which was Littler's Factory when Morris took over the Merton Abbey Works. The Morris Works are now covered by the Sainsbury's/M&S complex and on the west bank by Trellis House care home.

'At the Merton Abbey works, Morris paid his workers higher than average wages, supplied a library for their education, a dormitory for the apprentice boys and provided work in clean, healthy and pleasant surroundings,' according to *mertonabbeymills.org.uk*. Sadly, the works no longer exist. The company closed down in August 1940. They were then badly damaged during the war before the site was purchased by the New Merton Board Mills, who then demolished the building to make way for an extension to their mills. (Source *Wandle Industrial Museum*)

The *Tatler* reported on 13 November 1940 that there had been a great revival in tapestry work since the air raids began,

> as an artistic relaxation from the knitting and more prosaic forms of needlework connected with war comforts and supplies, to which so many hours are given. Needlework is a centuries-old remedy for nerves, and women standing by for night duties are stitching elaborate patterns like those worked by the ladies in medieval times while their men-folk fought on the battlefield.

New Merton Board Mills

New Merton Board Mills, adjacent to the Wandle, erected in 1923 and demolished in the 1980s, was one of the largest cardboard making firms in England. On 25 November 1942, a fire started at the Mills which burned for sixteen days. Fortunately, according to D. Timmins, a director, it had been confined to a waste paper store, so the main plant and mills were not affected and production continued as usual.

Movies at Merton

With the outbreak of war, production at Publicity Films, Kingston Road, Merton Park – or Merton Park Studios – went over to armed forces training material and to propaganda films. In 1943, the cutting rooms were extended to cope

Long Lodge, now offices, was the headquarters of Merton Park Film Studios. (Author)

with the volume of work required. No bombs fell on the studios, although there were incidents close by, notably a flying bomb at Cliveden Road, Wimbledon. At the end of the war, the studios continued with peacetime information and educational films and returned to advertising work. (*Merton and Morden The Official Guide*, Merton and Morden Urban District Council, 1957).

Smiths

In terms of aviation instruments and sparking plugs during the Second World War, Smiths contributed more to this effort than any other British firm, according to *A Long Time in Making: The History of Smiths* by James Nye. Smiths Industries bought KLG spark plug factory on the A3 (Portsmouth Road) at Putney Vale – between Wimbledon Common and Richmond Park – in 1927. In 1937, construction of a new and larger factory here commenced. A further Smiths factory was soon under way at Treforest, South Wales and in operation in early 1940. According to Mr Nye, 'The Putney Vale main factory was camouflaged from mid-1940. Though it was never hit, captured documents show that detailed target photographs were issued to Luftwaffe crews, and at least one high explosive bomb landed remarkably close'. More than 13 million spark plugs were made during the Second World War, many used in Hurricane, Spitfire and Lancaster aircraft (*Kingston Aviation Heritage Project – kingstonaviation.org*). The Putney Vale factory was demolished in 1989 and replaced by an Asda supermarket.

Vortexion

Vortexion of Wimbledon, formed in October 1936, was a notable British manufacturer of public address amplifiers, mixers and tape recorders. It traded from 182 The Broadway, Wimbledon and expanded a little further along the road into premises at 257-263 The Broadway. By 1937, its first portable amplifier was introduced under the Vortexion brand name, capable of operating from the mains. With the outbreak of war, Vortexion found itself under the direction of the government for war work (see *ferrographworld. com*). The original factory on the Broadway was disposed of in early 1976.

Early version of the Vortexion 'Wimbledon' amplifier. (ferrographworld.com)

CHAPTER NINE

The First Bombing of Wimbledon, 1940

During air raids, the ARP Wardens patrolled their areas. As soon as an incident occurred, they would report details to their ARP post, from which the information would be passed to the Control Centre at the Town Hall. Where fire was involved, they could call directly to the Fire Brigade. The work of the various services at the incident was usually coordinated by the warden. But when damage was widespread, an Incident Officer would be sent from the Town Hall to take charge. The report, known as an *ARP/M1* Wardens Message Form, gave the location, details of the incident, an estimate of the number of casualties, the extent of the damage and the services required. Fire-fighting equipment, ambulances and light and heavy equipment would then be sent as necessary. This process was later speeded up by the introduction of an *Express Report,* which preceded the *ARP/M1* and gave only the location of the incident and the need for ambulance or fire service.

Tuesday, 13 August 1940

• This was *Adlertag* (Eagle Day), the first day of the Luftwaffe's campaign to force Fighter Command out of the south-east corner of England within four days, and destroy the RAF within four weeks.

Thursday, 15 August 1940

• The Luftwaffe launched a series of raids aimed mainly at RAF bases.
• During the first bombing raid on Greater London, originally intended for RAF Kenley, Surrey, Croydon airfield (which at that time was a fighter drone) was hit. Neighbouring Purley Way factories took the worst of the bombing. The British NSF factory, which made electrical components, was almost entirely destroyed, and the Bourjois perfume factory gutted. The Rollason Aircraft Service factory was also hit and accounted for many of the sixty-two civilians killed. (There was a mass burial at Mitcham Road Cemetery, next to Mitcham Common).

From their observation post high on the roof of Wimbledon Town Hall, the ARP Wardens on duty could clearly see white vapour trails in the blue sky and then a massive pall of drifting smoke, during the 15 August attack on Croydon airfield.

(Source *Surrey at War*, Bob Ogley)

Colin Perry, an 18-year-old living with his parents and brother Judd in Wimbledon when the bombing began, wrote a war diary. It was published as

---

WARDEN'S REPORT FORM.

A.R.P./M.I.

Form of Report to Report Centres.

(Commence with the words)	**" AIR RAID DAMAGE "**

Designation of REPORTING AGENT
    (e.g., Warden's Sector Number)

POSITION of occurrence

TYPE of bombs :—H.E.   Incendiary   Poison Gas

Approx. No. of CASUALTIES :— .
    (If any trapped under wreckage, say so)

If FIRE say so :—

Damage to MAINS :—Water   Coal Gas   Overhead electric cables   Sewers

Names of ROADS BLOCKED

Position of any UNEXPLODED BOMBS

TIME of occurrence (approx.)

Services already ON THE SPOT or COMING :—

Remarks :—

(Finish with the words)	**" MESSAGE ENDS "**

ORIGINAL } These words are for use with a report sent by messenger.
DUPLICATE }   Delete whichever does not apply.

Form of Report to Report Centres.

Boy in the Blitz in 1972. The following was recorded by Colin, whose father was a journalist, on the evening of 15 August 1940:

> Overhead a hum of aircraft became audible, and I looked upwards into the slowly-setting sun thinking to see a 'Security Patrol'; then I saw three whirling planes, and Alan yelled, 'Look! See them, it's a German!' and by God it was. I tore hell for leather to the top of our block of flats, and standing on the window-sill of the hall-landing I looked out over Surrey. Yes, thunder alive, there over Croydon were a pack of planes, so tiny and practically invisible in the haze, and – by God! the Hun was bombing Croydon airport. I yelled down to Mother, roused the Court, 'Look, Croydon's being dive-bombed' and I rushed to commandeer my excellent vantage point. Machine-guns rattled over the still air, and there only a few miles away, bombs commenced to drop. At last, the war was here! At last I was seeing some excitement. Anti-aircraft guns threw a dark ring around the darting planes, Spitfires and Hurricanes roared to battle. A terrific cloud of smoke ascended from the town; two more fires, obviously slight, rose on the wind. Boy this was IT!
>
> I munched an apple and went out armed with my enviable story. I didn't get far though, for a whine, fluctuating, grew from affair to a sudden deafening crescendo. Only the air raid sirens. Hell, they were a bit behind time, the damn raid was over. Least I was convinced it was, and it happened I was proved right. Still people were not to know that, and all the milling throngs calmly drifted to their nearest shelter. The wail died away, and the roads, practically deserted, made way for a police car speeding along the Upper Tooting Road at something like 80 mph complete with a whirring, piercing siren. Just like G-men on the films, I thought. The wardens efficiently took up their action stations, and I, well as I still sat munching my apple on the steps, thinking well at last a bit of excitement had hit the everyday routine. My one regret was I had to be an onlooker; boy, if only I had been in one of those Spitfires – oh Hell! those planes got me; I must be a pilot!
>
> Well, I hardly imaged that my journal would ever bear such an interesting story. I would mention that I was absolutely the first person in the whole of our district to spot the raiders and definitely the first by far to witness the actual bombardment. Naturally, all the papers will be hot on the trail. By God why on earth didn't I phone to the *Express* an eye witness view of the bombing? Hells bells I might have got my name in the paper. Ah, well, it's too late now.

Friday, 16 August 1940

At 5.20pm on Friday, 16 August 1940, a number of German bombs were dropped along Merton High Street and Kingston Road, killing fourteen people and injuring fifty-nine.

(Source *The Wimbledon Society*, 16 August 2013)

The bombs were small, only 50kg, and they fell roughly along the line of Merton High Street and Kingston Road. Houses in Cecil Road and Montague Road were wrecked. In Palmerston Road, all houses from No 72 to 106 and from 101 to 115 were damaged. In Russell Road, No 86, 131 and 143 were hit by bombs and all houses from No 47 to 113 were damaged by blast. A car standing in the road burst into flames. Bombs falling in Gladstone Road caused damage to No 74 and No 84 to 116 and to houses on the other side of the road from 107 to 137.

(*Safe as Houses*, Norman Plastow)

Wimbledon Tyre Company, on the corner of Kingston Road and Montague Road, took a direct hit during a raid that day, and heavy clouds of black smoke were produced by the burning rubber. Another fire was started at the nearby Berne Motor Company premises in Kingston Road.

There was a direct hit on No 135 Hartfield Road, Merton Park; a doctors surgery and all the houses from No 131 to 157 and 158 to 168 were badly damaged. In Graham Road, No 120 and 122 were partly demolished. A 9-year-old girl, on her way home from Dundonald School, died from her wounds later that night. A 14-year-old boy returning to Graham Road also died from his wounds.

A bomb also fell on the railway line behind Kingswood Road, Merton Park. Electricity cables and gas and water mains were damaged and some roads were closed by craters or debris. Amid the chaos, the Civil Defence Service arrived to take victims to hospitals and first aid posts. Policing too was needed to fend off ghoulish sightseers and property looters. (Source *The Wimbledon Society*, 16 August 2013)

Auxiliary Fire Service fireman Charles Tompkins of Southfields lost his life at Bathurst Avenue. Wimbledon ARP Warden John Stacey (1888–1940) of Dorset Road, Merton Park died in Brisbane Avenue, and Wimbledon ARP Wardens George Cowin of Bayham Road, Morden and Percy Thomas Whisker (1891–1940) died on duty in High Path, South Wimbledon.

Thomas Arthur Whitaker of Rougemont Avenue, Morden was injured on 16 August at West Barnes Lane, New Malden. He died the same day at Wimbledon Hospital. Also on 16 August, George Warwick of Cannon Hill Lane, Merton Park died at Iron Foundry, Kingston Road, and Ronald Henry Victor Thompson, son of Mr and Mrs Thompson of Bournemouth Road, Merton Park, died at Kingston Road. Frederick James Brook died at 17 Kingston Road. Hilda Caunt died at 143 Russell Road. (*WWII Civilian Deaths* from CWGC database).

Many Wimbledon people who lost their homes, or had been evacuated from houses that were damaged or near unexploded bombs, were taken to the Rest Centre at the YMCA. Similar respite was offered at the Parochial Hall.

The ARP Wardens were wary about letting evacuated people back into their homes, for fear of delayed action bombs. At least two delayed bombs did blow up on Saturday morning (17 August 1940), but the locations of these were not reported. Other bombs failed to explode, one for example being found near the Tooting railway line outside Merton Park station on Sunday (18 August 1940). The Royal Engineers dealt with unexploded bombs, except in the case of parachute mines, which were handled by the Royal Navy. However, it was found that there were so many reports of suspected unexploded bombs that a great deal of time was wasted in investigating false alarms. It was decided, therefore, to form a corps of reconnaissance officers who were trained to recognise and identify unexploded and delayed action bombs. In Wimbledon, two ARP Wardens were trained as Qualified Reconnaissance Civil Defence (QRCD) officers: George Ball, the Chief warden who succeeded Sir Patrick Kelly in this post in 1940, and Mr Polak, a district warden.

CHAPTER TEN

Peter Kenneth Walley

Pilot Sergeant Peter Walley (1919–1940) went to school in Sutherlands Grove, Southfields where he became captain of the school rugby team. He was killed on Sunday, 18 August 1940 at 1.30pm when he steered his crashing Hurricane aircraft away from housing during an air battle and landed in Morden Park on the spot where South Thames College (Merton Campus) now stands.

Peter Walley's second cousin Mike Squires, who was born and grew up in Wales, knew Peter's mother Dorothy well. He said:

> Peter was my Aunt Dorothy's only son. Her husband, George Walley, [Peter's father] died as a long-term result of gassing in the First World War when Peter was only 13. Dorothy raised Peter in Croydon on her own. He was an apprentice and a very good sportsman.
>
> Peter was a member of 615 County of Surrey Squadron of the RAF and was stationed at Kenley from where he took off to defend the airfield against a German attack on the 18th of August 1940.
>
> He was shot down but instead of bailing out of his crippled aircraft he remained in it and tried to land it in Morden Park in order to prevent it from crashing on houses. He reached the park but by then the plane was out of power and speed and crashed heavily in the park, killing Peter. The site of his crash is only a matter of yards from where the new college was built and opened in 1972. Residents of the area voluntarily raised a subscription to have the bronze plaque made which commemorates Peter's act of bravery in order to spare others. It was unveiled in 1972 at the opening of South Merton Technical College by Group Captain Leonard Cheshire VC of Cheshire Homes fame. Peter's Mother, my Aunt Dorothy, was at the unveiling. Peter gave

Photo of Peter Kenneth Walley at 7 years of age. (Mike Squires)

Photo of Peter Walley after getting his 'Wings'. (Mike Squires)

his life for those on whom the plane would have crashed, possibly killing and injuring many others.

The events of 18 August 1940 were remembered in 1999 by Charlie Jenkins:

I remember the young Spitfire pilot, he was in the aircraft coming down and on fire and he crashed into Morden Park. I flew down there and it was burning. There was ammunition going off. I think he wasn't very old. I think he was about 21/22. He steered the aircraft to miss the estate; he stayed with us instead of bailing out.

(*Reminisces of St Helier Estate*,
St Helier Estate Reminisce Group,
1999)

In 2010, Mike Squires and his wife Glynis laid a wreath on Peter Walley's grave at Whyteleafe. There was already a wreath on his grave with a poignant

EWS, W/E May 19, 1972

ECHNICAL COLLEGE IS OFFICIALLY OPENED BY HESHIRE, VC

V £1 MILLION Merton Technical College, which was begun in 1969 its first students last September, was officially opened on Saturday Captain Leonard Cheshire, VC.

so unveiled a commemorative plaque to Sergeant Peter Kenneth he 19-years-old Battle of Britain pilot who bravely avoided houses n and crashed his plane, killing himself, near the college site in 'ark in August, 1940.

ash-landed
his death
others
ght live

The Mayor of Merton, Mr John Coombes, invites Group Captain Leonard Cheshire, to unveil the memorial plaque to Sgt Peter Walley. Pictured (from the right of the guard of honour) are the Rev Peter Dawson, Rector of Morden and College chaplain; Mr Scott; Mrs Dorothy Scott, Sgt Walley's mother; Group Captain Cheshire; the Mayor and the Mayoress, Miss Maureen Coombes.

Report of the unveiling of the plaque on 13 May 1972. (Mike Squires)

verse attached to it. Mike Squires said he and Glynis 'have met many people with whom we have become lifelong friends through our mutual pride in Peter'. Mike Squires laid flowers there again on 5 September 2016 and was accompanied at the grave by Tony Morris, who is his friend through their mutual interest in Peter.

The story of Peter Walley features in *Wings of Freedom* by Norman Franks (William Kimber & Co, 1980).

The letter below, from the Royal Ancient Order of Buffaloes (RAOB) Lodge, George Inn, Epsom Road, Lower Morden, is dated 9 October 1940,

R.A.O.B.

PRIDE OF MORDEN LODGE

GRAND LODGE OF ENGLAND.   No.7132.

Hon. Secretary.   George Inn,
                                                   Epsom Road, Morden.

                                                   August 21st, 1940.
Meeting every Monday at 7.45 p.m.

Sir Archibald Sinclair,
Secretary of State for Air.

Dear Sir,

          At a meeting of the above-named Lodge held on Monday August 20th which was attended by several Brothers resident in the Earl Haig Homes and L.C.C. houses (adjoining) I was instructed to write you, beseeching you to convey, or cause to be conveyed to the next-of-kin, their admiration and pride for the gallant Pilot of the Aeroplane which crashed on Sunday, August 19th at Morden.

          By what must have been to this gallant airman a super human effort, he managed to lift his crashing 'plane sufficient to miss by what seemed inches, the homes of the men maimed in the last war, and by his action avoided what might have proved to be a terrible calamity.

          To the relatives of this gallant Pilot, who we feel sure, gave his life in order that we might live, we extend our deepest sympathy and we would like them to know that all brothers on "The Link" reverently observed a two minute silence on behalf of this gallant soldier and gentleman.

                    On behalf of the above-named Lodge,
                       I remain,
                         Yours obediently,

                         (Sgd) H. Leake,

                            City Secretary.

A letter from the RAOB Lodge. (Mike Squires)

and it is in the possession of Mike Squires. It is addressed to Sir Archibald Sinclair, Secretary of State for Air and reads as follows:

> Dear Sir, At a meeting of the above-named Lodge held on Monday August 20th which was attended by several Brothers resident in the Earl Haig Homes and L.C.C. houses (adjoining) I was instructed to write you, beseeching you to convey, or cause to be conveyed to the next-of-kin, their admiration and pride for the gallant Pilot of the Aeroplane which crashed on Sunday, August 19th at Morden.
>
> By what must have been to this gallant airman a super human effort, he managed to lift his crashing 'plane sufficient to miss by what seemed inches, the homes of the men maimed in the last year, and by his action avoided what might have proved to be a terrible calamity.
>
> To the relatives of this gallant Pilot, who we feel sure, gave his life in order that we might live, we extend our deepest sympathy and we would like them to know that all brothers on 'The Link' reverently observed a two minute silence on behalf of this gallant soldier and gentleman.
>
> On behalf of the above-named Lodge,
> I remain,
>
> Yours obediently,
>
> (Sgd) H. Leake,
> City Secretary

Peter Walley was buried in Airman's Corner in St Luke's Churchyard, Whyteleafe, a village in the district of Tandridge, Surrey and is also commemorated on the war memorial in Rhyl, North Wales. Peter's grandfather, John Walley, lived in Elwy Street, Rhyl and this appears to be the reason why the names of both Peter and another grandson, Stuart Walley (who died in 1943), being on the memorial at Rhyl.

St Luke's Churchyard in Whyteleafe contains the graves of other airmen who were also stationed at nearby RAF Kenley and who died during the war. There were hopes (August 2016) for a new Airmen Memorial there.

(Peter Walley's details have now been added to *iwm.org*)

Flight Sergeant Leslie Riddy Milner (1910-1942) of Kingston was killed with his Pilot Officer Richard J. Stevens when his plane crashed in flames near Blennerhasset, northwest Cumbria on 23 September 1942. But they avoided all people and buildings in the village as they crashed. On 30 June 1943, memorial photographs of the two men were unveiled in Blennerhasset School presented by the parents of Stevens and Mollie Violet Milner, the widow of Milner. Milner is buried at Kingston-upon-Thames cemetery.

CHAPTER ELEVEN

The Blitz

The repeated bombing of London and its suburbs, 'the Blitz', lasted from 7 September 1940 to 11 May 1941. The first raids, towards the end of the afternoon on 7 September, were concentrated on the densely populated East End, along the river by London's docks. Wimbledon was struck on the night of Sunday, 8 September 1940. The bombs fell mainly around the station, the first landing on the District Line beside platform 1. Luckily, an approaching train managed to stop in time, although there were still nine casualties, including the driver. No 10 Railway Place, at the other side of the railway bridge, received a direct hit. Other bombs fell at the rear of Alexandra Road and Woodside.

The following night, Monday, 9 September, saw further bombing. An off-licence in Haydons Road, South Wimbledon received a direct hit, and seven people were killed. Another bomb fell at the rear of Haydons Road, while two bombs fell in Plough Lane near the junction with Durnsford Road. A football stadium (demolished in 2002) at the corner of Plough Lane and Haydons Road was the home ground of Wimbledon Football Club from September 1912 until May 1991.

Several other bombs fell on or near the railway track and in a garden at the rear of Queens Road, Merton Park, but these failed to explode. During the night of 10 September, bombs fell around White Cottage on Wimbledon Common – a private house within the woodland of the Common. Some houses in Haslemere Avenue and Dawlish Avenue were damaged by a delayed action bomb which fell in Wandsworth.

During the night raid of 11 September, incendiary bombs were dropped on Wimbledon Common. Anti-aircraft fire was exceptionally high during this raid. The Horse & Groom pub at 145 Haydons Road was hit by a shell. Other shells fell at Wimbledon County School for Girls in Merton Hall Road (Merton Park), at Wycliffe Road, and at the corner of Haydons Road and South Road. The following night, a bomb fell in Arthur Road, causing a crater and fracturing gas and water mains. Another fell nearby at Home Park Road. Other bombs that night fell in Crescent Gardens, Durnsford Road and in a playing field in Havana Road.

No bombs fell in Wimbledon on 13 September. However, anti-aircraft fire was again heavy. A number of shells fell, including at St Georges Road, opposite the Drill Hall. Two members of the Home Guard who were on duty at the Drill Hall were severely injured and died the following day (Saturday, 14 September) in Wimbledon Hospital. At the top of Wimbledon Hill, a shell landed at the junction with the Ridgeway and a fire was started at the Wimbledon Motor Works showroom. Two shells fell on Wimbledon Station. Shells also fell in gardens of houses in Victory Road and in Grove Road.

Terence Bertram Rosewell (1926–1940), son of Bertram Albert Rosewell and Mary Joan Rosewell, was a schoolboy killed in an air raid (his death was registered in September 1940). He was returning home from accompanying visitors to the bus stop when the siren went, and was killed while running back to his house. (Newspaper cuttings, photos and an article from the Wimbledon College magazine can be found at the Museum of Wimbledon, LDWIM00421).

On Sunday, 15 September – now known as Battle of Britain Day – the Luftwaffe launched two huge bombing raids on London. The RAF managed to scatter many of the German bomber formations, meaning that when the surviving bombers did drop their loads, they fell over a wide area and were less harmful. The RAF shot down sixty-one German planes and the RAF lost thirty-one planes. In Wimbledon, bombs fell in Gladstone Road and Palmerston Road, and two shops at the corner of Wimbledon Broadway and Stanley Road were demolished by bombs. A bomb fell in Effra Road and a shell fell near the corner of Haydons Road. Three shops in Haydons Road were destroyed (No 300 had been a baker's shop). Mr J.H. Young, an ARP Warden, was in Haydons Road at the time the bombs fell and helped people out of the debris. In recognition of his act of bravery on 15 September, he was awarded the George Medal, which had been instituted by King George VI in September 1940 to honour those who showed gallantry 'not in the face of the enemy'.

Also on 15 September, the south-west corner of Wimbledon Football Ground received a direct hit. Bombs also fell at the rear of Russell Road and Faraday Road, but without causing serious damage. An anti-aircraft shell fell through the roof of the public hall at Wimbledon Town Hall and exploded inside. Another exploded in the foyer of the Kings Cinema, Wimbledon Broadway.

On Monday, 16 September, several houses in Evelyn Road were caught in the blast of a bomb. Phillipe James Willoughby (1877–1940), an experienced musician, of Evelyn Road, and his wife Isabel Laura Willoughby (1878–1940) died at their home (No 53, according to CWGC). He was a musician in the J.H. Squire Celeste Octet. The *Manchester Evening News* reported on 23 September 1940:

A few days before, he had jocularly suggested to other members of the octet that if he were killed he hoped his friends would make a donation to a Spitfire fund rather than buy a wreath. His wish has been carried out and a donation of £3 has been sent to Lord Beaverbrook. When an air raid warning sounded, Mr and Mrs Willoughby decided to stay in the house. Their daughter went to a shelter. When the all-clear sounded, she found a huge crater where her parents' house had stood. He served in the Artillery in the last war. Though he was 63, he had pestered the War Office to take him back as an instructor. He was a man practically without fear.

During the war, *Gramophone* magazine, founded in 1923 and devoted to classical music, announced the deaths of many notable musicians. Regarding Phillipe Willoughby's death, it reported: 'An HE bomb destroyed his house in the night and nothing was found afterwards of Mr or Mrs Willoughby except part of his hand showing the indentations of violin strings on the tips of his fingers.'

Also on 16 September, Sarah Alice Bentley of 93 Gladstone Road died in an Anderson shelter at 93 Gladstone Road. In the evening of Tuesday, 17 September, a large bomb fell on the Lysol Chemical Works in Kingston Road, causing extensive damage, including destroying water and gas mains. A trench shelter belonging to the firm was hit and there were eight casualties. Houses over a wide area were damaged by the blast from this bomb.

An ARP Warden collapsed on his way to his post on Tuesday, 17 September at 3am, the *Wimbledon Boro' News* reported on Friday, 20 September 1940. Enoch Thomas Ollson of Manor Road, Merton was lying on the footway in Kingston Road. He was taken to The Nelson Hospital, Kingston Road, Merton but was dead on arrival. He was aged 50, and was apparently on his way to his post. The same issue reported that Malcolm McMillan and his wife Ursula McMillan (1893–1940), who had lived at 24 Albany Road, Wimbledon for a number of years, were buried at Fulham Old Palace Cemetery. They were two of the seven victims who were killed in the cellar of an off-licence during an air raid the previous week. They died at 308 Haydons Road.

There was considerable air activity on Wednesday, 18 September 1940: The first bombs fell on Cambridge Road, Wimbledon and people were evacuated to shelters in Holland Gardens, and a cluster of bombs fell around King's College School. A bomb landed in the garden of the headmaster's house at Woodhayes Road. In Alexandra Road, two petrol bombs started fires. Springfield Court in Springfield Road was hit by a bomb which demolished most of the blocks of four flats. Another bomb fell on the east sidings of the railway adjoining Alexandra Road. At the rear of Leopold Avenue, a bomb fell on open land. Small fires were started by incendiaries in the car park at Wimbledon Stadium, in Wandle Park and in Grove Road. On the night of

18 September, a land mine destroyed Wesleyan Methodist Church, Mitcham (*merton.gov.uk*). Because of the damage, the congregation joined that of the Cricket Green Church.

Bombing did not start until 11pm on 19 September when the first bombs fell at Melrose Avenue. Extensive damage was caused between Ashen Grove and Revelstoke Road by two bombs which landed in the road. In Queens Road, Merton Park, a bomb caused a large crater in the road and broke the mains. Nearby in Faraday Road, houses were wrecked by high-explosive bombs.

On 19/20 September, a Junkers 88 that had been hit by anti-aircraft fire flew low over South Wimbledon and crashed into two houses in Richmond Avenue, near the Nelson Hospital. Members of the local AFS watched the plane's descent, and had already set out before it reached the ground. They were on the scene within three minutes. While they worked on the flames, wardens marshalled residents of Richmond Avenue, Quintin Avenue in Merton Park and part of Kingston Road from their homes. The gunner, Wilhelm Schlake, had baled out and landed on a roof of a house in Clapham Park; the rest of the crew died and their bodies were never found. He surrendered and became a PoW. (*The National Archives*, Kew holds some records relating to enemy PoWs).

Immediately after the Junkers 88 crashed, a parachute and parts of the machine were collected and were placed on exhibition at a shop near Wimbledon Town Hall. Scores of people paid the 6d entrance fee towards the Spitfire Fund. Exhibits included the rear machine gun, with part of the turret attached, which fell in the garden of Woodside House, an oxygen helmet which was found in Gap Road, the parachute by which one of the airmen escaped from the burning machine, together with various other parts recovered from the wreckage.

On the night of 21 September, a high explosive-bomb fell on open ground at the junction of Hood Road and Beverley Avenue. Many hundreds of incendiary bombs were released in an area between Cottenham Park recreation ground and Wimbledon Common. Many failed to ignite, but the top floors of several houses were severely damaged by fire.

Nos 124 to 126 the Broadway received a direct hit on the night of 24 September 1940, destroying the buildings completely. Shops were badly damaged, as was the front of the Baptist Chapel, Palmerston Road. Incendiaries fell in the Durnsford Road recreation ground and on the banks of the Southern Railway adjoining. On 6/7 October, an oil bomb fell in a meadow on the south side of Barham Road. One high explosive and one oil bomb fell just before midnight on 8 October on the Royal Wimbledon golf course and four houses were damaged. On the night of 9 October, houses in Bathgate Road and Queensmere Road were damaged by bombs which fell in Wandsworth.

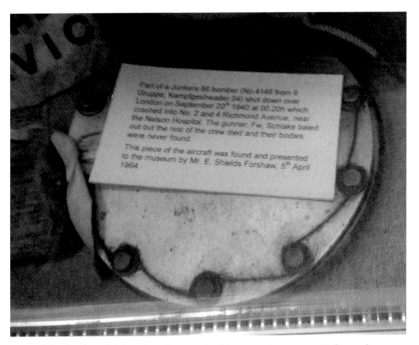

Part of the Junkers 88 bomber that crashed into two houses in Richmond
Avenue, found and presented to the Museum of Wimbledon on 5 April 1964.
(Author)

The major incident of the night of 10 October 1940 was caused by a parachute mine which fell at the rear of houses in Russell Road, damaging the buildings. High-explosive bombs fell at the rear of Haydon Park Road. Forty incendiaries fell in the Revelstoke Road area and a shell fell in Tennyson Road. St Mary's School was wrecked. Many houses in Pelham Road, the Broadway and Gladstone Road were damaged, and seven people were killed. ARP Warden Frank George Bird (d1940) died at 34A Russell Road (*WWII Civilian Deaths*). The bombers returned at 11pm on 11 October 1940, dropping their load on Florence Road and the rear of Faraday Road. In Compton Road, a bomb destroyed two houses. A bomb fell on a new block of maisonettes in Glendale Drive, Wimbledon Village, trapping five people. Two bombs fell at the All England Lawn Tennis Club, and high-explosive bombs fell in the Worple Road, Wimbledon area. All four ARP Wardens were seriously injured, and one died. Two other people were killed and eighteen injured. A bomb hit the Ironclad Mantle factory in Haslemere Avenue.

On Sunday, 13 October, the worst incident was at the United Dairies premises (now Dairy Crest), adjoining Gap Road Bridge. A large bomb fell close to the air raid shelter, trapping twenty-three people and killing four. Many people in Gap Road who were sheltering in basements were endangered by a large water main that burst under Gap Road cemetery. Altogether, fourteen people, including one warden, were killed and seven injured. On Wimbledon Common, a bomb fell in Cannizaro Park, south of Wimbledon Common, killing one person and injuring another. An oil bomb, which fell at the same time, landed in the grounds of Westside House, Wimbledon Village. Built in the early eighteenth century and now converted to flats, Westside House was the mansion house of Spencer Gore (1850–1906), first Wimbledon tennis champion in 1877.

Major George Arthur Edgar Panter was injured on 13 October at Canayaro Bungalow, Wimbledon Common, and died on 16 October at Wimbledon Hospital. His wife, Marguerite died on 13 October at Canayaro Bungalow. Edith and Gladys Ballard, Alice Beatrice Brownless, and Frederick Clyde Cartwright and Margaret Lilian Cartwright died at 59 Gap Road, and Victor Adey Beisley of Waldemar Road died at Gap Road. Alice Maud Mary Burrows died at Gap Road. (*WWII Civilian Deaths*)

On the night of 14 October 1940, Worple Road, Wimbledon was hit, and Railway Place received a direct hit. At the top of Wimbledon Hill, a bomb fell at the rear of Murray Road and another fell in the grounds of Lauriston House nearby. A delayed-action bomb, which landed on 14 October, exploded at

A plaque from the Gap Road premises of the Haygarth Witts Home which was saved from the building after it was bombed in 1940. It is in memory of Jane Lake Witts, Foundress of the Home. (Museum of Wimbledon)

midday on 15 October and destroyed a house in Oldfield Road. Oil bombs fell in Murray Road, Marryat Road, Dunmore Road and the grounds of the All England Tennis Club. These bombs detonated but did not ignite.

Soon after 7.30pm on 15 October, Worple Road was hit again. A bomb fell straight down one of the chimney stacks of the Southern Railway power station in Durnsford Road, demolishing it; fortunately the generators were not damaged. The power station supplied power to the Southern Railway's electric commuter trains. According to *Steaming to Victory: How Britain's Railways Won the War* by Michael Williams, the power station's capacity was reduced by 50 per cent as a result of that bomb: 'It was so badly damaged that it took 127 days to repair. Meanwhile, the trains had to run at even more of a snail's pace than usual, prolonging even further the journeys of commuters wearied by blackouts and bomb warnings.' An oil bomb landed in the grounds of Wimbledon High School; around 100 incendiary bombs fell in the area of Wimbledon Park and South Park and there was internal damage to the Haydons Road Baptist Church.

Shortly before midnight on 17 October, two bombs fell on the Sunlight Laundry premises in York Road, two at the rear of South Park Road, and another two on the Southern Railway Repair Shed (now the Wimbledon Traincare depot serving primarily South West Trains), off Durnsford Road alongside the Southern Railway power station.

On Saturday, 19 October, one high-explosive bomb fell on the Southern Railway main line, east of Durnsford Road bridge, derailing a train and killing one person. The next afternoon, bombs damaged properties in Merton High Street and Leyton Road. At 10.20pm, bombs fell in Cambridge Road. Bombs fell by the trench shelters in the children's area and the sports field of Cottenham Park recreation ground, West Wimbledon. These shelters were formed of concrete arches below ground level with an entrance which was approached by steps and screened by a blast wall. Timber-slatted benches lined the walls and the floor consisted of duckboards because of the water which seeped through. At the end of each shelter was an escape hatch reached by means of a steel ladder. These shelters still exist under the 3.2 hectare park which included tennis courts, although they have long since been covered over. Forty houses and two shops were destroyed in the area of Ashen Grove and Braemar Avenue, Southfields and houses were demolished in Revelstoke Road. Incendiary bombs fell again in the Haydons Road area, causing slight damage to St Peter's Church, a timber yard in Effra Road and several houses. The police had a problem recording the deaths that occurred during this raid, but Alice Emily Banks of Braemar Avenue died at 27 Alverstone Avenue, Southfields.

Bombs fell on the nights of 21, 22, and 24 October. On the night of 24 October, around 150 incendiary bombs fell in the Haydons Road area. Three high-explosive bombs fell on the Common. On 24 October, the funeral of ARP Warden Nicholas Joseph O'Dwyer (of Braemar Avenue), took place at Wimbledon Cemetery (Gap Road). O'Dwyer, formerly a member of the Royal Irish Constabulary, died while on duty as a warden. There was more activity on the night of 25 October. In Merton High Street, near the corner of Leyton Road, a large crater blocked the road, and gas and water mains were broken. Pieces of tramlines were hurled into the air. More bombs fell on 26 October: at the rear of Ridgway Place and at the rear of Kenilworth Avenue just before 10pm. A bomb fell in open ground close to Johnson Ward at the isolation hospital, Gap Road. Patients from two wards were evacuated to another part of the hospital. Many incendiaries fell in the area of Cannizaro, Westside, and Atkinson Morley Hospital, Copse Hill. On 1 November, a delayed-action bomb fell at 7.30pm in Burghley Road, Wimbledon Village. It exploded at 2.30am, killing two people. Bombs also fell that night in Wyke Road and at the junction of Montana Road and Arterberry Road. A bomb fell in the grounds of Margin House, Marryat Road. Bombs fell at the rear of Worple Road, Crescent Road and Lansdowne Road. Anti-aircraft shells fell on a path near Pitt Crescent and another in a garden at Wolsley Avenue.

CHAPTER TWELVE

The Single Worst Night of Bombing

Wimbledon's single worst night of bombing during the Second World War happened on 6 November 1940; no fewer than sixty-seven incendiaries fell within an hour. Each weighed a kilo (*Wimbledon Guardian*, 2 November 2012). Bombs fell on the Queens Road depot of Wimbledon Council, where a fire was started. Four ambulances, a mobile First Aid unit and three other vehicles were destroyed.

In Effra Road, Wimbledon, two bombs fell on Holy Trinity primary school, one passing through a first floor classroom and exploding on the ground floor. In the Broadway, a bomb landed in front of the Baptist Church at the corner of Palmerston Road, blowing away the front of the building. Almost directly opposite, in Stanley Road, one bomb destroyed a property and another scored a direct hit on the Seventh Day Adventist Church. In Haydons Road, two properties were destroyed by a bomb. A third bomb landed outside a doctor's surgery in Haydons Road. The Sunlight Laundry building was again hit and six bombs fell in the Haydons Road recreation ground.

A bomb fell in the front garden of a house in Cottenham Park Road; Christ Church, the church hall and surrounding houses were damaged. Three bombs fell in Copse Hill, south of Wimbledon Common. Six bombs fell in the grounds of Queen Alexandra's Court, St Mary's Road, Wimbledon Village, where residents were widows and unmarried daughters of servicemen. More bombs fell, one landing in Church Road, Wimbledon Village. Jane Emma Blesson and husband Louis Blesson died at 36 Faraday Road (*WWII Civilian Deaths*).

On Wimbledon Hill Road, two bombs fell simultaneously. A No. 200 single-decker bus was overturned by the blast and the driver, conductor and passengers were injured and taken to hospital. During the war, buses had to be borrowed from the provinces because hundreds of buses had been destroyed by air raids. Later, the government allowed a limited production of buses to re-commence. Because of the shortage of materials, however, the bus builders had to find ways of building adequate buses from low grade

Queen Alexandra's Court, Wimbledon, originally 'the homes for officers' widows and daughters'. Today, seen here, it is retirement property. Credit SSAFA

components. These 'utility' buses were built to strict austerity standards issued by the Ministry of Supply, a department of the government formed in 1939 to co-ordinate the supply of equipment to all three British armed forces, headed by the Minister of Supply. They were built using any available wood and metal left over from the war effort. Ken Blacker's *London's Utility Buses* (1999) tells the story of the 756 buses that made up the fleet of London's utility buses.

Not all the bombs that fell on the night of 6 November caused damage to property. A number fell on the Common near Westside House and another created a new bunker near the thirteenth green at the Wimbledon Park Golf Club, set around Wimbledon Park Lake, to the east of Wimbledon Common. A 1998 report from Glasspoole Thompson, commissioned by Merton Council, found it was silting up and the water was in an advanced state of eutrophication, according to Friends of Wimbledon Park. (For information about the Wimbledon Park Lake Project, visit *merton.gov.uk*).

On the night of 7 November, bombs fell on Wimbledon Common between Camp View and the woods by Warren Farm. A mixture of high explosives and incendiaries fell on the night of 10 November. The last bomb of the night landed on the piggery at Queensmere Road. Five incendiaries fell on Wimbledon on the night of 11 November. On 12 November, the first high explosive fell in Avebury Road, Merton Park. Two bombs which fell that night landed near Windmill Road and on Wimbledon Park golf course.

On 15 November, there were nine incidents involving incendiaries with high explosive attachments. Jane Ann Brayshay (d1940) died on 15 November at 6 Lindisfarne Road, Wimbledon (*WWII Civilian Deaths*); this house was completely demolished. Two bombs fell in Melville Avenue, Wimbledon. A bomb fell in a garden at Drax Avenue, Wimbledon, and two other bombs fell on Wimbledon Common. Brickfield Cottage, Wimbledon Common was wrecked. Anti-aircraft shells caused damage to properties in Springfield Road, Wimbledon and Glendale Drive,Wimbledon, and at the premises of Lighting Trades Limited in Ravensbury Terrace, Earlsfield.

Bombs fell at 6am on Sunday, 17 November and the worst incident was caused by two bombs that fell simultaneously. The first hit the front of a shop on Hartfield Road, Merton Park, which had been converted into a public air-raid shelter. The second fell in the roadway opposite, breaking a large gas main. Thirty-nine people had taken cover in the shelter; four were killed and another five seriously injured. Those who were not injured were taken to the shelter station at the Town Hall. On 19 November, bombs fell in South Park Road and Hamilton Road.

On 24 November, at 7.50pm, a bomb fell in Florence Road, and another at the junction of South Park Road and Haydons Road. Four properties on Haydons Road were wrecked, and there was damage to shops and houses in South Park and Cowper Roads. A bomb fell at the rear of North Road, and on allotments. Bombs fell again in the borough on the night of 3 December. Blast damage from a bomb on Wimbledon Park golf course was recorded in Home Park Road, Church Road, St Mary's Church and Vicarage, Arthur

The 2-ton bomb that failed to explode, 9 Dec 1940.

Road, Leopold Road, Wimbledon Hill Road, Somerset Road, Burghley Road and the High Street. Incendiaries also fell in Copse Hill.

Five high explosive bombs fell in Wimbledon on 8 December, including one that fell on Centre Court at the All England Tennis Club. Another fell on Gap Road Cemetery and at the rear of the Fire Station. Nearly 200 incendiaries fell on the headquarters of the rescue service at Queens Road School, damaging several ambulances. The nights were comparatively quiet after 8 December, except for the German 'Satan' 1,500kg bomb that failed to explode when dropped near Camp Road, Wimbledon on 9 December 1940 (see picture). On the night of 27 December, four bombs fell in the borough, and houses were destroyed and badly damaged. Two bombs fell on the Ark Engraving Company works at Ashcombe Road, Wimbledon. The two incidents on 29 December were caused by anti-aircraft shells; one fell down a chimney in Palmerston Road and exploded in a ground floor room. The sky that night was lit by the fires of London.

However, not all fatalities during air raids were caused directly by the bombing. Ernest Albert Rudman, aged 60, of South Road, Wimbledon, was crossing Wimbledon High Street on Friday, 13 September on his way to the air raid shelter when he was hit by a car and killed. Meanwhile, on the same day, the *Wimbledon Boro' News* reported that Mr Herbert, manager of the Odeon Cinema, Morden, stated that audiences had been well-maintained during the period of German air activity: 'Our practice, when an air raid warning is received, is to announce the fact to the audience by a statement on the screen pointing out that those who wish may remain, but that there is public shelter outside the cinema. Meanwhile, the show goes on.'

CHAPTER THIRTEEN

The Tower Creameries, 1941

There were no bombing incidents in Wimbledon throughout January 1941. A number of incendiaries fell in the north-eastern part of the borough on the evening of 17 February 1941. Small fires were started in Mount Road, Haslemere Avenue, Dawlish Avenue and Brooklands Avenue. Four weeks passed before there was any activity and then the incidents were caused by anti-aircraft shells. Again, a month passed with only occasional raids.

'B' Company 57th Surrey (Mitcham) Home Guard was based at Tower Creameries (still referred to today by some locals as 'the Margarine Factory') on Commonside East, Mitcham Common.

Three aircraft dropped bombs in the Tower Creameries area in swift succession, around 10.40pm on Wednesday, 16 April 1941, after a relatively quiet couple of weeks. One dropped a parachute mine, which landed in a back garden in Greenwood Road, close to the junction with Ivy Gardens, and fortunately failed to explode. The mine was defused by the Bomb Disposal Service (BDS) and removed by Admiralty workers on Thursday. Mr D. Atterbury, a senior ARP officer, was in Mitcham for much of the night. He was responsible for the Group 9 area, which included much of south-west London and north Surrey (from Kingston to Croydon) within No. 5 Defence Region, which covered London and its surroundings. He noted that 'unexploded bomb(s) necessitated the temporary evacuation of 3,000 persons from their homes. Rest Centres were called into operation and upwards of 1,200 persons catered for'.

A parachute mine fell on the Creameries, and thirteen members of the Mitcham Home Guard were killed: William Richard Aplin; Charles Albert Branch; James William Thomas Henson; William Jones (whose wife Clara returned to Whitehaven, Cumbria after his death); Joseph Stanley Kilbee; Charles James Labrum; Harold Francis Langbein; Frederick Albert Newstead; Frederick Thomas O'Brien; Walter Joseph Peacey; Richard John Sharman (who was just 17); George Stephen Taverner and Arthur Frederick White. The military gravestones to eleven of the men are in Mitcham Cemetery. Other 57th Surrey Home Guard members buried at Mitcham Cemetery are Sergeant Hugh Kenneth Forrester (born in Sutton and had also served in the First World War); and George Stephen Taverner, of 37 Lavender Cottages, Mitcham.

In memory of volunteer Frederick Albert Newstead who lived at 109 Abbotts Road, Mitcham. Photograph taken at Mitcham Cemetery, March 2017. (Author)

Two other men died at the Creameries: Aubrey Edgar Marriott, of 175 Wide Way, Mitcham, a member of the Red Cross Society, who was buried at Croydon Cemetery; and Frederick Percy Andrews, of 321 Commonside East, Mitcham, a fire watcher. Though not members of the Home Guard, they are accorded honorary membership of the 57th (Mitcham) Battalion, East Surrey Regiment, by their names being included on the bronze plaque erected to the memory of those who died that night.

Mr Atterbury said: 'The building caught fire immediately after the explosion, the margarine burning furiously, and the intense heat and ammonia fumes from the plant caused much distress and exhaustion to members of ARP services.' Under the heading 'Action of Services', he remarked that the incident was 'discovered immediately by wardens of post E1 who acted promptly and were instrumental in securing the release of the three survivors.' Strictly speaking, dashing into blazing buildings to rescue injured persons was the province of Rescue Parties and Fire Services, with their special equipment, and formed no part of an ARP Warden's brief.

The following is a personal account by William Bumstead, whose late twin brother John Bumstead was badly injured when the landmine fell on the Creameries:

> On Wednesday the 16th April 1941, during a tea time chat with my twin brother John, I asked if he was free that evening to join me at the 'shilling hop' in the Catholic School at the Cricket Green, with our mutual friend Teddy Smith. I even offered to pay his entrance fee!
>
> However, John had already agreed to stand in for a colleague on Home Guard duty at what was the Tower Creameries Factory (on Mitcham Common), and so sadly, he declined the offer to attend the dance.
>
> When John left school he started work at the Tower Creameries, Commonside East, and shortly after the Second World War began, John joined the newly formed Tower Creameries LDV (London Defence Volunteers), which eventually became known as 'B' Coy. 57th Surrey (Mitcham) Home Guard and Tower Creameries. He was a conscientious member of the unit always prepared to do his duty and to stand in for his colleagues.
>
> On that particular night John proceeded to the Tower Creameries, Ted Smith and I went on to the Wednesday 'Hop' dance, although times were not good, we still enjoyed ourselves amongst a host of good friends. Coincidently, John occasionally played the drums with a pianist named Len, backed up with gramophone records; there were no eight-piece brass bands available at the time.
>
> As the night progressed the air raid siren could be heard, in particular the one that was situated in the vicinity of the nearby police station, letting us know an air raid was about to take place. We were told by the organisers of the event to take shelter or make your way home.

I cannot be precise about the time we left the school hall to walk home; it would possibly have been between 10pm to 10.30pm. As we proceeded across the Cricket Green towards Cold Blows, I do recall there was little cloud in the sky; in fact it was a nice bright dry night only to be spoilt by the noise of the anti-aircraft guns having a shot at the enemy bombers and with the occasional whizz noise of shrapnel falling nearby. The anti-aircraft guns sited on Mitcham Common near Mitcham junction had come into operation, obviously, the German aircraft were in range and the likelihood of bombing taking place had intensified.

It was not long before the aircraft could be heard overhead, London and the surrounding suburbs were certainly in for a hard time that night.

Ted Smith and I proceeded along Cold blows pathway leading to Commonside West and crossed over to walk directly to the foot of Beehive Bridge. Before reaching the bridge, to the right hand side of the pathway there stood a huge tree, (quite magnificent) it was upon approaching the tree we spotted a parachute floating by, coming from the Cricket Green direction. As mentioned before it was a bright clear night sky and the visibility was good. The parachute passed over the train lines floating in the direction of Manor Road.

Ted and I, at the time, thought it was a parachutist bailing out from a plane that had been hit. That certainly was not the case, because one or two minutes later there was an explosion followed by a large red/orange ball of fire which appeared in the direction of the Tower Creameries site. Instinctively I knew that the Tower Creameries had been hit and naturally I was very concerned for the safety of my brother John.

Ted and I ran as quick as possible over the Beehive Bridge, Ted going into The Croft at the junction of Spencer Road where he lived. I continued along Commonside East finally reaching the factory, which was fully ablaze. The fire was being tackled by the Fire Brigade and Auxiliary Fire Brigade; indeed I take my hat off to those men, they did a tremendous job during those dark days, under very dangerous conditions.

I saw some of the victims being laid on the grass verge and footpath immediately in front of the houses that stood at the right hand corner of the site, quite separate from the main factory building. I was not able to find John. I asked somebody who was attending to the casualties if there had been anyone taken to the Wilson Hospital, he replied 'yes one or two'.

Unable to trace John, I immediately ran back along Commonside East to my home in Kings Road to break the news to our Mother and Father.

I explained what had taken place and said there is a chance that John may be one of those who had been taken to the Wilson Hospital. Straight away my Father and I hurried across Mitcham Common, the raid was continuing, the anti-aircraft guns still blasting away, with the occasional whistling noise of shrapnel hitting the ground around us as we made our way.

On reaching the hospital we made our way to the casualty department. As to be expected it was full of people; people on stretchers and trolleys, with doctors and nurses attending to the injured.

We looked around trying to find John, when suddenly I spotted someone on a stretcher having their head/face and arms bandaged, with great relief I said to my father 'that's John over there', pointing to the left hand corner of the ward. I recognised the colour of my shirt which he had borrowed that night to go on Home Guard duty.

My father walked towards the nurses as they starting pushing the trolley out of the casualty ward towards the main part of the hospital. He was allowed to see him for a short while then we had to leave, John was still unconscious.

We returned to the hospital the next day. John was able to talk a little; he had suffered severe injuries to his face, arms and legs which were heavily bandaged.

I learnt some time later, a lady colleague (I'm unable to recall her name) and John were on one of the Towers when the blast from the landmine explosion threw them on to the East side of Mitcham Common. It was at this location where First Aiders of the St. John's Brigade heard calls for help and went to their assistance. It was said at the time; as soon as a bomb explosion was heard the First Aiders would speed on their cycles to the area involved, arriving in a matter of minutes to render first aid. Through their promptness and dedication I feel sure this lady and John were able to survive. Unfortunately the injuries the lady sustained included the loss of her leg.

Sadly a Home Guard named Fredrick Arthur White who lay in a nearby bed to John died during the night. He was actually the Officer in charge of the 'B' Coy 57th Surrey (Mitcham) Home Guard and Tower Creameries.

Like many of the Home Guard personnel, John underwent surgical operations including skin grafting for quite a period of time. The injuries took their toll John suffered with ill health for the rest of his life. Nevertheless he made the best of things, enjoyed a joke, loved music and always helped people whenever he could.

Many local people were affected by the bombing on that night in April and I would like to refer to a letter written by Mrs L. J. Nicholls (surname formerly Bunce) which she wrote in response to a letter by Mr John Prince in the *Wimbledon Guardian* on 30 March 2000 entitled 'What happened the night the Creameries was bombed'.

Extract from Mrs L. J. Nicholls letter:

I was waiting for my husband to come home from the Army, as I was a very young woman with a baby and expecting another child, naturally I was very nervous. So the woman next door said come in with me. We stood on her doorstep looking up at the sky and we saw a plane's parachute coming down. Well I think the Home Guards thought it was a German soldier on the end of it; they went towards it but it was a land mine that caused the explosion and they were caught in the thick of it.

Incidentally, another parachuted landmine landed that same fateful night in Greenwood Road in close proximity to the Tower Creameries. Fortunately the chute was caught in a tree and the mine did not explode. The Army were able to diffuse the mine thereby saving a considerable amount of lives.

This all occurred over 70 years ago and yet for those who experienced these events they still remain very real. I know I speak for many who were there on that evening in April 1941; our hearts go out to all those who suffered that evening.

They will always be remembered. William Bumstead

The third aircraft dropped three big bombs without causing casualties: one on back gardens in Castleton Road, another on the Common south of the Creameries without exploding and a 500kg one not far from that one which did go off, leaving a crater 14m across and 3m deep in the gravel.

Tower Creameries was previously a telegram-cable factory – known in 1867 as the India Rubber Works – built before the Act of Parliament of 1891 that protected Mitcham Common. Tower Creameries was rebuilt in 1944 as part of the Windmill Trading Estate. The Mitcham Home Guard memorial plaque was unveiled in 1962 in the re-built Tower Creameries building entrance lobby by Colonel S.W. Barber, Deputy Lieutenant of Surrey.

The plaque commemorating the 15 killed was reinstated in St Mark's Road, Mitcham in December 2012.

After Tower Creameries ceased business on the site, the buildings had other light industrial uses. The buildings were completely empty in 1996 and, as a result of vandalism, the memorial plaque was removed and placed in the Royal British Legion building in St Mark's Road, Mitcham.

The whole site was demolished in 2009 for a current mixed tenure of housing apartments. The Notting Hill Housing Trust agreed to have a memorial wall at the front of the new development on the site of the Creameries. A plaque, a replica of the one in the Royal British Legion building, was unveiled by children of The Sherwood School and William Bumstead at a service on Friday, 14 December 2012.

Reverend Jane Roberts from the Ascension Church, Pollards Hill in the borough of Merton, led the service which opened with a short prayer. William Bumstead read his short history of the plaque and a representative

The plaque in April 2016. (Author)

from Notting Hill Housing gave a short speech about the building of the development.

Reverend Roberts read out the fifteen names on the plaque and Allan Barley from the British Legion read the Exhortation. This was followed by an affirmation by a pupil from Sherwood School. Richard Watts played the Last Post on the bugle and there was a minute's silence. This was followed by the laying of wreathes by Mayor of Merton David Williams, and Allan Barley. A wreath and twenty-four wooden poppy crosses were presented by the twenty-four pupils from the School Council of Sherwood School and the crosses were placed in two large wooden boxes that were placed underneath the plaque and Allan Barley recited the Kohima Epitaph: 'When you go home, tell them of us and say, for your tomorrow we gave our today'. The schoolchildren had composed and memorised the following poem which was then read out loud by them to the group:

On Duty At The Tower

The night was quiet
   And all were asleep,
   Except the Home Guard
   On duty at the Tower.

Something fell from the sky,
Something from another country,
Something not friendly.

Crash,
Bang,
Flash,
And the Tower was ablaze.

People shouted,
People screamed,
People helped,
People died.

We are here today to think of those
Who died that night,
The people of the Home Guard
On duty at the Tower.

Also on 16 February 1941, a bomb fell into a garden in Worple Road, Wimbledon; it failed to explode. At 9.25pm, a Heinkel bomber, heading in the direction of Wimbledon, was hit by anti-aircraft fire and burst into flames. The crew baled out over south London and the plane flew on until it dived into the garden of 15 Denmark Avenue. On 8 May, an aircraft crashed on the Royal Wimbledon golf course; the crew (four) did not survive.

The night of 10-11 May 1941 witnessed the most destruction on the capital throughout the Blitz. Over 1,000 tons of bombs were dropped on the capital, resulting in the loss of nearly 1,500 lives and destroying 11,000 houses. Many of the 2,000 fires blazed out of control as the low tide and fractured water mains deprived the firefighters of water.

Wimbledon escaped lightly with four people killed and six injured. A bomb which fell in Hartfield Crescent, Wimbledon demolished houses and wrecked railway carriages in the nearby sidings. Bombs fell at the rear of Burghley Road, Wimbledon Village and at the Burghley Road junction with Marryat Road. Two more bombs fell in the car park of the All England Lawn Tennis Club and another in Oakfield Road, Wimbledon, damaging several houses.

CHAPTER FOURTEEN

The Sinking of HMS *Hood*

Acting Flying Officer Dennis Alfred Briggs DFC lived in Lower Morden Lane. Early on 25 May 1941, the British forces lost contact with the German battleship *Bismarck* after she had sunk HMS *Hood* (24 May 1941) in the Battle of the Denmark Strait. She was rediscovered late morning on 26 May 1941 by Briggs, the captain of the *Catalina Z* flying boat, despite bad weather. Briggs's report to Coastal Command – 'Have sighted enemy battleship' – sent hope. At 7.24pm, the Admiralty sent an orientation on *Bismarck's* position to every officer, NCO and seaman on board the British warships that were in pursuit.

The DFC was awarded to Briggs in September 1941. The *Wimbledon Boro' News* reported on 3 October that the distinguished artist Maurice Codner (1888–1958) had painted Briggs's portrait, to be added to the *National Portrait Gallery*, and that he was one of three brothers serving with the Forces. 'His brother Basil is a captain in the RASC at Singapore, while his younger brother Rex is at present in Florida, USA, training as a pilot.' It is not known whether it actually went to the *National Portrait Gallery*, it does not appear to be there now.

The German Battleship Bismarck. Public domain.

The *Wimbledon Boro' News* of 3 September 1943 reported that Briggs had been awarded the Bar to his Distinguished Flying Cross: 'During convoy escort duty during March 1943, his prompt and daring action caused three Focke-Wulf Kurriers to break off an attack on the convoy without damage either to the ships nor to his own aircraft.'

In 1941, Ernest Leonard Harvey from Wimbledon volunteered for the Royal Marines, following a childhood interest in the Sea Cadets. He had always been drawn to the armed forces following in the footsteps of his brothers and father who had both served in the Army. Within months, he was drafted to HMS *Suffolk* and was aboard on the night that *Bismarck* was spotted. He recalled in 2015:

> *Bismarck* was sighted. The alarm sounded and all crew were informed. I was a gunner at the time, manning and alternating between the eight-inch and four-inch guns. We were all aware of the sinking of HMS *Hood* and the huge loss of life. I considered myself to be very fortunate that I was still alive.

Suffolk had radar and continued to shadow *Bismarck* and report her position. After the war, Ernest Leonard Harvey returned home and to Bennett's (picture framers) of Wimbledon. He had no problems obtaining employment or housing.

DFC Dennis Briggs. With thanks to John Asmussen.

This bell was recovered in August 2015 from the depths of the Denmark Straits and subsequently preserved for display at the National Museum of the Royal Navy. With thanks to HMS Hood *Association*

A special parade and presentation of a dark-blue beret was made by the Royal Marine Reserves (RMR) at Wandsworth Barracks in June 2015 to recognise him. Sadly he died just before Christmas 2015; he didn't quite make 96.

Of 1,415 *Hood* crew members, there were only three survivors. Petty Officer Alfred 'Ted' Edward Pryke Briggs MBE (1923–2008) of Derby, who settled in the south of England in 1973, was the longest living survivor. The others were Able Seaman Robert Tilburn (1921–1995) of Leeds, and Midmanship William John Dundas (1923–1965) of Perth, Scotland. They were rescued by the destroyer *Electra*. Many officers and men of *Hood* had given her five, ten or even twenty years of service, and the sinking was the Royal Navy's largest loss of life from a single vessel. There is a Book of Remembrance in St John the Baptist Church, Boldre, Hampshire.

Ordinary Seaman Herbert Reginald Dyment (1912–1941) of Arthur Road, Wimbledon Park was lost in the HMS *Hood* sinking. In his last letter home, he told his mother Helen he was having a very happy time, and he appeared to have a bright future before him in the navy. He was centre forward for the Authentic Football Club, which played at Craven Cottage (Fulham) in the late 20s and 30s. He also played in the Fulham & District Cricket League, and the Paddington & Kensington Cricket League. He was married a few months before the sinking of *Hood*. He and his wife, Louisa (Vera), had one son, Alan, who was born after the sinking of *Hood*.

Men lost in the *Hood* sinking also include:

- Able Seaman William George Cleeter (1897–1941) born in Merton to Frederick and Susan Cleeter and lived in Wimbledon (1911)
- Francis Bertram Coulthurst (1919–1941) married to Lizzie Coulthurst of Mitcham
- Wireman John Frederick Cox (1917–1941) born in Wimbledon (Victory Road) to Robert and Ruth Cox
- Chief Stoker Frederick James Hobbs (1895–1941) born in Mitcham to James and Alice Hobbs
- Leading Stoker George Frederick Keal (1912–1941) born in Wimbledon to Ernest and Hope Keal of Walton-on-Thames
- Stoker 2nd Class Edward Alfred Percy Moore (1916–1941) only son of Alfred and Lily Moore of Mitcham
- Frederick Charles Murray (1920–1941) born to Henry and Alice Murray of Earlsfield
- Able Seaman Jack Arthur Punter (1919–1941) whose family lived in Merton Park
- Ordnance Artificer 5th Class Noel Stevenson (1920–1941) born in Wimbledon
- Chief Petty Officer Edward Arthur Herbert Watts (1905–1941) born in Wimbledon to Ernest and Emily Watts, married to Elsie Watts of Fareham, Hampshire. His first service date was 12 August 1918; the first ship he served on was HMS *Ganges*.
- Ordinary Seaman John Verdun Wilson (1916–1941) married to M. Wilson of Mitcham

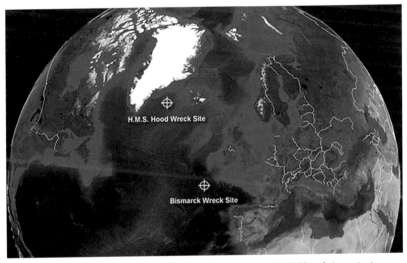

HMS Hood *and* Bismarck *wreck sites, with thanks to HMS* Hood *Association.*

The ROH plaque in its final resting place.

A Roll of Honour plaque, containing two specialised digital Rolls of Honour in Compact Disk format, serves as the grave marker for each of the 1,415 men who died. It was unveiled by David Mearns, an American-born UK-based marine scientist and oceanographer, at the May 2001 HMS *Hood* Association reunion. Ted Briggs, the last living survivor of *Hood's* sinking, pressed the button which released the plaque over the site of the *Hood's* last resting place.

On 26 June 2018, *Hood* veteran Commander Keith Evans (1919-2018) died, aged 98. He served on *Hood* from 1 January 1938 to 3 January 1939. He was a pupil at Pangbourne College in Berkshire and lived in Haslemere, West Sussex. He attended the unveiling of the ship's bell at The National Museum of the Royal Navy, Portsmouth in 2016.

CHAPTER FIFTEEN

Life Became Grim

Apart from a few anti-aircraft shells, no incidents were reported in Wimbledon between May 1941 and February 1944. Attitudes had hardened and life became grim; there were constant reminders of the raids. Most of the shop windows in Wimbledon Broadway had been blown out and had been replaced by plywood or boarding. The blackout was rigidly enforced and identity cards and gas masks had to be carried at all times. Petrol was strictly rationed and every journey on official business had to be accounted for and recorded. Almost all foods were rationed. Books were in short supply. The Civil Defence Services had to stay on the alert and all posts had to be manned.

In the Old Pound near the Wimbledon War Memorial, a concrete pillbox had been erected and rows of posts stood across open spaces to prevent aircraft or gliders from landing. Every week, the *Wimbledon Boro'News* listed people who had been fined for infringing blackout regulations.

British Restaurants – communal kitchens created in 1940 to help people who had been bombed out of their homes, had run out of ration coupons or otherwise needed help – were set up across the country. The first in Wimbledon was opened in Holy Trinity Church in October 1940, and reasonable meals could be had there for as little as a shilling. Miss C.M. Dolamore, born in 1919, was supervisor of the whole of the restaurants under control of Wimbledon Council. One was opened at 103 The Broadway by Lady Asquith on 22 May 1941. Meanwhile, housewives from St Helier were frequent visitors to the Food Advice Centre at North End, Croydon. The Ministry of Food's Advice Centres, which started opening on the main streets of larger towns from Spring 1941, offered free advice and wartime recipes. According to *Blood, Sweat, and Toil: Remaking the British Working Class, 1939–1945*, by Geoffrey G. Field (2011), Food Advice Centres got a 'mixed reception from working-class women who mostly lacked the time to attend the sessions; and those who did go often criticised the recommended dishes as too finicky and time-consuming and sometimes too expensive.'

Other British Restaurants in 1941 were located at 182 Merton High Street; 82 Coombe Lane, Raynes Park; the Day Nursery, Montague Road, South Wimbledon; South Wimbledon station; Legion Hall, Newminster

Road, St Helier; 138 Grand Drive, Raynes Park; and the large hall attached to the Congregational Church in Morden Road, South Wimbledon. (The church seems to have closed some time before 1957, possibly because of destruction during air raids in 1940).

The first British Restaurant in Mitcham was opened by Lady Robertson, wife of MP for Mitcham Sir Malcolm Robertson (1877–1951), and the kitchen was run by an instructress from the Wimbledon Technical College, according to *merton.gov.uk*. The Friar Tuck was one of the six British Restaurants set up in Mitcham during the war, and was decorated with murals depicting the various stories of Robin Hood and his Merry Men.

'Indoor Andersons Not Approved', read a headline in the *Sutton Times & Cheam Mail* on 1 March 1941:

> While the concreting of Anderson shelters is proceeding at Merton and Morden, it was reported at a Council meeting on Friday that a number of applications had been received for Anderson shelters to be erected indoors. In view of the report that the shelters would not have the same effectiveness if erected in this way, the Civil Defence Committee confirmed the Surveyor's proposal that this work should not be undertaken by the Council. The Committee agreed that where the shelters have already been erected indoors by householders, a special inspection is to be made in order that instruction may be given with regard to the proper use of the shelters.

Housewives queuing for eggs outside Gardner's Butchers shop, Arthur Road, Wimbledon Park, c 1941.

The Morrison shelter, introduced in March 1941, was the result of the realisation that due to the lack of house cellars it was necessary to develop an effective type of indoor shelter. The shelters came in assembly kits, to be bolted together inside the home.

CHAPTER SIXTEEN

1942 and 1943

The *Wimbledon Boro' News* reported on 9 January 1942 that Wimbledon's Warship Week's aim was 'to raise the purchase price of HMS *Havelock* (1939)'. *Havelock* was an H-class destroyer, built in Cowes, that had originally been ordered by the Brazilian navy on 8 December 1937, but was bought by the Royal Navy after the beginning of the war. She survived the war but was approved for scrapping on 18 February 1946.

A British Restaurant was opened in January 1942 at Wimbledon Park Hall (a community hall), Arthur Road, by Lady Woolton, whose husband Lord Woolton (1883–1964) was Minister of Food between 1940 and 1943.

Soap rationing came into force on 9 February 1942 with an allowance of 4oz of household soap or 2oz of toilet soap per person per month.

As a result of the air raid on Sunday, 10 January 1943 (the first German night raid on London since 10/11 May 1941), there was a return to the Tube shelter at South Wimbledon station. On Monday, 11 January 1943, forty people were already there, including several children; many brought their bedding with them. Although the underground trains were going past at regular intervals, they were peacefully asleep.

The *Wimbledon Boro' News* of 7 May 1943 reported that Wimbledon had won a trophy for best NAAFI (Navy, Army and Air Force Institutes) canteen. The canteen was a Nissen hut (location not given). The Wimbledon Civil Defence Service Trophy was won by Miss W. N. Hines, a Civil Defence auxiliary nurse at the Club First Aid Post, 1943.

A salvage exhibition was held on a Saturday in February 1943 at Elys, showing how waste material from home, office and

Lord Woolton, the man who fed wartime Britain.

Wimbledon Park Hall, Arthur Road today.

Women line up outside a butcher shop to buy meat on London Road, North Cheam, south of Wimbledon, on 17 April 1942, near the present-day Sainsbury's supermarket.

factory could be converted into munitions. It was organised by Wimbledon Corporation and showed, for example, how discarded pots and pans might form parts of the planes which carry bombs to Germany. The *Merton and Morden News* reported on 19 March 1943 that ARP worker Mr H. Wheeler of Kingsbridge Road, Morden made a model steamroller from waste. It was awaiting transport to the London Region Civil Defence Exhibition from 20 to 27 April. A pram wheel served as a driving wheel.

In May 1943, a British Restaurant was opened at Ivy House, Motspur Park. Opening the restaurant, actress and theatrical manager Phyllis Neilson-Terry (1892–1977) said: 'Tell your friends to come to these restaurants; it will save you trouble, time, food and fuel. You will be able to sit down and relax, have a nice meal and get that rest which will give you extra energy to go on with your war effort.'

Also in May 1943, Wimbledon 'Wings for Victory' week had the target of £350,000 enough to purchase seventy fighter planes. By midweek, £356,504 had been raised, and the final total was £730,000. When Councillor Drake sent Sir Stafford Cripps the last £400 of the £500 for a Spitfire, he was told it would be called *Wimbledon*.

The *Wimbledon Boro' News* of 25 June 1943 reported that an old couple who lost all their belongings by enemy action (and who have been living in an institution) were among the new arrivals at Wimbledon Home for Old People, 6 The Downs.

CHAPTER SEVENTEEN

1944 and the First Flying Bomb

The raid that occurred on 4 February 1944 in Wimbledon came as a shock. It had been so long since there had been any serious air raids that everyone was taken by surprise. Only five bombs fell and one of those, which landed at the rear of All Saints' Church, Wimbledon, failed to explode. But they were large bombs and damage was widespread. Twenty-seven houses were destroyed, forty-eight seriously damaged, with a further 320 suffering minor damage. This was the first of the hit-and-run-raids. They generally involved only one or two aircraft that flew over, dropped their bombs and fled for the coast.

On 18 February 1944, a bomb scored a direct hit on Nos 5 and 6 The Downs, Catholic homes of rest for the elderly. All available rescue teams were called in and they worked in four-hour shifts throughout the night. More ambulances arrived from the Richmond area. In the early hours of the morning, the rescue workers were stunned to see a group of nuns from St Teresa's Hospital, further down the road, arriving to help. Each nun had the hem of her habit tucked into heavy rubber boots and was wearing a steel helmet. The following day, rescue teams from Mitcham were called in to help. Five of the residents had been killed and another twenty-two injured. Local Girl Guides helped to salvage wheelchairs and personal belongings.

The shockwaves were so great that several of Wimbledon College's windows were shattered, doors were broken, and the ceiling of the swimming pool caved in. In summer 1944, therefore, it was arranged that candidates for the Higher Certificate and School Certificate would take their exams in Mount St Mary's College, Derbyshire. According to the BBC's *World War Two People's War* archive, the college was the only school in the Wimbledon area whose pupils in 1944 actually sat and passed their High Certificate and School Certificate.

King's College was hit on the night of 18/19 February 1944. The bomb destroyed a hut housing the Junior School Library, severely damaged the gymnasium and caused the loss of much of the glass in Great Hall and South Hayes. Mr Dann, the housemaster of Glencairn wrote: 'Not a boy was hurt as much as a scratch, I have always believed in miracles.'

On the night of 19 February 1944, a bomb fell on the grass verge at the edge of the Common and demolished Oakholm, an eighteenth-century house on Southside conveyed to Joseph Arthur Burrell (1849–1926) in 1890. The

Damage at King's College. (Author)

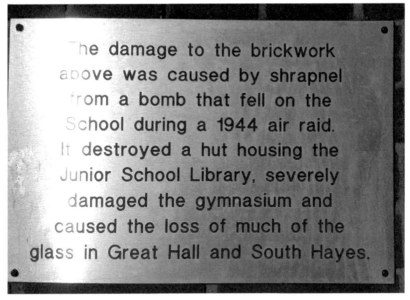

The damage to the brickwork above was caused by shrapnel from a bomb that fell on the School during a 1944 air raid. It destroyed a hut housing the Junior School Library, severely damaged the gymnasium and caused the loss of much of the glass in Great Hall and South Hayes.

Plaque outside King's College. (Author)

house was not occupied at the time. Firewatcher Gavin Berry died at 1 Inner Park Road. Winifred Mary Brooks and Elizabeth Brown died at 5 The Downs. William Herbert Carter of Raynes Park was injured at Oakholm Cottage and died the same day at Wimbledon Hospital (*WWII Civilian Deaths*). He may have been the gardener.

The following, written on 21 February 1944, is taken from the wartime diary of Fred French, born in 1888 in North Lambeth, of Chestnut Drive, Raynes Park and is entitled 'Wimbledon High Street bombed'. His diary was blogged seventy years later by nephew Tony.

> Very cold, very dull, driving bitter east wind. Warning from 3.25 to 3.55am. The Wimbledon Common guns fired a few rounds at very long range in an easterly direction. An enemy plane came down in last night's raid at Selhurst Station. Bombs fell in Wimbledon High Street last night. I cycled to Wimbledon to buy fish, haricot beans and window fasteners, the latter have been missing since the bombing. While there, I saw signs of blast but did not see where the bombs actually dropped. Mr Luccock called to make arrangements for a prayer meeting here on Wednesday evening.

Shortly before 10pm on 24 February, an anti-aircraft shell exploded in the forecourt of Wimbledon station. Shortly after midnight, Mr Ball, the Chief ARP Warden, was called out to investigate a suspected unexploded bomb that

*The nameplate from Oakholm (No 11 Southside) at the Museum of Wimbledon.
(Author)*

had fallen in the army campsite near the Windmill (the sails turned on occasions until the beginning of the Second World War). He found a crater around 6ft deep and 15ft diameter. From scraps of evidence found in the crater, he was able to establish that it was an unexploded 1,000kg bomb.

Mile End was hit by the first V1 flying bomb to strike London.

'Some debris from a bomb on the nearby golf course actually landed on the Centre Court,' said an official of the All England Tennis Club on 23 March 1944, 'but it was soon cleared away and no damage was done to the rich turf. Windows were smashed in the Royal room and clubhouse.' Another bomb made a small hole well clear of the courts. (*Lincolnshire Echo*, 23 March 1944)

On Tuesday, 27 March 2012, a brother and sister with metal detectors unearthed an unexploded Second World War pineapple hand grenade, without its locking pin, near to the Windmill. Bomb disposal experts carried out a controlled explosion.

The first V1 missile or V1 flying bomb – also known to the Allies as the buzz bomb or doodlebug – fell on London on Tuesday, 13 June 1944. It hit the railway bridge which carried the Great Eastern Railway across Grove Road, Mile End, East London. The bridge was badly damaged, as was the railway track. A number of houses were demolished and six people were killed. The V1 itself was a small aircraft, constructed almost entirely from thin sheet steel, which produced a characteristic stuttering roar when running. The airflow over its nose turned a small windmill. After this had rotated a pre-set number of times, the fuel line to the engine was cut and the missile fell to earth, where its 850kg warhead exploded. John Clark, who contributed to the BBC's *WW2 People's War* archive in 2003, said:

I can remember the first day of the doodlebug attacks on London and the south-east of England absolutely clearly because it was one of the two occasions during the war on which I was really frightened. I was on Wimbledon Common with two friends when the sirens went. We didn't take much notice as there hadn't been a daylight raid for years; we thought it must be a false alarm. Then we heard a very odd aircraft engine noise and suddenly all was let loose. By this time London had enormous numbers of anti-aircraft gun and rocket batteries all over it, including a naval gun turret on the Common a few hundred yards from where we were. It seemed as though every gun and rocket in London was firing at this 'attacker' but the really frightening thing was the sound of the shrapnel from the spent anti-aircraft shells hissing through the air all round us. We dived into a ditch and lay there with our hands over our heads for what seemed ages.

The strange engine noise became louder and then suddenly stopped. We looked up in time to see an odd looking plane dive into the ground a mile or so away with a huge explosion. We heard on the news that night that large numbers of people had been injured by shrapnel – many more than the bomb. It was soon realised that it was no good trying to shoot the V1s down over London as they'd explode when they crashed anyway, so rapidly all the moveable guns were taken to the south coast to try to catch them over the sea.

My second moment of terror was one evening when a friend and I were out on our bikes. We heard a doodlebug and set off towards the nearest public shelter. Just before we got there, the engine cut and we were certain it was right overhead. We hurled ourselves through the door of the shelter on to the floor followed by a man with the same conviction. Fortunately for us, the V1 fell about half a mile away and we were only shaken.

Victor Spink told me:

In June 1944, we children were blissfully unaware of the V1s which were about to change our lives. The war had been quiet on the home front for some time and my friends and I would play in the deserted side road of Craven Gardens, Wimbledon. I was the youngest at 6 years old. When the shock of the doodlebugs came later in that month, our school in Trinity Church Infants School in Effra Road was closed until further notice because of the bombardment.

At this point I would like to pay a tribute to the many men and women who ran the organisations responsible for the air raid warning systems. These people have been largely overlooked by history, but their prompt actions saved so many lives by giving us children enough time to run from playing in the streets to our shelters. For 24 hours a day they activated the air raid sirens with the 'alert', and the welcome 'all clear'. We just took it for granted that someone was looking after our welfare.

Some of the mums in our road went out and did part time jobs, so the arrangement was that the mums who were home would leave their front doors open so we kids playing in the road could run into the first open door near to where we were playing, and dive under the steel Morrison table shelter in the dining room, dog and all. The mothers who were off work would just naturally look after all of the streets kids who played together.

The 1944 V1 attacks persuaded many families to leave Merton. John Clark (then aged 14 or 15) and his brother Michael were once again evacuated to

Part of a V1 flying bomb (middle right) which fell in Wimbledon. (Wimbledon Museum)

their grandparents, who were then living at Abergavenny in Monmouthshire. In June 1944, Ronald Weeden (then aged 11) and his family were evacuated (his second experience) from Monkleigh Road, to Harrogate in Yorkshire. They returned to Merton when hostilities quietened down.

There were intense V1 raids on Saturday 17 June 1944; sixteen people were killed in Cliveden Road, including Edith Florence Brice, WVS. At 1.17am on 18 June 1944, a V1 damaged the Vickers Armstrong works on Belgrave Road, Mitcham. Almost all the casualties occurred in five adjacent houses in Homewood Road. A special investigation was made as aircraft components formed its entire output. Employing 230 people on night and day shifts, all production was lost for two days, due to the corrugated asbestos roofs having been demolished. There was no other damage to structure or machinery. There was another investigation when a V1 fell at 10.03am on 20 July 1944 near the Bryant Cartons factory in Church Road, opposite Aberdeen Road, which made cardboard packing cartons for the Ministry of Supply and the Ministry of Aircraft Production. With about 200 employees, there were no casualties to staff, who were in shelters, having received an 'Immediate Danger' warning from the roof spotter. The main damage was to the roof and the machinery was not damaged. Victor Spink, who lived at 65 Craven Gardens, told me:

In the middle of one particular bright morning my mother was a few doors up at No 61 (Craven Gardens) with an old lady called Mrs Adams whom she was comforting because of the frequency of the over flights of V1s. There was hardly any time at all between the 'All Clear' and the next 'Alert' sirens, and this went on for 24 hours a day. This was the period before the ACK guns were moved down en masse to the Kent coast. On this morning the air raid siren was sounding the 'Alert' from the roof of the Police Station in Queens Road. We kids were playing British and Germans in the street, so we ran directly to our doorway but not to inside the house because mum was not there to call us in.

Then we heard the racket of a V1 coming up from the direction of Mitcham. Four of us still stood on the front door step and as the noise got louder we covered our ears. We watched it as it swiftly appeared over the roof tops on the other side of Craven Gardens, and as it had just passed over our heads my mother came running down the pavement like mums do on school sports day parents races. She had her skirt lifted up showing her knees and thighs which I had not seen before. She swept us all up into the back room and under our Morrison shelter as the bomb stopped. Her head was under the table with us but her rear poked out in the room as there was not enough room for her as our Alsatian dog had got in under first. This bomb exploded next to the main railway line near to Gap Road Bridge and damaged terraced houses at the end of Landgrove Road. Our back windows were blown out, and all our family knickknacks fell off the Edwardian fireplace and broke. After she had calmed us down, Mum got some brandy which was kept in a medicine bottle with sticky paper round the cork and took that up to Mrs Adams.

The Nazis knew of Hore-Belisha's hideaway at Old Warren Farm and 'Lord Haw-Haw' promised to bomb it. In June 1944, when RAF pilots shot down two flying bombs, the second one hit the farm, landing on Hore-Belisha's bed. Then on 19 July, a V1 rocket damaged most of the buildings. He and his young wife Cynthia, a volunteer ambulance driver who had previously been captured by the Germans in France and imprisoned for four years, were away at the time.

St Helier Hospital was struck twice. A V1 landed in the morning on 21 June 1944 and injured many nurses who then became patients in their hospital. Six days later, another V1 struck the hospital and two died. St Matthew's Church, Durham Road, West Wimbledon received a direct hit and was destroyed at 8.55pm on 29 June 1944. The Reverend at the time was Robert Eke. Designed by Sebastian Comper, St Matthew's Church was built after the war to replace the earlier church.

In his wartime diary, Rutlish pupil Derek Pugh wrote on 1 July 1944: 'Spent as much time as possible revising Solid Geomatry theoreums [sic] (for Matriculation). It has also been a hectic day for 'doodle bugs', and as I write this four have come over together.' On 13 July 1944, he wrote: 'Chemistry

Bomb damage at the St Helier estate, 1944. (Merton Heritage and Local Studies Centre)

Practical Exam, in the Chemistry Lab – doodle bugs only slightly affected my work.' A month later, the Science Building was destroyed by a V1 direct hit. The chemicals in the Science Building kept the fire burning for three days.

A V1 fell in Southey Road on 10 July 1944; one girl was killed and seventy people injured. On 14 July 1944, a V1 destroyed the home of Albert Dunning (8) in Fortescue Road. In his book *Childhood Memories of Colliers*

Wood and Somerset, Albert Dunning wrote: 'Luckily we all managed to get into the Morrison shelter in the front room and this saved our lives. We stayed at the rest centre at Mitcham Baths until the authorities decided to evacuate us again.' This time they went to Mr and Mrs Wheatcroft in Carlton, a suburb of Nottingham, where they stayed until the end of the war in Europe.

On 17 July, Victor Spink and his brother Grahame were evacuated to an unknown destination 'Up North', which turned out to be Keighley. Many buses took children from Effra School and other schools, 600 children in total, from Wimbledon Station and from the top end of Alexander Road opposite Maynard's confectionary and tobacconist shop to King's Cross. The train journey from King's Cross to Bradford took five hours and, after another bus ride, the children ended up in a school hall in Keighley. Following a bad start for a couple of weeks on a council estate, Victor and his brother were transferred to Leeds. Victor Spink told me:

> At Kings Cross, we said goodbye to our mother who had come with us (Victor and Grahame) to see us off. The organisers were very wary of so many children in one place because there were doodlebugs about, and no shelter. Grahame was 11 and I was 6. Off course we did not want to go because my Aunt Gladys worked in the Foreign Office as a typist, and our lodger Jack Smith worked in the top secret bombproof Naval Citadel on Horseguards Parade as an electrical mechanic, so we got to hear of the war news from Whitehall at our Sunday afternoon tea sessions.
>
> We arrived at Bradford and were bussed to Keighley. My mother had given Grahame strict instructions that we must not be parted. We were

Some of the congregation of St Matthew's Church holding an open air service in front of the ruined church. (Merton Heritage and Local Studies Centre)

put in a school hall with beds, and some children were fetched off to their billets that evening. We were taken the next morning to 4 Braithwaite Avenue, Keighley, on a council estate where we were billeted for about a fortnight or three weeks. I have no recollection of the people there which has been blotted from my memory. We were allowed to run wild and separately while they went out to work. Bed wetting was normal. I came back one day mid-afternoon and was locked out. I was busting to go to the toilet so I defecated in the back garden and was barked at by next door's dog while doing so.

I must have been seen by neighbours and reported because we were taken from there by the billeting officer and taken to 39 Granby Drive, Riddlesden, near Keighley, to Arthur and Mary Bottomley who were a childless Christian couple and who had an adopted teenage girl called Brenda Spinks. The billeting officer persuaded Mrs Bottomley on the doorstep that as she already had one Spinks she might like to take two more.

We were treated with great kindness by all concerned. The house garden backed onto the Leeds and Liverpool Canal, and we were taught to fish in it by 'Uncle Arthur' using a jam jar and bread. Mother came up for a few days over the Christmas period. Bed wetting was still the norm. We skated down the frozen canal in the severe winter of 1945. We must have gone to the local school in Riddlesden but I have little recollection of it except we used slate boards to write on.

Arthur had been in the Home Guard and would walk us up to Rombolds Moor and show us where the field telephones were housed in the stone walls and where beacons were built and lit on the high grounds at night to confuse the Luftwaffe. Arthur was a foreman in a local wool mill and I went to see him on the mill floor at work with the clatter of the giant machines, and I took home some hard wooden bobbins which looked like peashooters. Uncle Arthur was a better father to me than my old man, and could not have been nicer. He was a veteran of the Great War, and we would polish his collection of army badges from that era. He would make us toys and take us by bus to Bradford to have tea at 'Busbys' department store. I think one of the Bottomleys cut our hair because when we got home our family complained of our pudding basin haircuts. We returned home just before VE Day.

I regarded and still regard the Bottomleys with great affection. In 1946, I went up and saw them again during the summer holidays. We kept in touch until Brenda got married when we were sent wedding photos, and we exchanged Christmas cards for a few years after that. I only know of one other evacuee and who is older than myself, and she is now senile.

Six people were killed on 21 July 1944 when a V1 destroyed many houses in Wilton Crescent. On 22 July 1944, Frances Caroline Anker, WVS, and husband Henry George Anker died at 9 Wilton Crescent.

Today, the name Spring House is attached to a group of flats on the north side of Kingston Road between Mayfield Road and Wilton Grove. Until 1935, the title belonged to an early Georgian brick house of five bays standing opposite Church Lane. Mayor of Wimbledon, Alderman T.J. Daniel, had a lucky escape on 27 July 1944, according to *Spring House in Merton* by John Wallace (1996). Daniel's house (Llanderis) was the second up from Spring House on the west side of Mayfield House. Passing from his scullery, he heard a V1 in the distance and shortly afterwards saw it glide into the flats (Spring House flats, formerly Spring House). All the ceilings in the house fell in and the mayor was hit on the head by a falling floorboard. He then found his garden under water because the large mains had burst. The bomb hit as people were returning from work, but how many casualties occurred is not known. At least four people were killed; Joseph Henry Simpson's body was recovered from flat 8 at 7pm. The following day, Eric Victor Ireland, his wife Lilian and daughter Barbara were found dead in the wreckage of the shelter at the back of the flats.

An old lady was killed in the Whatley Avenue bombing on 10 August 1944. Fred French wrote in his diary: 'She was one who would never go into a shelter, yet Anderson shelters in the gardens of houses completely destroyed are intact. There are still people who think they are safer in houses than in shelters.'

Overall, between 16 June and 28 August 1944, the total casualties were lighter than expected – 36 killed and 252 injured, but nearly half the houses in the borough had been damaged. (*Wimbledon Past*, Richard Milward, 1998)

On 28 September 1944, two V1s fell only 100yds apart in Havelock Road. Four people were killed and many houses destroyed.

At 8.30am on 19 November 1944, a V2 – the world's first long-range guided ballistic missile – landed on the site of the Hazelhurst estate, on the border of Wimbledon and Tooting. In total, at least 35 people were killed and more than 100 injured.

There was an exceptionally cold snap in January 1945, quickly followed by a very mild spell. The *Merton and Morden News* reported in January 1945 that the cold weather had claimed the lives of seven old people. In the 12 January edition, a letter headlined 'Housing Problem', and signed C.R.F. Morden read as follows:

> With reference to the acute housing shortage and the allocation of temporary housing to newly married couples etc., I would like to state my own case: I have been invalided out of the Navy (with approximately 80 per cent disability pension), married, with a son aged seven years. While in the Service, my wife and son (owing to the blitz of 1941) had to leave the flat we had at that time to seek the only available accommodation

with her relatives. That worked satisfactorily until I entered 'Civvy Street'. Apart from overcrowding I could not agree with the in-laws, consequently, to prevent further trouble, I had to find digs, while at the same time frantically searching, unsuccessfully, for an unfurnished house or flat. The result is that for nearly a year I have lived apart from my wife and son. The only opportunity I have of seeing them is for a couple of hours on the one day a week I have off from work. I have written to the L.C.C. [London County Council] and the local council, and from the latter have been told (rightly or wrongly) that they cannot cater for inadequately housed people. I have tried everything possible to try to secure a flat or small house without success, so it will appear that my family will have to live apart until a few years hence. I quite understand that I am far from being an isolated case. I surely think that ex-Servicemen, in similar circumstances, should also be included in the priority list when they do eventually allocate these temporary houses.

Also in January 1945 (14 January), a V1 hit the railway embankment south of Caesar's Walk, Hatton Gardens, Mitcham. This cut both tracks of the Wimbledon & (West) Croydon railway line and the adjacent telephone wires. Trains operated to either side of the obstruction and were linked by buses. This may serve as an example of keeping life moving during the worst days of the Second World War, and that the effect on the London transport network was more one of disruption than physical damage.

On Friday, 9 November 1945, the *Surrey Mirror* 'extracted and collated some of the figures relating to the effects of enemy bombardment on various

The Hazelhurst estate after the V2 bomb hit. (summerstown182.wordpress.com)

local Government areas in the county'. It said that the worst sufferers among the local government areas in the administrative county was the Borough of Wimbledon, which had 649 people killed and 587 buildings demolished, and the Urban District of Merton and Malden, with 142 fatal casualties and 525 buildings demolished.

CHAPTER EIGHTEEN

Happier Times with Brighter Prospects

20th April 1945: blackout to end – no more raids expected.

20 Fri. Very mild, a fresh breeze, lovely sunshine all day. Got a nice piece of beef to-day also other provisions locally. Erected a frame to accommodate runner beans; planted same – Champion Scarlet. Bought a paper at Morden. It is announced that the blackout restrictions will be completely suspended from Monday onwards. It is thought there will be no more raids; what a relief.

(*Fred French's diary, 20 April 1945*)

The blackout restrictions were fully suspended on 23 April 1945; it was thought there would be no more raids. Victory in Europe Day, generally known as VE Day, was the public holiday celebrated on 8 May 1945 to mark the formal acceptance by the Allies of Nazi Germany's unconditional surrender of its armed forces. It thus marked the end of the Second World War in Europe. In Wimbledon and all over Britain, people held street parties to celebrate and began taking down their Anderson shelters.

Winifred Whitehead, author of *Wimbledon 1885–1965*, lived with her parents and three sisters in Worple Road, Wimbledon. She wrote: 'The victory came at last and relief, and an ordinary life with its ordinary joys and sorrows.'

Ray Cobbett, who lived in Ridley Road in South Wimbledon and left Wimbledon in 1967, said that the whole of Ridley Road came out to celebrate with a mammoth street party. There was a very large bonfire which he was terrified of – he thought it might set the houses on fire it was so large. There were pianos and, of course, there was bunting and community singing.

Fred French wrote in his diary on 9 May 1945:

The Victory celebrations continue. A large bonfire was lit at night at the Kingston Road end of Chestnut Road. A piano was brought out and dance music played while people including Chas and Doris danced and sang. Hundreds of searchlights swirled and waved their long arms about in the sky in a bewildering manner, at other times forming up into a huge concentration.

A street party celebration in Leyton Road, Wimbledon. (Wimbledon Guardian)

Victor Spink remembers:

> After VE day in May 1945, there was a victory street party outside our
> house which was crowded with us happy returned evacuees back from
> "Up north" sporting our home cut "pudding basin" haircuts. The night
> before on VE Day, we had burnt an effigy of Hitler on top of a bonfire
> round the corner in the middle of the road with the makings from what
> was left of Mr Bretson's house and shed which had been bombed out on
> the corner of Craven Gardens and Queens Road in 1940.
>
>   It is one of my abiding memories of the war that relations, friends, and
> neighbours pulled together without reserve. But already the atmosphere
> was changing and there was a subtle but perceptible differing in the way
> people treated each other. This change was even more predominate after
> VJ Day. From then on people were decidedly less likely to help each
> other out.
>
>   Back to our street party in Craven Gardens. The next afternoon after
> VE Day, we children sat down on builders boards supported on dining
> room chairs. We were surrounded by mostly mums who had prepared
> the tables with Union flag bunting and served us with a moderate fare
> of thin jam sandwiches sliced from rationed "national" bread spread
> with unlabelled margarine. Also on offer were in this outdoor feast were
> plain rock cakes and rich tea biscuits. To drink was tepid lemon squash
> made from crystals, accompanied by half set jelly, blancmange, and to
> finish with a few lovely lovely sugared almonds issued from large flat

cardboard boxes. The sweets in between layers of tissue paper, and were a gift from the people of Australia, and oh yes, a sixpenny piece for surviving the war to take home with you, that is if you had a home to go to which had not been bombed.

Although the fighting was over in Europe, the war against Japan continued for another three months. It finally ended after the US dropped atomic bombs on the Japanese cities of Hiroshima and Nagasaki. In Britain, VJ Day parties (Victory against Japan), were held on 15 August 1945. These were a bit more low key than the VE Day celebrations, as people reflected on all the damage that had been done and all the people who had died during six years of war.

Fred French wrote in his diary on 5 June 1946: 'We received to-day the cheque for covering the war damage done to our home (66 Chestnut Road) and the matter is settled save for buying the required articles, some replacements and repairs are already done.' On 16 August, he wrote that he had seen two Raleigh bikes in a shop window, the finest since pre-war days. It cheered him to see such signs of a return to less austere times. On 8 August 1946, he bought (in Morden) his first bananas for six years.

CHAPTER NINETEEN

Lost Hospitals of the Second World War

Atkinson Morley Hospital, a convalescent home for the poor and needy at Copse Hill, was provided by Atkinson Morley (1780–1858), who was born in Westminster. During the Second World War, it was used for general acute work and was upgraded to 120 beds. Possil House (previously Ormond House), in a three-acre site at 23 Copse Hill, was bought for £9,000 for use as a Nurses' Home. In 1942, the surgical wards were taken over for neurosurgery, and the Home became the Atkinson Morley Emergency Hospital. In 1944, a V1 exploded nearby, but only a few windows were damaged.

After the war, there was a major change of use for the hospital, when it became an internationally recognised neuroscience centre. In 1949, the Department of Psychiatry was established, as well as an X-ray Department specialising in neuroradiology. A Sleep Laboratory was established in 1972.

By the beginning of the twenty-first century, the building was considered too old and out-of-date; the hospital closed in 2003 and services transferred to the new neuroscience wing – Atkinson Morley Wing – on the St George's Hospital campus at Tooting. The former hospital has been converted into apartments and townhouses.

The Wimbledon Cottage Hospital/Wimbledon Hospital

The Wimbledon Cottage Hospital, Copse Hill, opened in 1870 with eight beds. The Hospital – just across the lane from Atkinson Morley's – was closed in 1911. The new building, with a central administration block and two wings, opened in 1912. It had thirty-seven beds and four cots and was simply renamed the Wimbledon Hospital. During the First World War, it was one of the first smaller hospitals to offer treatment for sick and wounded servicemen. It became an auxiliary military hospital to the Horton War Hospital, Epsom, with the first twenty casualties arriving from France in October 1914.

The Memorial Wing in May 2017. (Author)

By 1938, Wimbledon Hospital had seventy-four beds: eighteen for males, twenty-six for females and eighteen for children, and twelve private rooms. During the Second World War, it became part of the Emergency Medical Service, with thirty extra casualty beds. The Emergency Hospital Service – later EMS – was introduced as soon as war broke out, and gave central government, the Ministry of Health, a right of direction over both voluntary and municipal hospitals which it had never before possessed. One of the challenges for the EMS was to deal with the 'normal' population of sick people while freeing-up capacity to deal with injuries attributed to air raids or other attacks. At that point, there was no NHS and there were many public hospitals, private hospitals, convalescent homes of varying competence and capacity.

By 1945, Wimbledon Hospital had ninety-three beds, including the EMS beds (but these were reduced to fifteen, then ten, in 1946). Wimbledon Hospital joined the NHS in 1948 under the control of the South West Metropolitan Regional Health Board. In October 1981, the decision was made to close Wimbledon Hospital, and closure finally took place in 1983. Services moved to The Nelson Hospital, Kingston Road, Merton.

The Nelson Hospital opened in May 1900 as the South Wimbledon, Merton and District Cottage Hospital. In 1911, a wall plaque was dedicated to the service of the people of the district and in memory of Admiral Lord Nelson, a former resident of Merton. A new hospital was opened in 1912 and a new wing was added in 1922 to commemorate Merton soldiers killed during the First World War. Above the Memorial Wing is a plaque that reads: 'In honour of all who went from this district and in loving memory of all who fell 1914–1918'.

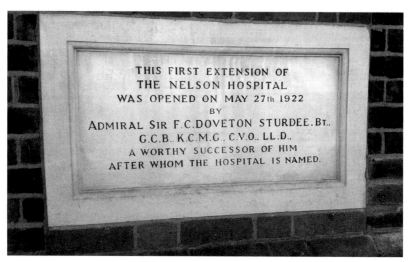

The first extension of the Nelson Hospital was opened on 27 May 1922 by Admiral F.C. Doveton Sturdee. (Author)

This stone was laid on 17 July 1911 by Her Grace the Duchess of Sutherland.
(Author)

The Wilson Hospital

The Wilson Cottage Hospital, Cranmer Road, Mitcham was gifted to the community by local businessman Sir Issac Wilson in the 1920s; it officially opened in 1928 and became the Wilson Hospital in 1933. On 14 January 1945, one ward was destroyed by a bomb; by 1952, the hospital had sixty-six beds and the bomb-damaged ward was still awaiting repair. In 1956, the ward was rebuilt and opened as the physiotherapy department. The Wilson Hospital – or The Wilson – is now mainly empty, but partially used as offices for the Merton, Sutton & Wandsworth District Health Authority.

The Grove Hospital, Tooting

Civilian air raid casualties were admitted to Tooting Fever Hospital/the Grove Hospital during the Second World War, as well as patients with infectious diseases. Most of the Grove Hospital buildings were demolished in the 1970s. The surviving ward blocks are now the Knightsbridge Wing of St George's Hospital Tooting (founded in 1976 at its current site), used for offices, wards and outpatients.

Lake in the grounds of Margin House, Marryat Road. The lake was used for boating, bathing, and fishing. (merton.gov.uk)

Margin House, Windyridge and Deepdale

Margin House and Windyridge, both in Marryat Road, Wimbledon Village, and Deepdale in Calonne Road, Wimbledon Village were large properties vacated by their owners and requisitioned for the war effort. They were used variously by the army for offices, temporary housing and as a hospital, and the grand interiors of all three fell into disrepair. By 1953, all three were empty and were bought for development. The lake was drained and modest houses with generous gardens were built on plots laid out on the extended Parkside Avenue and new roads named Margin Drive, Windy Ridge Close and Deepdale were created. More recently, the post-war houses have largely been replaced by larger homes with smaller gardens.

South Middlesex Fever Hospital

The Mogden Isolation Hospital, Isleworth, Middlesex, opened in 1898 and closed in 1991, was renamed the South Middlesex Fever Hospital in 1938. At the outbreak of the Second World War, the large pavilion wards were taken over by the EMS. Resident medical staff were seconded from St George's Hospital and the West London Hospital, Hammersmith (closed 1993).

Dr Seton Robert Tristram Headley – known as Bobby (1915–2013), was anaesthetist to the South Middlesex Fever Hospital from 30 August 1939. In an interview for the Museum of Wimbledon, he said:

We had a little theatre on a bank at the back in a separate little area. Patients had to be taken on in the open air. We had a sort of great big half cylinder can which was placed on the patients. If they had to be brought up during an air raid the shrapnel and stuff wouldn't do them any harm. In an air raid all this anti-aircraft fire – you may not realise this – there were a lot of falling bits and even if they didn't hit they would fall back and this could be fatal. It wasn't very nice for the patients to be taken there but they needed to be taken and all the porters wore tin hats. We had to give the anaesthetic.

We were slightly to the west of London. Most of the heavy bombing occurred from the east up the river in the docklands area, and in the middle of London stuff was very bad. West of London it wasn't really.

Dr Headley joined the Royal Army Medical Corps (RAMC) in December 1939 and he was sent to the RAMC Aldershot depot, Hampshire for military training. Then he went to another depot not far away where he did medical hygiene. On 1 January 1940, he was transferred to a casualty clearing station on the Isle of Man, the Onchan Head Hotel on a cliff overlooking Douglas, which had been made into a hospital. His job was to take care of the sick there. He was posted to No 29 General Hospital, Ormskirk, Lancashire.

He said: 'It wasn't very long before we embarked from Liverpool on 29 May 1942. The chaps went on a ship called the *Orontes*.' Dr Headley arrived in Suez on 22 July 1942. Then, after two weeks, he went to Freetown, West Africa. There was a British military hospital there. He set off from there after three days and eventually pulled up in Cape Town, South Africa for three or four days. Dr Headley said:

Then part of the convoy went to Madagascar. Half of the convoy went to Durban, half to Madagascar. They decided Madagascar was hostile and had decided to admit German submarines. So we landed part of our army there in disguise. It didn't take very long and there we were. That was a minor battle of the war that went on. It only lasted a few days. Madagascar was still a lovely place. We had some people going along to look at all the lemurs and interesting animals. A haven for rare animals and birds because it was a long way from anywhere.

We went straight to Aden, refuelled and then went up the Red Sea and arrived at Suez. Our luggage was unloaded at Suez and we were taken up by train to Ismailiya. That's the actual Suez Canal. We were then taken to a military camp in the middle of the desert for training in how to live in the desert.

He joined another unit: No 1 Mobile Military Hospital in the Nile Delta. It was a mobile surgical unit that had been paid for by the Friends Ambulance Unit (FAU), a volunteer ambulance service founded by Quakers. Dr Headley described it as 'an operating theatre on a sort of platform built up on a

HMHS Somersetshire. *In 1948, she was decommissioned and rebuilt by Harland & Wolff, Belfast to a passenger ship. (Uboat.net)*

frame.' Author Kate Adie, in *Corsets to Camouflage: Women and War*, wrote: 'In slacks and battle blouses, eight nursing sisters of the No 1 Mobile Military Hospital slogged through sandstorms and battlefield debris as part of the expeditionary force, covering well over 1,000 miles in seven weeks.' Dr Headley and the men spent Christmas 1942 in Benghazi, before eventually arriving in Tripoli, where they saw Churchill on 4 February 1943 on his visit to inspect the British 8th Army.

In 1943, Dr Headley was posted on HMHS *Somersetshire*, a British hospital ship with 507 beds, 118 medical staff and 171 crew members. He said: 'We set off from Alexandria. Then we began to realise we were going to Sicily where we understood the war had started.'

Dr Headley did not return to England until the end of the war, and returned by train. Then, armed with a testimonial from his commanding officer, he was able to obtain the position of consultant anaesthetist at St George's Hospital. In the late 1940s, the family moved from a flat in Barons Court to Wimbledon. Their first house was on the corner of Cottenham Park Road and Durham Road. His three children, Nigel, Charles and Angela, all attended Wimbledon schools.

Further research

Detailed information about Dr Headley's war work can be found on *wimbledonmuseum.org.uk*

U-453 hit HMHS *Somersetshire*, by mistake, on 7 April 1942 with three torpedoes (she was not recognised as a hospital ship by *U-453*); seven people died and there were 180 survivors. The ship was not carrying any patients. The crew later reboarded *Somersetshire* and managed to reach Alexandria. The remaining survivors were picked up by a Greek destroyer. *Somersetshire* was the first hospital ship to arrive from the Far East; 348 wounded and sick military personnel, including 116 PoWs, embarked from Liverpool on 21 November 1945. *U-453* was sunk by Royal Navy surface warships on 21 May 1944 off the south coast of Italy. A German hospital ship, *Tuebingen*, was sunk by mistake by the RAF in the Gulf of Venice on 18 November 1944.

CHAPTER TWENTY

We Will Not Go to War

Under the 1939 National Service Act, all eligible men aged 18 to 41 had to register at their local labour (employment) exchange for service in one of the armed forces. Some people were in reserved occupations – these were jobs that were so important to the war effort that workers could not be spared to join the armed forces. Some people were also too old, or too young, to fight. Conscientious objectors (COs) also had to register, but they applied to be put on a special register. Not only was registration the first step for a CO, but it was also often the first time a man publicly declared his intention to be a CO. Tribunals were set up to deal with claims for exemption. The waiting period between registration and being summoned to appear before a tribunal varied.

In a letter published in the *Wimbledon Boro' News* on 5 January 1940, Councillor Norman E. Edwards of Melrose Avenue, Wimbledon wrote:

> Let us admit that the German people are not degraded creatures; let us remember that they are very much like ourselves; and that they do not want this war more than we do. The war should be stopped and a world conference convened to tackle world problems. In such a conference, the richest nations should be prepared to set the best example.

Stating that his conscience was 'first awakened to the evils of militarism' while he was serving with the Officers' Training Corps (OTC) at school, Henry Arthur Gosden of Gordondale Road, Wimbledon, applied for exemption from military service at the London COs tribunal at Fulham Town Hall in January 1940. Gosden, an actuarial clerk, was prepared to work under civil control as long as it did not affect his conscience or principles. Evidence as to the sincerity of his views was given by Councillor Edwards. Olive Owen, also speaking for the applicant, said he addressed meetings in connection with the Peace Pledge Union (PPU) every Sunday at Wimbledon Common. The tribunal was satisfied that Gosden had a genuine conscientious objection.

Michael O'Reilly Nash, a shipping clerk, of Aboyne Drive, West Wimbledon, applied for exemption from military service, the *Wimbledon & Boro' News* reported on 2 February 1940. He had at one time applied for commission in the RAF because he had 'rather a boring job', but tendered his resignation after a few days on a course at a civil aerodrome (March 1938). He said this was because he would feel unable to fulfil the duties required of him by the Air Force in the event of war. He was registered as a CO on condition he remained in his current occupation or took up full-time ambulance work.

The *Wimbledon Boro' News* of 19 July 1940 reported that a clerk who had been discharged by the Wimbledon Borough Council because he was CO appeared before the Tribunal of Southwark. Wilfred Beaumont Lindsey, aged 24, of Amity Grove, West Wimbledon, told the Tribunal that, since his dismissal, he had endeavoured to find other clerical work, without success. He was now employed by the Hampshire War Agricultural Committee. His objection to war service was on religious grounds, and he had been a member of the PPU for four years. He was registered as a CO, provided he took up work in agriculture or forestry. The PPU is the oldest non-sectarian pacifist organisation in Britain, according to *ppu.org.uk*.

An article in the *Wimbledon Boro' News* on Friday, 21 June 1940 carried the headline 'Only 14 Objectors', referring to the fact that of the 900 men who had attended the Wimbledon Employment Exchange on Saturday, 15 June, only fourteen had registered themselves as COs.

Today, Wimbledon Disarmament Coaltion/CND holds a Remembrance Sunday Ceremony at Wimbledon Common, followed by the laying of a wreath containing white poppies on the Wimbledon Village War Memorial. In its November 2015 newsletter, the organisation stated: 'The white poppy is a symbol of personal commitment to working for a world where conflicts are settled with justice and without resort to violence, in contrast to the red poppy which has increasingly become a symbol of support for today's armed forces and a militarised society.'

Further research

Information about Eric Farley (1919–1989), who joined the Wimbledon Group of the PPU, can be found in Ann Kramer's book *Conscientious Objectors of the Second World War*. He appeared before a tribunal in May 1940.

According to the PPU, there were 61,000 COs in Britain during the Second World War. The organisation is currently compiling a database of every known CO.

CHAPTER TWENTY-ONE

Military Deception

London War Letters of a Separated Family: 1940–1945 by Christine Vassar Tall (b1928), a paperback published in 2007, is the story of an ordinary family living 'one block from the area next to Morden, Cheam and Sutton' during the war years: 21 Rustington Walk, Morden (between Morden Park and Sutton Common Recreation Ground, and within the St Helier ward). It is a story told through letters from Christine's mother Kathleen Vassar to Christine.

Kathleen Vassar wrote to Vassar College, Poughkeepsie, New York asking if anyone at Vassar could give sanctuary to a British evacuee named Christine Vassar. The telegram read (no date): 'Would you offer sanctuary duration war Christine Mary Vassar age thirteen English public school girl Father army Mother business Unimpeachable references Urgent need'.

The reply, dated 26 June 1940, from Harry MacCracken, the President of Vassar College, read: 'References desired'. A later reply (no date), following a reference (25 July) from the headmistress of City of London Girls School, Miss Winters, from Harry MacCracken read: 'Offer sanctuary one year will meet her New York'.

Christine sailed for America on the *Duchess of Atholl*, a steam passenger ship, with many other British children (evacuees) on 8 August 1940. (*Duchess of Atholl* was sunk by *U-178* on 10 October 1942, 200 miles east-north-east of Ascension Island. Four died and 821 survived). She was evacuated to the home of Harry MacCracken on 8 August 1940, at the age of 13.

Marjorie MacCracken (1909–2012), a graduate of Vassar College, became Christine's foster mother. Some of those letters took up to ten weeks to arrive and sometimes they were heavily censored. Others may have been lost at sea, according to *London War Letters of a Separated Family: 1940–1945*.

A letter from Kathleen Vassar to Mrs MacCracken written on 25 February 1944 stated that 'a few nights ago, Lord Haw-Haw said that Wimbledon had been razed to the ground. This is untrue! I have my office in Wimbledon so I can testify to the falseness of his statement. But there, we all know he is a liar!'

The letter is in a metal box given to Special Collections at Vassar College, with other letters from Christine's parents and family. Christine originally came to Poughkeepsie to stay for a few months, but stayed with the MacCracken family as the war continued and went on to graduate from Vassar. In 2007, she lived in Cheshire, Connecticut.

William Joyce (1906–1946), better known as Lord Haw-Haw, was a notorious broadcaster of Nazi propaganda to the UK during the Second World War. His announcement 'Germany calling, Germany calling' was a familiar sound across the airwaves, introducing threats and misinformation which he broadcast from his Hamburg base. Hore-Belisha was subjected to anti-Semitic propaganda from the Nazis through the radio broadcasts of Lord Haw-Haw, who promised to bomb his 'hideaway' at Old Warren Farm.

In the *War Decided* (1985), Joan Hartley wrote:

> Great fun was derived from tuning into Lord Haw-Haw. His Oxford accent earned him this name. His broadcasts were treated by the British as a humorous diversion from the serious business of war. The Germans never did understand British humour. Hitler's broadcasts were listened to in the same frame of mind. He just shouted and raved like a lunatic, which indeed he was.

Joyce was originally an American citizen, born in the US of Roman-Catholic Irish parents. He came to England in 1921 and briefly attended King's College School. At Birkbeck College of the University of London, he developed an interest in fascism. Shortly before war was declared, Joyce and his wife Margaret fled to Germany and he became a naturalised German citizen in 1940. On 28 May 1945, Joyce was captured by British forces at Flensburg, near the German border with Denmark. He was taken to London and convicted of three counts of high treason. He was executed on 3 January 1946 at Wandsworth Prison and his remains were buried in an unmarked grave within the walls of HMP Wandsworth. Joyce was reinterred in 1976 at the New Cemetery in Bohermore, County Galway, Ireland.

Ian Goodhope Colvin

Ian Goodhope Colvin (1912–1975), journalist and author, lived in the top floor flat of 17 Lingfield Road, Wimbledon Village, from which he broadcast propaganda to Germany during the war.

He began his career on the *News Chronicle* in Berlin as a journalist, from where he was expelled by the Nazis in 1939. Churchill, in *The War Memoirs of Winston Churchill: The Gathering Storm* (1948), wrote that Ian Colvin 'delved deeply into German Affairs and maintained contacts of a secret nature with the German Generals'. During the 1950s and 1960s, Colvin worked for the *Daily Telegraph* as a foreign correspondent in Africa and the Middle East. In 1975, he was the *Telegraph's* chief leader writer and roving foreign correspondent. His books include The *Unknown Courier* (1953),

Chief of Intelligence (1951), *Vansittart in Office* (1964) and *The Chamberlain Cabinet* (1971). The *Unknown Courier* is about Operation Mincemeat, a British Intelligence plan to mislead the German High Command by planting papers on a corpse washed up on the coast of Spain. According to *Biteback Publishing* (2017), 'Colvin's account looks beyond the military machinations to explore the identity of this 'unknown courier', the dead man who changed the course of the war.'

His father Ian Duncan Colvin (1877–1938), also a journalist and author, published *The Germans in England 1066–1598* (1915). In this he claimed the Hanseatic League (an economic and defensive alliance) had tried to control Europe through a mixture of peaceful and violent means. He followed this with *The Unseen Hand in English History* (1917). He wrote, in the book, that it was the purpose of the book, 'to show, by examining a segment of our history, from the reign of Elizabeth to the end of the eighteenth century, that England is most happy when the national interest and the government work together, and least happy when our government is controlled by the unseen hand of the foreigner.'

Klaus Hoffman

Klaus Hoffman, born in 1922, was 18 and a house prefect at King's College School (December 1940). He was charged at Wimbledon on 13 December 1940 with being an alien, a German citizen, and having 'in his possession or under his control a bicycle without a police permit'. 'I really forgot I am an alien,' Hoffman told the court. 'I am boarded out with other students, and as the bicycle was there I took it and rode it to a shop.' The headmaster of the school at the time, H.J. Dixon, was instrumental in getting Hoffman released from an internment camp. The chairman said that the charge would be dismissed on payment of 40*s* costs.

(Source *Daily Mirror*, 14 December 1940)

CHAPTER TWENTY-TWO

Women Remembered

The WAAF was the female auxiliary of the RAF, established on 28 June 1939. Rates of pay were revealed by the Air Ministry on 9 September 1939 in the following announcement: 'Women between the ages of 18 and 43 are required for the Women's Auxiliary Air Force which is now called out for service. Those with previous service, however, will be accepted up to 50. Applicants who are accepted will be enrolled as cooks, mess orderlies, equipment assistants, motor transport drivers, clerks, telephone and teleprinter operators and fabric workers, and will be expected to report for duty immediately.' At its peak strength in 1943, WAAF numbers exceeded 180,000, with more than 2,000 women enlisting per week. They did not participate in active combat. Miss Paddy Barr was an officer in the WAAF, Wimbledon. The wedding took place at Wimbledon on 9 June 1943 of Wing Commander Peter Billyeald MBE DFC, a native of Nottingham, and Miss Barr. (*Nottingham Journal*, 10 June 1943)

Gladys Eva from Wimbledon, who said in *The Secret Life of Fighter Command* by Sinclair McKay (Aurum Press, 2015) 'I'm a Wimbledon girl', was a Filter Officer in the WAAF, and in 2015 lived on the Dorset coast. She worked in the Filter Room at RAF Bentley Priory, north London. Bentley Priory, a mansion house, played a pivotal role during the Battle of Britain (10 July–31 October 1940) as Headquarters Fighter Command, according to Bentley Priory Museum in Stanmore, north London.

> In 1940, Great Britain had the world's first radar-directed air defence system. It consisted of two parallel chains of radar stations extending along the southern and eastern coasts, as well as around major industrial centres and ports on the west coast. In other words, the British were able to spot German aircraft almost all the way to Rotterdam, Brussels or Paris, provided that they flew high enough. The nerve centre of the system was the so-called Filter Room at Fighter Command's headquarters at Bentley Priory near Stanmore. All sightings at radar stations of incoming signals were forwarded to the Filter Room by means of a direct telephone line.
>
> The radar was supplemented with the Royal Observer Corps' well-developed network of air observation posts, which were scattered across the UK. Any observation of what could be hostile aircraft was also reported via telephone to Bentley Priory.
>
> (*Battle of Britain: An Epic Conflict Revisited*, Christer Bergström)

Gladys was one of the first women posted to the underground bunker beneath the Italianate gardens of Bentley Priory just before the Battle of Britain. It was a grossly unhealthy place. She told the Royal Air Forces Association (RAFA) in an interview in 2015: 'Basically they dug a hole in the ground. You never met anyone who did not smoke and lots of people had chest problems after working down there. But we felt safe as it was so deep down. We were bombed but could not hear anything. It was well-built – we did not have dust and debris falling on us as you see in the films.'

During her time off, Gladys went home to her parents in Wimbledon or up to the West End. One evening in March 1941, she and a friend were near the Café de Paris, off Piccadilly, when it was bombed, killing more than thirty people. Gladys returned to her car to find it unscathed but with a bomb crater on either side. She told RAFA that she had many memories of travelling back to work on the London Underground in the evenings and seeing station platforms filling up with families taking shelter ahead of the German bombing.

RAFA said: 'Not long before Gladys left Bentley Priory, she remembers plotting three aircraft over the Thames Estuary. The three suddenly became two – and she discovered later that the missing aircraft was being flown by Hull-born Amy Johnson (1903–1941), whose body was never found.' Amy Johnson flew in the Second World War as part of the Air Transport Auxiliary and died during a ferry flight.

The model of the old Filter Room at Bentley Priory Museum. (Bentley Priory Museum)

Gladys left Bentley Priory in May 1941 as a Flight Sergeant and was posted to Watnall near Nottingham. From here, she helped plot the 1,000 bomber raids as they set off from Lincolnshire and East Anglia. After the war, Gladys left the RAF and worked in her father's business before marrying and having a family. She attended the opening of the Bentley Priory Museum in September 2013 and was introduced to the Prince of Wales and the Duchess of Cornwall.

Joan Viney Jones-Francis of Monkleigh Road, Morden was an LACW wireless operator in the RAF. While serving, she met Sergeant Arthur Edward North, a wireless operation in the RAF. They married in April 1943 at St Mary's Church, Merton Park.

Wimbledon Mayor Herbert Aubrey Crowe said at the Chamber of Commerce at St George's Hall in March 1941 that there were too many women under 30 doing nothing. 'I would rather they be conscripted,' he said. In a letter published in the *Wimbledon Boro' News* of 4 April 1941, Gertrude Hunt of Merton Road wrote:

> For several weeks past I have read in newspapers arguments for conscripting women. How is it then that the Labour Exchange is still full of women and girls seeking work and unable to get it? A friend of mine who was 'put off' at one factory went to the Exchange for a job, and after being there three hours was told she must get a release form. Returning, she spent five hours at the same Exchange, only to be told they had no work to offer her. Why conscript the women when crowds are ready for work?

Gladys Eva. (RAFA)

Ernest Bevin, Minister of Labour and National Security, said regarding women in a June 1941 speech at Wimbledon: 'We want you in radio and technical work and all kinds of occupations. It is wrong to assume all we want you for is washing up dishes.' On 8 May 1942, part-time work became compulsory for women between the ages of 18 and 45, except for mothers looking after their own children under 14.

Her statue at the Bentley Priory Museum.

The Silver Thimble Fund's headquarters was at 17 High Street, Wimbledon. The idea was to collect old thimbles and other broken silver articles and sell them to buy life-saving equipment. A report in the *Yorkshire Post and Leeds Intelligencer* on 30 May 1941 said that the fund, organised by Miss Hope-Clarke, had authorised collectors over the world. 'So far in this war they have collected 25,000 thimbles and raised £45,000. With this they have provided all sorts of ambulance and hospital equipment'.

By December 1941, manpower was in such short supply that a Bill making unmarried women between the ages of 20 and 30 liable for conscription was announced in the House of Commons. They could choose between service in one of the armed forces, the nursing services, the Women's Land Army (WLA), Civil Defence, transport or factory work. COs often volunteered for fire-watching or work on the land. Two years later, as military casualty lists grew, the age of conscription for women was lowered to 19 and extended to 50. Mothers with a child under 14 were exempt and the great majority of women remained in the home caring for their families.

The WLA had originally been set up in 1917, but was disbanded at the end of the First World War. It reformed in June 1939 and by autumn 1941, more than 20,000 women – often known as Land Girls – had volunteered to serve, with a third of these volunteers having lived in London or another large city (source *iwm.org.uk*). They did a wide variety of jobs on the land, worked in all weathers and conditions, and could be directed to work anywhere in the country. The botanic gardens in Kew, Surrey also employed Land Girls. Rosemary Thomas, originally from Wallington, Surrey, had won the Ladies' Singles at Wimbledon in 1938, 1939 and 1947. She joined the WLA and on 6 September 1939, the *Sketch (*a weekly journal that focused on high society and the aristocracy) printed photographs of her at work learning to drive a tractor, wield a hayfork, handle a pig and balance a couple of buckets. The images were taken on a farm near Tunbridge Wells, Kent.

Irene Jean Chapman

Irene Jean Chapman, only daughter of Mr and Mrs Frank Chapman of New Malden, served with the Women's Royal Naval Service. The *Merton and Morden News* of 1 January 1943 reported that she married Lieutenant William Menzies of the Royal Naval Air Service. They met while both serving with the

Members of Wimbledon Red Cross pictured in 1943. Copyright International Committee of the Red Cross (ICRC)

forces at Winchester and married at St Saviour's, Raynes Park. Meanwhile, the *Merton and Morden News* of 15 January 1943 reported the marriage of Kathleen Moore of the Women's Auxiliary Air Force (WAAF) and Douglas Tubbs of the Royal Fusiliers. He was the son of Mr and Mrs Tubbs of Grove Road, Wimbledon. (He re-married in 1954).

Marion Dumas

Marion Dumas (b1921), an old girl of Wimbledon High School, second daughter of Lieutenant Colonel Dumas MC of Belvedere Drive, was parachuted into France and was captured and tortured by the Gestapo. She was awarded the Croix de Guerre for her bravery. The *Wimbledon High School News Sheet* of June 1945 quoted the Citation of Award as follows, adding that Marion was making progress but was still undergoing hospital treatment:

> [A] Young liaison officer, who in all circumstances did her duty with such calm and devotion that she won the esteem and admiration not only of her companions and higher officers but also of all the Refugees and wounded whom she had to handle. Wounded for the first time at Caen, when she was evacuating Refugees under shell fire, she was again wounded (this time very

grievously) on 6 August 1944, whilst trying to get into a town where she wanted to carry on with her work, but which was still occupied by the enemy.

Lady Prudence Cradock-Hartopp

Lady Prudence Cradock-Hartopp, a writer and former journalist who has lived in West Wimbledon since 1955, spoke to the Museum of Wimbledon about her wartime experience. In 1943, she decided she had had enough of London and she joined the Wrens (Women's Royal Naval Service), completing a gunnery course in Portsmouth and attending a training base in Southend. She said there was not enough to do, so she worked in an office there as a typist. She became a cypher officer, had various postings in the UK and then went out to India for a short time.

Cecilia Emily Maud Gummow MBE

Cecilia Emily Maud Gummow (1907–2008), born in Croydon, daughter of Frederich Richard Gummow (1871–1943) and Eliza Gummow (1872–1958), was a member of the National Savings movement, established in 1916 to encourage the people to 'save and prosper'. In 1911, she lived at Falhoun, Branksome Road, Merton Park, and, from around 1930, the family lived at 14 Melrose Road, Merton Park. She was engaged in various war work, including assessing bomb damage to local houses, overseeing emergency food storage, and organising the ARP Wardens on night-duty watching for bombs. She was an officer in the council offices – then the Urban District of Merton and Morden – at Morden Hall when they were severely damaged by a bomb. After the war, while still working for the Council, she became involved in the National Savings movement and in January 1956 was awarded the MBE (Civil Division) for her work as chairman of the movement's mid-Surrey branch. The report of this event in the local press also states that at this time she was chairman (for the sixth year) of the National Streets and Villages Committee, and a member of the regional conference. She also became UK chairman of the Soroptimists Club, a worldwide organisation for women in management and the professions, working to advance human rights and the status of women. She died on 30 June 2007 and her ashes were interred in her parents' grave in the churchyard of St Mary the Virgin, Merton Park.

Mrs Keene

Mrs E. Keene of Poplar Road, Wimbledon received the Distinguished War Service Badge of the Red Cross Society from the Queen, the *Wimbledon Boro' News* reported on 7 May 1943. Mrs Keene had commanded the

Surrey II Detachment in the Wimbledon Division of the British Red Cross since 1939 and was equally well-known for her work in Wimbledon's Civil Defence Department.

The war dead buried at Mitcham Cemetery include:

Pauline Margaret Blackwell, Aircraftwoman 2nd Class, WAAF (RAF Henlow in Bedfordshire), daughter of Alfred Blackwell and Edna Blackwell of Mitcham, who died on 2 August 1945, aged 19. Plot 30. Grave 2394.

Private Betty Violet Williams, Auxiliary Territorial Service, daughter of George Arthur Williams and Edith Louisa Williams of Mitcham, who died on 24 February 1944, aged 23. Plot 30. Grave 2274.

Further research

The Wimbledon High School News Sheet from 1945 lists the following old girls: Mary Abel, Officer in Charge of the Church Army Canteen at Wimbledon; Joan Couchman, a Petty Officer in the WRNS; Joan Flack, a VAD, nursing in Scotland; Diana Jones (Matthew) in the WAAF working in the Messing Office with rank of corporal, stationed at Biggin Hill, Greater London; Kathleen Ogden, Sister in Charge of a training ward of a war hospital for African patients; Patricia Patten, serving in the WRNS, stationed in the Orkneys.

TALKED WITH THE QUEEN

After Receiving War Badge

Mrs E. Keene received a war badge from the Queen. (Wimbledon Boro' News)

Women's Voluntary Services Roll of Honour 1939-1945 by Matthew McMurray (2016) lists 'these members of the women's voluntary services whose names are written in this book and others of whom there is no record, gave their lives in the service of their country during the Second World War.' The following women are on the Merton and Morden listing:

GB Beretta (Cycle Corps Messenger)
Elsie Burrows (Billeting Officer, Housewives Service)
Amy Corbett (Housewives Service)
Minnie Lillian Hallet (Aid House Worker)
Elsie Maud McEleny (Salvage Steward)
Emily Maud Packwood (Housewives Service)
Winifred Violet Sanderson (Emergency Feeding Centre).

Gladys Bertha June Beretta (1907-1940), a serving member of the WVS, was killed at home in Kenley Road, Merton Park on 27 September 1940 by a high explosive, referred to as HE by McMurray, which demolished the house. Her husband Leonard Beretta (1901-1940), a tools buyer for a cycle company, also died. Elsie Elizabeth Burrows (1889-1944) was killed at home on 21 July 1944 by a flying bomb/V1. Amy Sarah Corbett (1881-1944) was killed at home on 10 July 1944 by a flying bomb/V1. Hallet died in hospital on 21 July 1944 from injuries received when her house was destroyed by a flying bomb/V1. McEleny was killed at home by a flying bomb/V1 on 10 July 1944. Packwood (1886-1944) was killed by a flying bomb/V1 on 3 July 1944. Sanderson died on 27 September 1940.

The following are on McMurray's Wimbledon listing:

Frances Anker (Housewives Service), see page 120

Edith Brice (Housewives Service Canteen Worker and Helper at a First Aid Clinic), see page 116

Jessie Cavey (Housewives Service)

Winifred Walker (Salvage Steward, Housewives Service).

Anker was killed in her own home by a V1 on 22 July 1944. Edith Florence Brice (1885-1944) had just returned from duty at the Pelham Road Canteen when she was killed in her home, 54 Cliveden Road, by a bomb on 17 June 1944. Cavey (1881-1944) was killed in her own home, 133 Cambridge Road, by a flying bomb/V1 on 20 June 1944. Winifred Florence Walker (1911-1944), husband of Albert Walker, was killed by a direct hit on her home, 52 Elm Walk, Raynes Park, on 23 July 1944. She died with her two children, a three-year-old boy and a girl aged three months. The next night, in Raynes Park, a bomb fell at the Bushey Road end of Chestnut Road. That area was hit again on 14 August 1944 when a large number of houses were destroyed in Vernon Avenue and Carlton Park Avenue.

Violette Reine Elizabeth Szabo (nee Bushell) (1921-1945) sent her baby to childminders while she worked at the Rotax aircraft factory in Morden where her father was stationed. During this time, she was informed of her husband's death in action at the beginning of the Second Battle of El Alamein. In 1943, she became a secret agent. On her second mission into occupied France, she was captured by the German army, interrogated, tortured and deported to Ravensbruck concentration camp in northern Germany, where she was executed. Visit *violetteszabomuseum.org.uk*. Ravensbruck was a German concentration camp exclusively for women from 1939 to 1945. The largest single national group consisted of 40,000 Polish women.

In memory of Pauline Margaret Blackwell at Mitcham Cemetery. (Author)

CHAPTER TWENTY-THREE

VC Winners

Ian Bazalgette

Squadron Leader Ian Willoughby Bazalgette VC, DFC (1918–1944), born in Calgary, Alberta, Canada grew up in New Malden and attended Rokeby Preparatory School in Wimbledon from 1927 to 1932 and then Beverley Boys Secondary School, New Malden. Sir Joseph William Bazalgette CB (1819–1891), his great-grandfather, was the designer and engineer responsible for Putney Bridge and the Victoria, Albert and Chelsea Embankments, whose major achievement was the creation of a sewer network for central London. His great-great grandfather, Joseph William Bazelgette (1783–1849), was a Royal Navy captain. On the other side of the family, Ian Willoughby Bazalgette was great-grandson of John Boustead whose home was Cannizaro, Wimbledon Common.

When war was declared, Ian Bazalgette enlisted in the Royal Artillery, being commissioned as a Second Lieutenant in 1940. After serving in the Searchlight Section as an instructor, he transferred to the RAF Volunteer Reserve. He soloed within a week of beginning his flight training at RAF Cranwell and swiftly completed his ab initio (from the beginning) flying by 24 January 1942, given the rank of Pilot Officer. His first posting was to 25 Operational Training Unit (OTU). But by September 1942, he had joined an operational bomber squadron, No 115 Squadron RAF at RAF Mildenhall, Suffolk. Flying the Vickers Wellington bomber, 'Baz' was sent out initially on 'gardening' sorties, laying mines in the North Sea. After thirteen operations, Bazalgette and his squadron transitioned to the Avro Lancaster, completing their training in March 1943.

After completing ten more operations successfully on raids against heavily defended targets – Berlin, Essen, Kiel and St Nazaire – and surviving some harrowing escapes, including a crash landing, Bazalgette was awarded the Distinguished Flying Cross on 29 May 1943. Within the end of his tour of twenty-eight operations, he was posted as an instructor and Flight Commander to 20 OTU in Lossiemouth, Scotland, before he was 'recruited' for the Pathfinders. He transferred in April 1944 to No 635 Squadron RAF No 8 (Pathfinder Force) Group, based at RAF Downham Market in Norfolk.

He was killed in air operations at Senantes, France on 4 August 1944, aged 25. He was the pilot of a Lancaster bomber on a daylight raid on a *V1* storage depot. Nearing his target, his aircraft came under heavy anti-aircraft fire, setting the fuselage alight and both starboard engines out of action. In spite of this, he managed the target before the burning aircraft turned away in a slow spin. Gaining some control, he flew for thirty minutes before ordering the crew to bale out. Landing in a field, the plane immediately exploded killing him and two other crew members.

There are memorials to him at Bazalgette Gardens, New Malden; St Mary's Church, Wimbledon Village; St Clement Danes Church, the Strand, London; the Nanton Lancaster Society Museum, Canada; and the Ian Bazalgette Junior High School, Canada. There is a painting of him at New Malden library. His name is on the RAF Memorial at St Clement Dane's Church, central London, and his medals at the Royal Air Force Museum. Interestingly, he also has a memorial at Bexwell Church, Downham Market, Norfolk.

Eugene Esmonde VC

Lieutenant Commander Eugene Esmonde VC DSO (1909–1942), a pupil of Wimbledon College in the 1920s, joined the RAF in 1925 on a five-year

Bazalgette Gardens in New Malden, where he attended Beverley Boys School, was named in his honour in the early 1950s.

On 4 August 2015, Maldens & Coombe Heritage Society laid a wreath at the New Malden War Memorial in remembrance of the sacrifice of Bazalgette in the attempt to prevent the use of V1 bombs on Britain. (Maldens & Coombe Heritage Society)

Headstone to Bazalgette at Senantes Churchyard Cemetery, Oise, France.

commission and was killed in action in the Straits of Dover on 12 February 1942. He was posthumously awarded the VC on 28 February 1942 for his actions while in command of a British Fleet Air Arm (responsible for the operation of naval aircraft) torpedo bomber squadron.

In February 1942, German warships *Scharnhorst*, *Gneisenau* and *Prinz Eugen* planned to sail from northern France through the English Channel to their German home port. Commanded by Esmonde, 825 Squadron had been sent to RAF Manston, Kent, in anticipation of this move by the German navy. Esmonde's orders were to attack the convoy before it got beyond Calais.

On 12 February, after the fleet was spotted in the English Channel, Esmonde and six Swordfish took off from Manston at 12.25 and circled over Ramsgate waiting for the escort of five squadrons of Spitfires they had been promised. Only ten Spitfires, from No. 72 Squadron, appeared. Fearing that if he waited any longer the German battle fleet would be out of range, Esmonde pressed on. 825 Squadron was hopelessly outmatched. The German fleet had 400 aircraft assigned to it, with more than 100 in the air at any one time,

A painting of Esmonde. (With thanks to Wimbledon College)

including the Focke Wulf 190. As Esmonde made for the *Prinz Eugen*, a shell burst in front of his plane, blowing off his lower port wing. Esmonde desperately pulled up the nose of the Swordfish, releasing the torpedo, but a direct hit destroyed the plane.

The German battlecruisers got through in what became known as the Channel Dash. All six Swordfish were lost, and only five out of the eighteen airmen who left Manston survived.

Esmonde had already survived the sinking of HMS *Courageous* in 1939 and had been waiting to take off from when she was torpedoed by *U-29*. Esmonde had been awarded the Distinguished Service Order (DSO) for his role in the *Bismarck* raid on 26 May 1941. The following morning, *Bismarck* sank with heavy loss of life. The wreck was located 'upright and in good shape' in the bottom of the Atlantic Ocean 470 miles of Brest in June 1989. The crew of the *Bismarck* may have scuttled her to avoid capture.

Esmonde, son of Dr John Joseph and Eily Esmonde of Tipperary, Ireland, was born in the village of Thurgoland near Barnsley, Yorkshire with a twin brother in 1909, in a family of eight brothers and three sisters. Dr John Joseph Esmonde (1862–1915), in temporary general practice in Thurgoland, was an Irish nationalist MP for North Tipperary from 1910 to 1915, and died on 17 April 1915 while serving as captain in the Royal Army Medical Corps. Eugene Esmonde's brother, Patrick Esmonde, was awarded the Military Cross whilst serving in the Royal Army Medical Corps at the Rhine in 1944. His great uncle, Thomas Esmonde (1829–1873), was an Irish recipient of the VC for his courage during the Crimean War.

Esmonde was buried at Woodlands Cemetery, Gillingham, Kent on 30 April 1942. He is commemorated on Wimbledon College War Memorial and on the Royal Navy Memorial, Portsmouth.

Robert Ryder

Captain Robert Edward Dudley Ryder VC (1908–1986) was MP for Merton and Morden between 1950 and 1955 after retiring from the navy. He was born in India and had two brothers; both were killed in the Second World War. Major Lisle Charles Dudley Ryder, Royal Norfolk Regiment, died in the Le Paradis massacre of 1940 in France, while Major Ernie Terrick Dudley Ryder, 1st King George V's Own Gurkha Rifles, died in captivity after the defence of Singapore in 1942. When the Second World War started, Robert Ryder was serving as a lieutenant commander on HMS *Warspite*. In 1940, he was promoted to commander of the Q-ship HMS *Edgehill* which was sunk by a torpedo from *U-51* in the Atlantic, 200 miles west of Ireland; sixty-seven died and twenty-five survived. Ryder was adrift for four days before rescue. According to *uboat.net*, 'the commander rescued himself on a piece of flotsam and was rescued by a passing ship on 2 July and eventually landed at Plymouth. Another crew member was also rescued from a piece of debris on 6 July.'

In 1941, he went on to captain the *Prince Philippe*, a cross-channel steamer converted to a Commando ship, which sank after a collision in the Firth of Clyde on 15 July 1941. Ryder fought in the successful St Nazaire Raid, or 'Operation Chariot', on 27 March 1942, where he commanded HMS *Campbeltown*. The stated aim of the operation was to deny large German ships, particularly the German battleship *Tirpitz*, a base on the Atlantic coast. After the raid, 228 men of the force of 611 returned to Britain; 169 were killed and 215 became PoWs. German casualties were over 360 dead.

The official citation for his award reads as follows:

> For great gallantry in the attack on St Nazaire. He commanded a force of small unprotected ships in an attack on a heavily defended port and led HMS *Campbeltown* in under intense fire from short range weapons at point blank range. Though the main object of the expedition had been accomplished in the beaching of *Campbeltown*, he remained on the spot conducting operations, evacuating men from *Campbeltown* and dealing with strong points and close range weapons while exposed to heavy fire for one hour and sixteen minutes, and did not withdraw till it was certain that his ship could be of no use in rescuing any of the Commando Troops who were still ashore. That his Motor Gun Boat, now full of dead and wounded, should have survived and should have been able to withdraw through an intense barrage of close range fire was almost a miracle.

For his actions during his operation, he was one of five people awarded the VC. Ryder's medal is held by the Imperial War Museum. He died on 29 June 1986 on board a yacht off Guernsey (*thepeerage.com*). There is a portrait of the Ryder family (1936) at the National Portrait Gallery.

Arthur Scarf

Squadron Leader Arthur Stewart King Scarf VC (1913–1941) was born in Wimbledon and attended King's College School between 1922 and 1930. He joined the RAF in 1936, and was accepted for pilot training. On gaining his wings, he was posted to No 9 Squadron, operating the Handley Page Heyford biplane bomber of the 1930s. He was a squadron leader in 62 Squadron, RAF during the Second World War when he was awarded the (posthumous) VC. A painting by Edward Neatby at King's College School, unveiled in 1947, is in memory of Scarf.

On 9 December 1941, in Malaya, near the Siam border, all available aircraft had been ordered to make a daylight raid on Singora (where the Japanese Army was invading) in Siam. Squadron Leader Scarf, as leader of the raid, had just taken off from the base at Butterworth, Penang, Malaysia, when enemy aircraft swept in destroying or disabling the rest of the machines. Scarf decided nevertheless to fly alone to Singora. Despite attacks from roving fighters, he completed the bombing run and was on his way back when his aircraft became riddled with bullets and he was severely wounded. His left arm had been shattered, he had a large hole in his back and was drifting in and out of consciousness. He managed to crash-land the Blenheim at Alor Setar, a city and the state capital of Kedah, Malaysia, without causing any injury to his crew, and was rushed to hospital where he died two hours later. Scarf's wife Elizabeth Scarf (later Gunn), known as Sally, was a nurse at the General Hospital in Alor Setar. But during the previous day, she had left Alor Setar, so Scarf died without seeing her again.

Phyllis Thom (1908–2008), or Phyllis Briggs as she was then, was one of four nursing sisters at the General Hospital in Alor Setar. She told the BBC, on 29 December 2004, of her memories at the beginning of December 1941:

> I was determined that Pongo (Scarf) would be buried properly. We managed to get a coffin from the jail. Another sister came with me in my Morris 8 and we followed the ambulance bearing his coffin to the local cemetery, where a grave had been dug. On our way, we met two Army padres driving towards us. I stopped the car and asked if they would come with us to say a prayer.

Scarf's VC was not gazetted until June 1946. The facts concerning his actions were not known until after the war because of the chaotic nature of the Malayan campaign. His VC is displayed at the RAF Museum, London. He was buried at Taiping War Cemetery in Malaysia, which was created by the Army after the defeat of Japan. There are now 864 Second World War Commonwealth casualties and one Dutch casualty in this site, more than 500 of whom are unidentified.

The *London Daily Mail* of 22 June 1946 printed a comment by one of the masters of King's College School: 'A pleasant boy, maybe not frightfully bracing, but a fine ordinary chap. He never reached the Rugger 15, but played a steady unsensational game in the second team and he was mad about aeroplanes.'

CHAPTER TWENTY-FOUR

Lord Dowding, the Airman who Saved Britain

Air Chief Marshal Lord Hugh Caswall Tremenheere Dowding (1882–1970) was head of the Royal Air Force's Fighter Command during the Battle of Britain and three-times a Wimbledon resident. From April to October 1940, his pilots had resisted the German Luftwaffe using a system he himself had developed before the war. While it was happening, he was controlling all the resources behind the scene, replacing lost men and aircraft, and maintaining a significant reserve force so that the numbers committed to battle never exceeded half of the total available.

The invasion threat had eased by the time Hugh Dowding moved to 3 St Mary's Road, Wimbledon Village, in 1941, Hitler having switched his attentions to Russia after the Battle of Britain. Dowding lived at the house until 1951, but the man who had just masterminded the most critical defence strategy in British history had also lived in Wimbledon earlier in his life: first at 8 Lansdowne Road around 1900 and later, from 1917, at 65 Wimbledon Hill Road with his first wife Clarice, who died after just two years, leaving him to care for their young son.

He relinquished his post at Fighter Command unwillingly in November 1940 after internal RAF policy differences and he retired altogether in July 1942, honoured with a peerage the following year as Baron Dowding of Bentley Priory.

His book, *Twelve Legions of Angels*, was suppressed until after the war because the Government thought it contained information that might be of use to the Germans.

It was a strange fate for such a significant military figure in wartime, but Dowding was always controversial. He had taken over Fighter Command at its formation in 1936 and introduced the 'Dowding System' for air defence including radar (then a novelty), the Royal Observer Corps, raid plotting, and radio control of aircraft. The system was unified by dedicated bomb-proof telephone links beneath the ground and commanded from RAF Bentley Priory, a country house north of London.

3 St Mary's Road in 2015.

Dowding had also introduced the Spitfire and the Hurricane to the RAF before the war, and fought the Air Ministry to ensure that fighter planes were fitted with bullet-proof windscreens. He had reached the rank of Air Chief Marshal in 1937 and had been due to retire in June 1939, but remained in command throughout the Battle of Britain despite some internal hostility at senior levels.

Known to his men as 'Stuffy', he refused to sacrifice aircraft and pilots to support the ill-fated British Expeditionary Force before the fall of France – although he did organise cover for the Dunkirk evacuation – and always took a particularly caring approach to his own men. This dated back to his days in the First World War when, as a pilot in the Royal Flying Corps, he had clashed with the commander, Lord Trenchard, over the need to rest pilots exhausted by non-stop duty. He had been sent home for the rest of the war as a result, although he had then gone on to a distinguished career in the newly-formed RAF.

This caring attitude continued after his retirement and, with his second wife Muriel, he became a vegetarian and campaigner for the humane treatment of animals. They both opposed cruel laboratory experiments on living animals and the Lord Dowding Fund for Humane Research was established after his death. When he died on 15 February 1970 a memorial service was held at Westminster Abbey and his ashes were laid to rest below the Battle of Britain Memorial Window.

English Heritage erected a blue plaque on 3 St Mary's Road, Wimbledon Village in April 2000, but it was removed and stored when the house was demolished in 2009. It could not be put on either of Dowding's earlier homes in Wimbledon Hill Road or Lansdowne Road because they too were gone. A new house was built at 3 St Mary's Road, but as English Heritage only allows its plaques on original buildings, the owners of the property remedied matters by putting up their own.

This is a replacement for the English Heritage plaque, marking the residency in the previous house. Copyright English Heritage.

CHAPTER TWENTY-FIVE

Major Malcolm Munthe

Major Malcolm Pennington Mellor Munthe (1910–1995), a writer and artist, devoted himself to seventeenth-century Southside House, Woodhayes Road, Wimbledon Common after returning from the Second World War with post-traumatic stress disorder (PTSD). He wanted to go back pre-war when he took refuge, to a world of chivalry and monarchy.

Southside House was once the principal manor house in the area, using the Crooked Billet and Hand in Hand pubs as its outbuildings and stables. The house passed from the Penningtons to the Munthe family when Hilda Pennington Mellor (1882–1967), a descendant of Robert Pennington, married Axel Munthe (1857–1949), a Swedish doctor, animal rights activist and writer, in 1907. They had two sons, Peter and Malcolm. Southside was taken over by the once-wealthy cotton merchant Pennington Mellor family from Biarritz

Southside House contains many examples of seventeenth-century furniture, and memorabilia connected to the Pennington family.

in the 1930s. Their wealth came from their business activities in the cotton and shipping industries. In May 1941, the ceiling of the seventeenth-century house was damaged by German bombs. The preservation of the house was left to Hilda Pennington Munthe, who did not live there during the war, and Malcolm Munthe. Many of the valuables and family portraits were sent to caves in Wales.

His Wimbledon links dated back to his boyhood when his mother Hilda – then divorced from Axel Munthe – occupied a property on Spencer Hill, and he and his elder brother Peter attended King's College School. Malcolm Munthe was brought up between the Swedish court, Italy, and Britain. He became a British citizen at the outbreak of the Second World War in order to fight, since Sweden would be neutral throughout the war. He was assigned to the Gordon Highlanders for no other reason than his first name's (Malcolm) Scottish roots.

In September 1939, he was asked if he would be interested in a 'volunteer job'. Agreeing, he found himself a part of Military Intelligence (Research), which was responsible for irregular warfare.

During the 'Winter War' (November 1939–March 1940) between the Soviet Union and Finland, Munthe (who spoke Swedish) was tasked with conveying equipment through neutral Norway and Sweden to the Swedish Volunteer Corps in Finland, and instructing the volunteers. The equipment, labelled as farming machinery, actually included Matilda tanks, artillery pieces, explosives, anti-tank mines and grenades. Strictly against orders, Munthe took an active part in missions against the Red Army (the army and the air force of the Russian Soviet Federative Socialist Republic).

In early April 1940, in anticipation of a German invasion of Norway, Munthe was appointed Liaison Officer to the Norwegian Army, and was in Stavanger, a city and municipality in Norway, when the invasion took place. He was captured by German soldiers after being wounded in both legs by shrapnel from a German artillery round. Taken to a hospital in Stavenger, he promptly escaped and managed to recuperate with Norwegian help. He tried to get to Sweden by various arduous routes over the next three months, eventually succeeding.

The Special Operations Executive (SOE) was a British Second World War organisation, also known as 'Churchill's Secret Army' or the 'Ministry of Ungentlemanly Warfare'. For the next year, Munthe was the SOE's representative in Sweden and trained Norwegian exiles in sabotage. He was finally asked to leave in July 1941 because of his involvement in a plot to assassinate Heinrich Himmler (1900–1945), head of the Nazi SS, in Oslo.

On the day he left Stockholm, news came through of an explosion of a German train of five cars in transit loaded with ammunition at Krylbo in the middle of Sweden. The train exploded at 4.20am on 19 July 1941 while standing at the Krylbo railway station. Although Munthe never acknowledged

A statue of John Axel Viking (Peter) Pennington Munthe (1908–1976), brother of Malcolm Munthe, which stands in the front courtyard of Southside House. (Author)

any responsibility for this action, it is widely assumed that it was his farewell gesture aimed at the Swedish government. According to *Sweden, the Swastika and Stalin: The Swedish experience in the Second World War* by John Gilmour, pencil bombs had been placed on the German ammunition train and the explosion injured twenty-four Swedes. Gilmour said: 'The fears of the Swedish Cabinet of reprisals by Britain, expressed during their decision to allow transit, had now been realised.' Neutral Sweden allowed Nazis to use their railways to occupy Norway. Munthe was disgusted with Swedes helping Nazis, though became Swedish later.

He was put in charge of SOE's activities in Southern Italy, where he participated in the Anzio landings on 22 January 1944. After months of desperate fighting, the Allies managed to break out of the beachhead and liberate Rome on 4 June 1944. The Allies suffered 43,000 casualties, of whom 7,000 died and 36,000 were wounded or missing. The Germans suffered similar losses. Munthe suffered severe injuries at Anzio and was left with shrapnel lodged in his head. The music room at Southside contains a photograph of his friend, Captain John Michael McVean Gubbins, Queen's Own Cameron Highlanders, SOE at Anzio beach head. He died on 6 February 1944, and is commemorated on Cassino Memorial, Italy and the Harrold War Memorial, Bedfordshire.

Krylbo explosion.

In Scandinavia, Munthe had established a network of 'Friends' which he called the 'Red Horse', an imitation of the Baroness Orczy's *Scarlet Pimpernel*, a fictional English dandy who leads a secret life saving French aristocrats from the guillotine. In southern Italy, he took the mimicry further, dressing as a large old lady to smuggle a radio transmitter past Nazi lines and coordinate SOE activity in the occupied zone.

Munthe was also instrumental in the rescue of liberal philosopher Benedetto Croce and his family, who were being held captive in the Villa Tritone at Sorrento, Italy, and their flight to Capri where his father Axel Munthe's house Villa San Michele – which had a stunning view over the harbour and the blue bay – provided shelter.

Among the litter of antiquities, Etruscan pots, Roman marble and Greek statuary at Villa San Michele, Royal Navy Lieutenant Commander Quintin Riley (1905–1980) got hold of the visitors' book and ruled off a new section, which he headed 'September 13, 1943 – Liberation by the English'. 'What about the Scots?' asked Malcolm Munthe, indicating the kilt of his regiment, the Gordon Highlanders. All the commandos signed their names. After the war, Munthe published *Sweet is War*, a memoir of his wartime experiences.

Major Munthe was decorated with the Military Cross for bravery. The reclusive Major eventually retreated to Southside House. He was so convinced his family and home were under threat from attack that he slept in the basement to keep watch. The Second World War differed from previous wars in its bigger field weapons and bombs. PTSD is an anxiety disorder caused by very stressful, frightening of distressing events. Someone with PTSD often relives the traumatic event through nightmares and flashbacks, and may experience feelings of isolation, irritability and guilt. They may also have problems sleeping and find concentrating difficult. Cases of PTSD were first documented during the First World War when soldiers developed shell shock as a result of the harrowing conditions in the trenches. But the condition was not officially recognised as a mental health condition until 1980.

New objects uncovered at the house include maps from Norway marking the places where German munitions trains were blown up. They are on the piano in the Music Room.

Munthe started giving tours of the house while he was still alive, but many of his stories – such as one of Lord Nelson's lover Emma Hamilton dressing up as Greek deities in a guess-who game in the music room – were proven to be unfounded after his death. When parking charges were introduced in London, Malcolm went there on his horse. He made additions to the house, including a chapel, and claimed they had been damaged in the Blitz. Described by Sir Angus Ogilvy (1928–2004), the husband of Princess Alexandra of Kent, as 'the last true English eccentric', he died at Southside House in November 1995.

In November 2010, firefighters saved artwork worth millions of pounds from a blaze at Southside House. On 15 April 2011, during the restoration, a cache of weapons was discovered in a hidden room, which was discovered after a hearthstone in the dining room fireplace was removed to reveal wooden steps. Weapons discovered in the secret basement included a Colt 45 pistol, a Sten sub-machine gun and magazines for an M1 carbine rifle. Workmen and residents from the area were evacuated and the weapons were taken away by the Metropolitan Police, but they are due to go on display at The Guards Museum, London.

Appendix

If you are researching your family history, you may discover that one of your ancestors was a soldier in the Second World War. The following may assist your research or inspire further research. Information has been cross-checked with family members where possible.

Short Biographies from the Wartime Seas

The Battle of the River Plate, which took place on 13 December 1939 in the South Atlantic, was the first major naval battle of the Second World War. Two Wimbledon men were heroes of the battle, in which the *Graf Spee* was driven to seek shelter in the harbour of Montevideo and was scuttled to avoid continuance of the battle. The men honoured were Gunner <u>Reginald Charles Biggs</u> (1909–1977), whose home was at Haydon's Road and who was awarded the DSC, and Chief Petty Officer <u>Ronald Palmer Burges</u> (1904–1969).

<u>Frank Clifford Hopkins</u> (1893–1943) was born in Wimbledon and lived on West Drive, Cheam. He was in command of HMS *Fandango* from 3 July 1940 to 4 November 1940, HMS *Hyacinth* from 4 November 1940 to mid-1942, and HMS *La Flore* from 29 June 1942 to 22 October 1942. Hopkins, who was a captain of the P&O steamship company, died on 8 April 1943 in Queen Mary Hospital, Roehampton, Surrey.

Steam merchant *Harpalyce* was carrying a cargo of 8,000 tons of steel from North America to Hull when she was torpedoed by *U-124* without warning and sunk 23 miles north of the Butt of Lewis, Hebrides on 25 August 1940. Thirty-seven of the forty-two crew were lost, including Second Engineer <u>David West Harris</u> (1914–1940), son of Sir Sidney West Harris and Emily Mary Harris, of Wimbledon. He was at Charterhouse school and studied engineering at Cambridge. He is commemorated in London on the Tower Hill Memorial, panel fifty-five.

Lieutenant <u>George Robson Colvin</u> (1932–1943), Royal Navy, of Lingfield Road, Wimbledon Village, was one of three brothers serving with HM Forces. In command of HMS *Sunfish*, a Royal Navy S-class submarine launched in September 1936, he torpedoed and sank the Finnish cargo ship *Oscar Midling* (under German control) off the coast of Norway on 5 December 1940. On 18 November 1941, commanding HMS *Sealion*, he sank the Norwegian tanker *Vesco* and on 5 December 1941 torpedoed and sank the Norwegian merchant ship *Island*. On 6 December 1942, commanding HMS *Tigris*, he sunk an Italian submarine, *Porfido*, off the coast of Algeria, and, on 21 January 1943, torpedoed and sank the Italian merchant *Citta di Genova* off Saseno Island. HMS *Tigris* was sunk by a German submarine chaser, *Uj-2210*, off Naples on 27 February 1943. Each year, there is a Remembrance Service for the submarine and the crew (sixty-three) lost at St Nicholas Church, Newbury, Berkshire (Newbury adopted *Tigris* as part of a national scheme to raise money for the Navy during The Second World War).

SS Jura, in convoy from Huelva, Spain to Aberdeen with ore, was bombed and sunk by German FW200 Kondor aircraft on 9 February 1941. Fifteen-year-old Cabin Boy <u>Frank Dennis Hope</u> was one of thirteen recorded as lost, and is remembered at Tower Hill Memorial, London (panel fifty-nine). He was the foster-son of Alice Burns (nee Summers) of Morden.

Cargo ship *Siamese Prince*, en route from New York to Liverpool, was torpedoed and sunk by *U-69* on 17 February 1941. Nine people were lost from a crew of fifty-eight, including <u>Robert Edwin Strachan</u> (1901–1941) of Wimbledon.

Ordinary seaman <u>William Percy Jessup</u> (1920–1941) of Merton lost his life on ocean boarding vessel HMS *Manistee*, sunk by *U-107* on 23 February 1941 south of Iceland while under the command of U-boat ace Gunther Hessler (1909–1968). After the war, Hessler spent more than a year in Allied captivity. In 1947, he was commissioned by the British Royal Navy to write *The U-Boat War in the Atlantic* (completed 1951), a definitive account of the German U-boat offensive.

Ordinary Seaman <u>Robert George Hill</u> (1921–1941) of South Road, Wimbledon survived the sinking of *Empire Endurance* by *U-73* on 20 April 1941, but died of exposure (7 May 1941) in a lifeboat found by the British motor passenger ship *Highland Brigade* on 9 May 1941. Only seven crew members were still alive. Two of them died shortly after being picked up and another died in a hospital at Liverpool where the men were landed on 11 May 1941. Hill is remembered on the Tower Hill Memorial. He was an old boy of Haydons Road School, Wimbledon. (The school building on Haydons Road closed down in the 1980s – as the school had moved to a new site – but was reopened, and the school is now divided between two locations).

Early in the Second World War, light cruiser HMS *Dunedin* was involved in the hunt for the German warships *Scharnhorst* and *Gneisenau* after the sinking of HMS *Rawalpindi*, a converted passenger ship intended to raid and sink enemy merchant shipping, on 23 November 1939. *Dunedin* was sunk north-east of Recife, Brazil on 24 November 1941 by *U-124*. Only 4 officers and 63 men survived out of *Dunedin's* crew of 486 officers and men. <u>William Robert Frost</u> (1924–1941) of Wimbledon died.

<u>Stanley Harry Ernest Hubbard</u>, from Wimbledon was killed when HMS *Barham* was hit by *U-331* on 25 November 1941. In an effort to conceal

the sinking from the Germans and to protect British morale, the Board of Admiralty censored all news of *Barham*'s sinking. After a delay of several weeks, the War Office notified the next of kin. The notification letters included a warning not to discuss the loss of the ship with anyone but close relatives. Two men from Morden survived the HMS *Barham* sinking: Corporal Edward AW Sullivan (1913–1995) and Signalman Donald Charles Featherstone.

On 27 November 1941, *U-559*'s torpedo hit HMAS *Parramatta* of the Royal Australian Navy off the Libyan coast. Only those on deck had a chance to escape. One hundred and thirty-eight lost their lives, including Ordinary Seaman Albert Edward Cash (1917–1941) of Wimbledon.

Steam tanker *Refast* was torpedoed by *U-582* on 26 January 1942 south of St John's, a city on Newfoundland Island, off Canada's Atlantic coast. Ten crew members were lost, including Cabin Boy Donald Lewis Davie (1924–1942), son of William John and Ada Mary Davie, of Wimbledon. The master, twenty-seven crew members and four gunners were picked up by the British steam merchant *Mariposa* and landed at Halifax, Canada the next day.

Able Seaman Edward Henry McPherson (1921–1942) of Wimbledon was one of the crew of HMS *Belmont*. *Belmont* was torpedoed by *U-82* south of Newfoundland on 31 January 1942. There were no survivors.

Motor tanker *Anadara* was sunk by *U-558* on 24 February 1942 east of Halifax. Sixty-two died, including Third Radio Officer Basil Williams (1924–1942) of Wimbledon.

HMS *Bedouin* was lost on 15 June 1942 south of Pantellaria in the Mediterranean Sea when the convoy in which she was sailing was intercepted by an Italian cruiser and destroyer force led by the cruisers Eugenio di Savoia and Montecuccoli. She was completely disabled. Eventually, it was an Italian aircraft which finished off *Bedouin* with a torpedo. She sank with the loss of twenty-eight men, including Leading Stoker A.S. Gough of South Park Road, Wimbledon. At dusk, an Italian floatplane and a little Italian hospital ship picked up 213 survivors who were taken as PoWs. (Source *wartimememoriesproject.com*)

SS *Ocean Crusader* was completed on 13 November 1942 and sailed from Portland, Maine to New York to load general cargo for the UK. On 26 November 1942 in the North Atlantic, north-east of Newfoundland, she was intercepted by *U-262*. *Ocean Crusader* transmitted two distress signals reporting U-boat activity, and nothing more was heard. The ship was torpedoed and sunk. Ordinary seaman Cyril Edwin Braxton (1925–1942), son of Cyril Edwin Braxton (formerly Stoker 1st Class, Royal Navy) and Rosetta Mabel Braxton, of Wimbledon, was lost in the sinking. He is commemorated on the Tower Hill Memorial.

On 3 November 1942, ocean liner *Ceramic*, the largest ship until P&O introduced RMS *Hooltan* in 1923, left Liverpool for Australia. At midnight on 6-7 December 1942, *U-515* attacked *Ceramic*. Ernest Murray Norrie

(1919–1942) of Wimbledon Park was one of the passengers who went down with the ship.

Landing craft HMS *LC1 (L)-162* was sunk on 7 February 1943 by *U-596* 25 miles north-north-east of Mostaganem, Algeria. Eighteen died, including Motor Mechanic Percy Thomas Phillips (1907–1943) of Wimbledon. Seven surviors were picked up by HMS *LCI (L)-7* and HMS *LCI (L)-2010*, which were en route with the landing craft.

Whilst defending Convoy HX 228 – a North Atlantic convoy of the HX series that ran during the Battle of the Atlantic – on 3 March 1943, HMS *Harvester* forced *U-444* to the surface and then rammed it. The next day, *Harvester* was torpedoed by *U-432* and broke in half. Nine officers and 136 ratings were lost, including William John Stanley Furner (1921–1943) of Wimbledon Park. The French corvette *Aconit* rammed and sank *U-432* herself and then rescued *Harvester's* few survivors.

On 9 April 1943, HMS *Beverley* was seriously damaged in a collision with the British steam merchant *Cairnvalona* and took station in the rear of the convoy, until she was torpedoed 30 hours later by *U-188*. George William James Reeves (1921–1943), son of George William James and Ellen Reeves, husband of Emily Caroline Reeves, of Morden, died. There were only four survivors out of a crew of 155.

HMS *Holcombe* was torpedoed and sunk on 12 December 1943 by *U-593* whilst on duty in the Mediterranean with the loss of eighty-five men, including Ordinary Seaman Peter Alder (1924–1943), son of Henry and Emily Florence Alder, of Wimbledon, and Leading Seaman Charles Reginald Gallop (1912–1943) of Wimbledon. Earlier that day, *U-593* sunk HMS *Tynedale*.

Light cruiser HMS *Penelope* was torpedoed and sunk by *U-410* on 18 February 1944 near Naples. Four hundred and seventeen of the crew, including the captain, went down with the ship, including Sub-Lieutenant Edward Ernest Draper (1924–1944) of Wimbledon Chase and George Charles Francis (1912–1944) of Wimbledon; 206 survived. A memorial plaque commemorating those lost is in St Ann's Church, HM Dockyard, Portsmouth. British writer C.S. Forester published his novel *The Ship* in May 1943. He dedicated the book 'with the deepest respect to the officers and crew of HMS *Penelope*'.

Hell ships

After invading many countries in the Far East, Japan found itself with a large amount of prisoners. Japan decided to use them as slave labour to help their war effort, the majority being transported by ship to new destinations. These ships were not built for transporting the large numbers involved and were without correct markings, leaving them open to attack by the Allies as legitimate targets, as they had no knowledge of what the ships contained. These ships became known as Hell Ships.

The *Harugika Maru*, which left port on 25 June 1944 with 730 prisoners, was sunk on 26 June 1944 by a torpedo fired from HMS *Truculent,* just south of Balawan. Lance Sergeant Donald Frederick Twiddy, Royal Corps of Signals, husband of E. Twiddy of Morden, and Corporal Desmond Charles Keats, East Surrey Regiment, died with another 175 prisoners in the sinking. Keats was a Japanese PoW being transported in the *Harugika Maru* from Belawan in Sumatra to Pakanbaroe in Sumatra.

Hofuku Maru (also named *Toyofuku Maru*) was sunk by an American carrier aircraft 80 miles north of Corregidor on 21 September 1944, while carrying 1,289 British and Dutch PoWs; 1,047 died. Private Robert George Shepherd, son of Ernest Gordon Shepherd and Fanny Louisa Shepherd of Merton, died and is named on Column seventy of the Singapore Memorial. His brother, Albert Gordon Shepherd also died on active service, on 12 December 1941, and is also named on Column seventy of the Singapore Memorial. Private Dennis Fitzpatrick, 5th Battalion, Royal Norfolk Regiment, husband of Catherine Fitzpatrick of Wimbledon, died when *Hofuku Maru* was sunk.

In 1946, it was decided that the Japanese PoW camp at Kranji, northwestern Singapore, would be designated as Singapore's War Cemetery. The Singapore Memorial, dedicated to the men and women from the UK, Australia, Canada, Sri Lanka, India, Malaya, the Netherlands and New Zealand who died defending Singapore and Malaya against the invading Japanese forces, stands over Kranji War Cemetery. Corporal Oswald Robert Riddle (1915–1942), East Surrey Regiment, husband of Emmeline Hannah Riddle of West Wimbledon, is listed on Column sixty-eight.

Further Research

Anthony Kenneth Stanley Philips (1922-1987), born in Wimbledon, and Ronald Franklin Seddon (1917-1998) of Merton were Royal Naval Volunteer Reserve (RNVR) officers. Philips, son of Walter Charles Stanley Philips (1881-1968) and Kathleen Elizabeth Hankinson (1891-1988), served at HMS Lochailort from 24 August 1942 to 7 December 1942, a Combined Operations training establishment not far from Fort William in Scotland. From 10 January 1943 to 30 October 1943, he served at HMS Wescliff, Southend, Essex. He was sent to HMS Salsette in India, and served there from October 1943 to April 1944. He was stationed at HMS Braganza in Bombay, India from 1 April 1944 to 12 October 1945. Seddon was Commanding Officer of HM Motor Launch 145 in 1943, and Commanding Officer of HM Motor Torpedo Boat 718 from 20 January 1944 to 1945. A motor launch (ML) is a small military vessel in Royal Navy service. It was designed for harbour defence and submarine chasing, or for armed high speed air-sea rescue.

Tracing Wimbledon, Morden and Merton Soldiers

Corporal <u>John Dennis Allison</u> (d1947), East Surrey Regiment, son of Henry John and Bessie Allison of Morden, is buried at Fayid War Cemetery, Egypt. The cemetery was opened in June 1941 for war burials from the numerous military hospitals in the area.

<u>Carl Askloff</u> (d1940) of Wolsley Crescent, Morden, died in 1940 in a hospital at Dover after his ship was struck by a bomb during an enemy aerial attack. He was so badly wounded that he died two days later. The *Wimbledon Boro' News* of 2 August 1940 reported that 'A particularly sad circumstance is that his son, Private <u>Albert Askloff</u>, who was one of the BEF who took part in the fighting round Dunkirk, has been reported missing.'

Flying-Officer <u>Edgar William Bennee</u> (1912–1996), 101 Squadron, of Waldemar Road, Wimbledon, attended Merton Park Central School and was awarded the Distinguished Flying Cross. In August 1942, one engine of his aircraft failed when over Belgium, but he flew back safely to base on the remaining engine.

Acting Sergeant <u>Ronald Cuthbert Besant</u> DFM, 51st Squadron, who went to Emanuel School, Battersea Rise and lived with his mother at Ashen Grove, Wimbledon Park. Before joining the RAF in March 1939, he worked for caterers Messrs Lyons. At the time of his death (11 August 1943), he was in 192 Squadron and went missing with another pilot over the Bay of Biscay. He is remembered on the Air Forces Memorial at Runnymede, Surrey.

Squadron-Leader <u>Norman Maxwell Boffee</u> DFC, an old Pelham Road Primary, Wimbledon schoolboy, whose mother lived in Hardy Road, gained the rank of Wing Commander in the service of the RAF. He was decorated with the award of DFC. In 1953, he married Iris Leslie Pepys. She gained the rank of Flying Officer between 1940 and 1953 in the service of the Women's Royal Air Force.

Air Chief Marshall <u>Sir Brian Burnett</u> (1913–2011), All England Tennis Club chairman from 1974 to 1984, joined the RAF in 1934. Throughout the Second World War, he served as Commander of No 51 Whitley Squadron. After seven months in command, he was awarded the Distinguished Flying Cross and left for Canada as Commander of No 33 Air Navigation School. In 1984, he wrote his memoirs, *A Pilot at Wimbledon.*

Lieutenant Colonel <u>Reginald Edward Hawke 'Buzzer' Hadingham</u> (1915–2004), All England Tennis Club chairman from 1984 to 1989, was born in Holland, and lived in Wimbledon after the First World War. He served the Second World War as a gunnery officer in North Africa and Italy, where he took part in the Anzio and Salerno landings.

Lieutenant <u>Kenneth Benjamin Culley</u>, Royal Canadian Naval Volunteer Force, at Rutlish School from 1925 to 1929, was mentioned in dispatches for gallant services in an action with a U-boat while serving on Canadian corvette *Oak Villa*. The *Wimbledon Boro' News* reported on 1 January 1943 that during the action, two of the crew of the corvette jumped on the deck of the submarine, killed several of the crew and forced the remainder over the side.

The *Wimbledon Boro' News* of 2 August 1940 recorded the death of Leading Aircraftman <u>W. Roy Driscoll</u>, general manager of Kennards and second son of Mr and Mrs R.A. Driscoll of New Church Road, Hove. He was 25. His business acumen at an early age marked him as the youngest managing director in the country.

Private <u>Ernest Charles Grafton</u> (d1942), 1st Battalion Middlesex Regiment, son of Wallis Henry and Elizabeth Grafton of Morden, is on the Yokohama War Cemetery ROH, Japan.

<u>Anthony Lawrence</u> (1912–2013) started life at 34 Effra Road, Wimbledon and attended King's College School. He joined the *Wimbledon Advertiser* as a reporter in 1930 and worked for several London weeklies in the mid-1930s when his parents moved to Thornton Road, Wimbledon Village. When the Second World War broke out, he enlisted in the Royal Artillery, reached the rank of captain, married his first wife Sylvia, and led his men in battle across France and Germany after D-Day in 1944. His press experience came in useful in the war's immediate aftermath as he was assigned to the Army's Information Control Unit and he played an important role in founding the new post-war German newspaper *Die Zeit*. Sylvia had been killed by German bombing while in a shelter for expectant mothers but, in Germany, Lawrence met his second wife, Irmgard. They were married in 1946. Returning to London, he joined the BBC World Service and soon became a supervising editor.

Flying Officer <u>Donald Sinclair Margach</u> (1911–1944), RAFVR, No 106 Squadron, whose home was in West Wimbledon, enlisted in the RAFVR in 1940. He was commissioned in 1942, and was awarded the DFC for accurate bombing. The citation stated: 'Flying Officer Margach has completed nineteen operational sorties, during which his accuracy in bomb-aiming has been outstanding. He has been engaged in attacks on a wide range of the enemy's objectives and in a mine-laying sortie, when he calmly laid mines only a very short distance from a warship. This officer's steadiness and coolness in the face of the fiercest opposition have been demonstrated by the excellent photographs he has obtained. The success which has attended his untiring efforts has been a fine example to other air bombers.'

Margach died on 29 July 1944. He took off from Little Staughton at 10.30pm and crashed south of Heimerdingen. The aircraft was thought to have exploded, although the pilot, Squadron Leader V. F. Coleman ejected and was taken prisoner. The rest of the crew was killed.

Lieutenant Colonel <u>Bernard Donald Ogden</u> MC TD (1887–1961), East Surrey Regiment, of School House, Church Lane, Merton (1938) had been a soldier for thirty-eight years. He was awarded the Military Cross and Bar during the Great War, and commanded the 5th Battalion, East Surrey Regiment from 1934 to 1938. He commanded the Battalion in England and Northern Ireland from May 1940 to February 1941.

Colonel Reginald Nowel Parker, who died in 2009, of Merton Mansions, Bushey Road was awarded the Military Medal for gallantry on the field while serving with the Queen's Royal Regiment, West Surrey Regiment in Egypt and Libya. He was employed by Lysol prior to joining the forces in 1939. He took park in heavy fighting which preceded the evacuation of Dunkirk, prior to which his regiment did one of the longest route marches on record, seventy miles. His brother Jack Parker was a telegraphist on a minesweeper in the Mediterranean. His sister, Private Constance Parker, served with the Auxiliary Territorial Service (ATS) – the women's branch of the British Army – on an anti-aircraft gun team. His brother Private Norman Parker was a member of the Home Guard. Reginald Nowel Parker's wife, Margo Adela Parker (nee Lloyd) (1917–2007), became a nurse in 1941 and joined a section of the VAD that was nursing soldiers and prisoners on the Isle of Wight.

Private George Penford (d1941), East Surrey Regiment, son of Thomas William and Edith Penford of Merton Park, died in Malaya on 17 December 1941. He is buried at Kranji War Cemetery, Singapore, and listed on Column 70 of the Singapore Memorial in Kranji. There are now more than 4,460 Commonwealth casualties of the Second World War buried or commemorated at Kranji War Cemetery.

Airman Flight-Sergeant Frank Cecil Petts of Spencer Road, Cottenham Park was mentioned in dispatches for his part in the Battle of the Heligoland Bight (1939). Five German planes were brought down by the crew of the bomber he was piloting.

Lance Corporal Claude Richardson, Welsh Guards, died in 1944, and his brother Aircraftman 1st Class Edward Norman Richardson died in 1941. They are buried at Wimbledon (Gap Road) Cemetery. Edward Norman Richardson is listed in *Flight Magazine* of 25 September 1941 as 'Died on Active Service'. His death seems not to be aircraft related and could have been due to an illness or accident.

Major General Gilbert Szlumper (1884–1969), born in Kew and educated at King's College School, was assistant general manager of the Southern Railway. He left the Southern Railway for war service in 1939, becoming Director General of Transportation & Movements, War Office (1939–1940); Railway Control Officer, Ministry of Transport (1940–1941) and Director General of Supply Services, Ministry of Supply (1942–1945).

Sapper Ernest Arthur Tompkins (1912–1941) of the Royal Engineers took an enemy incendiary bomb to the house of his step-brother in Merton and attempted to dismantle it. He died on 20 April 1941 at the Nelson Hospital as a result of the injuries and burns sustained in his attempt. His nephew, niece

MARGACH,   Donald Sinclair   Flight Lieutenant 115985. Air Bomber. 582
DFC   Sqdn., Royal Air Force Volunteer Reserve. Died
                                                  Saturday 29 July 1944. Age 32. Son of William
                                                  and Janet Sinclair Margach, of Edinburgh;
                                                  husband of Margaret Sivess Sinclair Margach, of
                                                  Blackhall, Edinburgh. Buried: DURNBACH WAR
                                                  CEMETERY, Bad Tolz, Bayern, Germany. Ref. 11.
                                                  E. 26.

28 / 29 July 1944

Took off from Little Staughton at 22.30. Crashed south of Heimerdingen. The aircraft is
thought to have exploded, the Pilot, Squadron Leader V G F Coleman ejecting, and being
taken prisoner. However S/L Coleman appears as kia in the Memorial Book. The rest of
the crew were killed

AWARDED D.F.C.

Flying Officer Donald Sinclair
Margach,
who has been awarded the D.F.C.
for accurate bombing.
    Flying Officer Margach, who is
an air bomber in No. 106
Squadron, is the second son of Mr
and Mrs W. Margach, 36 Miller
Crescent, Edinburgh, and was
born in 1911. He is a former
Heriotee, and before joining the
R.A.F.V.R. was with the North of
Scotland Bank, first in Edinburgh
and from 1935 at their London
office. His home is at West
Wimbledon, and he enlisted in the
R.A.F.V.R. in 1940, and was commissioned last year.
    Flying Officer Margach (states
the citation) has completed 19
operational sorties, during which
his accuracy in bomb-aiming has
been outstanding. He has been
engaged in attacks on a wide
range of the enemy's objectives,
and in a mine-laying sortie, when
he calmly laid mines only a very
short distance from a warship
    The citation adds: — "This
officer's steadiness and coolness
in the face of the fiercest opposition have been demonstrated by
the excellent photographs he has
obtained. The success which has
attended his untiring efforts has

been a fine example to other air
bombers."
    Flying Officer Margach is at
present on leave in Edinburgh
with his wife, and the first intima-
tion he had of the gazetting of
the award was a telegram of con-
gratulations from a relative in
London.

Donald Sinclair Margach. With thanks to his family.

and a friend of theirs were also injured by the explosion. At the inquest, the Wimbledon Coroner said: 'Everybody knows, or ought to know, that it is the duty of everybody, whether soldier or civilian, on finding any sort of bomb or anything that might conceivably still be explosive to report it to the police. Then in turn will report it to the bomb disposal unit to deal with.' Tompkins is buried in Morden Cemetery. The *Western Morning News* on 24 April 1941 reported that the bomb contained a very sensitive explosive pellet and that Tompkins was trying with a hammer and chisel to knock the top off the bomb.

Flight Sergeant George Albert Wood of Thornton Road, Wimbledon was reported missing and believed killed. However, on 3 September 1943 the *Wimbledon Boro' News* reported the good news that, 'The other day, greatly to the joy of his parents, he walked into his home alive and well, arriving hard on the heels of a telegram which announced his safety.'

Wimbledon War Memorials

The Wimbledon War Memorial, a square tapered pillar set on a square plinth on a five-stepped base, is located on the boundary between Wimbledon Village and the Common. It was unveiled on 5 November 1921. On the west side is a second inscription added in 1947: 'In honoured memory of the men and women who gave their lives serving in his Majesty's forces during the Second World War 1939–1945, and those killed in other conflicts'. There are no names on the memorial. It was designed by Sir Thomas Graham Jackson (1835–1924), manufactured by Messrs Dove Bros, and unveiled by the local MP Sir Joseph Hood. Sir Thomas was an architect who saved Eagle House from development in 1886 and restored it as a home.

St Mary's Church, St Mary's Road is a large church in Wimbledon Village. The first record of a church building on the site of St Mary's can be found in the Domesday Book in 1086, where the survey simply says 'there is a church'. Inside, its Warrior Chapel was dedicated to the men of Wimbledon who died in the First World War, and to the memory of Grant Govan, RAF Pilot, and people everywhere who were killed during or died as a result of the Second World War.

Second-Lieutenant George Grant Govan (1914–1942) of Belvedere Grove, Wimbledon Village was the son of George Ernest and Margaret McQueen Grant Govan of Wimbledon. His dead body was found on 25 May 1942 and he died on war service, according to the *National Probate Calendar*. He was buried at Ipswich New Cemetery, Suffolk. At the entrance of the Warrior Chapel is a flag that was flown in action by HMS *Inflexible*, Battle of Jutland on 31 May 1916.

Inset in the oak-panelled walls in the Warrior Chapel are the individual bronze tablets bearing the name and rank of men of Wimbledon who gave their lives. The memorial above the Lynchnoscope (pictured) – a low-side

Wimbledon War Memorial. The Wimbledon Society has been keeping the site in good order. (Author)

The Great War inscription is on the left and the Second World War inscription on the right. (Author)

window revealed in 1919 during the building of the Warrior Chapel – is in memory of Squadron Leader <u>Ian Willoughby Bazalgette</u> VC, DFC, killed in 1944.

There is a tablet to Captain <u>Andrew Francis William Parsons</u> (1913– 1942), Queen's Royal Regiment (West Surrey). He, the elder son of Richard Godfrey Parsons who served in three dioceses including the See of Southwark (1932–1941), died of wounds at El Alamein, in the Siege of Tobruk, on 25 October 1942. There is also a ROH, in chronological order, at the church in a wooden case.

There is an ornate, brass font cover at the church to remember Second Lieutenant <u>Arthur Denis Caswall Dowding</u> (1917–1940), 4th Royal Tank Regiment. Dowding, only son of Vice-Admiral Sir Arthur Ninian Dowding

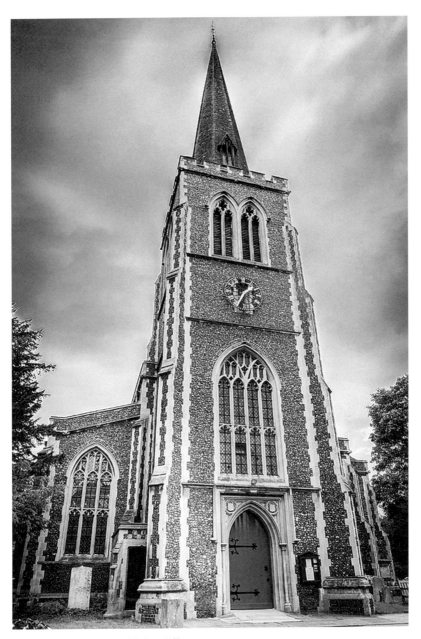

St Mary's Church, Wimbledon Village.

The tablets inside the Warrior Chapel of men of Wimbledon who gave their lives in the First and Second World Wars. (Author)

The wooden case holding the ROH within St Mary's, Wimbledon. The pages appear to be turned over on a daily basis, or as often as possible. (Author)

(1886–1966) and Kathleen Charlotte Hamilton Dowding of Wimbledon Hill Road, died of wounds in France between 22 and 26 May 1940. He, nephew of Sir Hugh Dowding, was buried at Wormhout, Departement du Nord, Nord-Pas-Calais. He was at Charterhouse school, Godalming, Surrey from 1931 to 1935 and his name is on the school's Memorial Chapel panels. His brother-in-law Flight Sergeant TE Anthony was killed on active service on 1 February 1945.

William Wilberforce is buried at St Mary's. Wilberforce, who lived at Lauriston House which stood on Southside facing the Common, took the leading part in the abolition of the slave trade. Lauriston House was demolished in 1967.

St Mary's Church, Merton Park

St Mary's Church, Merton Park dates from the fourteenth century. To the west of the church is a Norman archway leading to the vicarage. This is believed to have been the gateway to the guest house at Merton Priory. A free standing war memorial located on Church Path next to the wall of the church was unveiled on 25 September 1921. It is in memory of the men of Merton who gave their lives in 1914–1918 and 1939–1945, and the design is by H.P. Burke (1864–1947), a local architect. There are twenty-six graves in the churchyard

War memorial next to the wall of St Mary's Church, Merton Park, photographed in December 2016.(Author)

The car registration number of the local vicar is at the bottom-right on the right pane. (Author)

Memorials to the dead of the two world wars can be found in the Baptistry and the Augustine Chapel, off the south aisle. (Author)

The window in memory of Laky Piers taken from outside the church, December 2016. (Author)

Remembering Caroline Bond, Mary Ann Bond and Alfred Bond. (Author)

that hold servicemen, eleven of whom died in the Second World War.

The original east window in the chancel was destroyed by a flying bomb in 1944. The replacement was dedicated in 1950 and has some quirky details, including the car registration number of the local vicar.

A modern window representing Christ and the children and a Greek shepherd with staff was given in memory of Laky Piers (1897–1954), a parishioner of Greek origin, for his work in helping Greek refugees. Theodore Laky John Piers, (formerly Theodore Laky John Pispiris), lived in Grasmere Avenue, Merton Park, and was president of the Morden Rotary Club (1952).

The grave of Caroline Bond, who died in 1940, is at St Mary's, Merton Park. The tribute from her fellow workers is separate, so it can be considered a memorial. She lived in the caravans of the Bond family of fairground showmen, a family which today can boast of six generations in the fairground business. Three bombs fell in open ground between the Pincott Road junction and the railway on 16 August 1940, where the caravans were parked. Caroline Bond was killed and her mother, May Anne Bond, injured. Caroline, who was 19, was a night-shift worker at Venner Time Switches factory on the A3 near Shannon Corner (where the workers had shelters). Caroline's cousin Amy has laid flowers every year on the Bond family graves at St Mary's, Merton Park.

The tribute from her fellow workers. (Author)

King's College School

Five marble panels, with the school crest on the centre panel, were unveiled in the school's Great Hall on 2 November 1949 and dedicated on 2 November 1949 at a ceremony attended by the Archbishop of Canterbury. There are 147 names on the Second World War memorial. There were 294 pupils at King's College Wimbledon in 1914; 789 pupils served; 159 were killed; the percentage killed was 20.2 (*Public Schools and the Great War*, Anthony Seldon and David Walsh).

Squadron Leader <u>William Denys Butterworth Ruth</u> DFC (1918–1944), educated at King's College School and Rutlish School, and whose parents lived in Worple Road, Wimbledon, was awarded the DFC on 22 November 1940 for 'gallantry displayed in flying operations against the enemy'. He had taken part in nearly forty raids on Norway, Germany and the occupied territories in France and Holland. He died on 11 June 1944, and is named on the 1939–1945 War Memorial inside St Mary's Church, Cofton, Dawlish, Devon. He is also named on the Rutlish 1939–1945 memorial.

Lieutenant <u>Charles Francis 'Chuggie' Sutcliffe</u> of the Royal Irish Fusiliers, son of Dr William Sutcliffe and Mrs Sutcliffe of Trinity Road, Wimbledon, was killed in fighting in North Africa, the *Wimbledon Boro' News* of 29 January 1943 reported. He was to have proceeded to Cambridge. When called up, he was studying to be a doctor.

Lieutenant <u>Cecil Francis Thunder</u> (1910–1942) of Rostrevor Road, Wimbledon Village, a chartered accountant of Wimbledon and son of Major Andrew Fitzgerald Thunder (South Wales Borderers) and Margaret Thunder (nee Brough), died when HMS *Fidelity*, a Special Service Vessel, was torpedoed and sunk by *U-435* while north of the Azores on 30 December 1942 with the loss of 274 crew, 51 Marines and 44 survivors from SS *Empire Shackleton*. The only survivors were the eight crew of the motor torpedo boat, detached on anti-submarine patrol, who were later picked up by HMCS *Woodstock*, and two crewmen of a seaplane that had crashed on take off on 28 December and had been picked up by HMCS *St Laurent* (H83). Thunder had served in the East and was for eighteen months at Freetown, Sierra Leone. He was buried at Barnoon Cemetery, St Ives, Cornwall and commemorated on the Portsmouth Naval Memorial.

Veteran airman <u>Leonard Arthur Vaughan</u> DFC, DSO (1900–1942), son of Mrs E. Vaughan of Lennox House, Mostyn Road, Merton Park, was, on 5 January 1943, posthumously awarded the Distinguished Service Order (DSO). He joined the Honorable Artillery Company in 1915. His mother said on 5 January 1943: 'He was only 15 when he joined the army in the last war. We tried to stop him going, but he put up his age and was in France in three months. We tried to get him out because of his age and, after a lot of pressure and when he had served for ten months, he was discharged. We put him back

War memorial at King's College School, which was refurbished and moved into a centre stage location in 2015. This image was taken in November 2016. (Author)

Memorial within Great Hall, November 2016. (Author)

to school again, but he hated being out of the army and would not stop there, so we shipped him off to the Argentine. But as soon as he was 18 he came back to England and joined the RAF and won his wings. When this war broke out, he was in the RAF again as soon as he could get there.' When he won the Distinguished Flying Cross (DFC) in December 1941, he was stated to have 'shown contempt of danger during fifty-four raids on the enemy'. Vaughan, a sugar planter, died in Zeitun, Malta on 17 December 1942, and was buried in Malta Naval Cemetery. His son was psychiatrist and politician Sir Gerard Leonard Folliott Vaughan (1923–2003), who was born and educated in what is now Mozambique and reached ministerial rank during the Thatcher administration.

Cofton Second World War memorial, Devon remembers William Ruth. (warmemorialsonline)

Morden Cemetery

(Battersea New) Morden Cemetery, Lower Morden, originally called Battersea New Cemetery, was set up by Battersea Burial Board in 1891, when it was clear that the old Battersea Cemetery would be inadequate. The Crematorium (North East Surrey Crematorium), was opened at Morden Cemetery in 1958. A Cross of Sacrifice, a Commonwealth war memorial, is erected near the

The Cross of Sacrifice at Morden Cemetery was erected near the chapels.
(Author)

Behind the Stone Cross: the poppy on the right remembers former PoW Harry Tracey. The one on the left remembers Dennis Lambert. (Author)

chapels in the middle of Morden Cemetery and a Screen Wall records the names of those graves which are not marked by a headstone. It reads:

THIS STONE CROSS OF SACRIFICE IS ONE IN DESIGN AND INTENTION WITH THOSE WHICH HAVE BEEN SET UP IN FRANCE AND BELGIUM AND OTHER PLACES THROUGHOUT THE WORLD WHERE OUR DEAD OF THE GREAT WAR ARE LAID TO REST. THEIR NAME LIVETH FOR EVERMORE.

1914–1918   1939–1945

THESE MEMBERS OF HER MAJESTY'S FORCES DIED IN THE SERVICE OF THEIR COUNTRY AND LIE BURIED ELSEWHERE IN THIS CEMETERY.

The Battersea Garden of Remembrance (above), located within Morden Cemetery, is dedicated to the memory of those who died in Battersea through enemy action in the Second World War. There is a bench memorial at the entrance to the garden, to the right, in memory of three members of the Morris family, including Herbert Edward Morris (1911–1945) who died on 21 February 1945. According to the CWGC, there were 583 civilian casualties in Battersea.

The Chelsea Second World War civilians' garden at Morden Cemetery is next to the Battersea Garden of Remembrance. There are 39 names on the memorial set into the brick wall. Chelsea lost 462 civilians through enemy

Battersea Garden of Remembrance at Morden Cemetery. (Author)

The plaque in the middle reads 'To the memory of those buried in this cemetery who died in Battersea through enemy action in the Second World War. (Author)

The Chelsea Second World War civilians garden. (Author)

The five members of the Dennis family, with Christina Fay and William Fay beneath. (Author)

action. The CWGC does not give their burial locations, so the memorial is important in terms of these 39 people.

Guinness Buildings

Guinness Buildings were lodging houses built in 1890 by Sir Edward Guinness to improve the living conditions of the London poor. They were single rooms plus the use of a club room, shared bathroom facilities with hot and cold water baths and access to hot and cold water all day. The first estate was at Brandon Street, Walworth, south-east London. At the outbreak of the Second World War, there were 10,085 persons living in the 3,682 dwellings provided by the Guinness Trust in the County of London. The Trust's properties suffered heavy damage from enemy air attacks. Eight of the twelve London Estates received one or more direct hits. The worst incident occurred on 23 February 1944, when all the 160 flats comprising the Estate at King's Road, Chelsea were rendered uninhabitable. Chimney sweep Anthony Smith (1894–1964) worked all night to free victims and recover bodies. In 1944, he was awarded the George Cross.

Albert Edward Littlejohn BEM was honoured for his role in the same rescue. Agnes Fletcher (nee Rogers) lost her parents, Walter and Agnes that night in the destroyed block of flats. In 2005, Agnes Fletcher said she wanted to bring the Morden Cemetery to the attention of anyone who was interested.

Further Memorials

All England Lawn Tennis and Croquet Club Memorial

A plaque with the club crest at the top is at the entrance to the All England Lawn Tennis Club, Church Road, Wimbledon. It is in memory of members who gave their lives for their country in the two World Wars. Four club members were killed serving in the Second World War: Air Commodore HRH, the Duke of Kent, Royal Air Force; Colonel Victor Alexander Cazalet MC MP, Captain F.W. Findlay, Royal East Kent Regiment; and War Correspondent Kenneth Cecil Gandar Dower.

Prince George, Duke of Kent (1902–1942), the fifth child of King George V and Queen Mary, died on 25 August 1942, at the age of 39, along with fourteen others, on board RAF Short Sunderland flying boat *W4026*, which crashed into a hillside near Dunbeath, Caithness, Scotland while flying to Iceland on non-operational duties. The occupants of the flying-boat in which the Duke was travelling numbered fifteen. There was one survivor of the accident, Flight Sergeant Andrew Simpson Wilson Jack, born in 1921, of

The Wimbledon tennis memorial. With thanks to Sarah Fransden of the Wimbledon Lawn Tennis Museum, March 2017.

The Duke and Duchess, Princess Marina, in 1934.

Grangemouth, Scotland, the rear gunner in the plane. A memorial cross was erected at the crash site.

Colonel Victor Alexander Cazalet MC (1896–1943), a Conservative MP, was commissioned into the Queen's Own West Kent Yeomanry in 1915 and reached the rank of Captain, winning the Military Cross in 1917. He was killed on 4 July 1943 when his plane from Gibraltar to Britain crashed seconds after take off. The B-24 Liberator II LB-30 *AL523* was also carrying the Polish General Wladyslaw Sikorski (1881–1943) and fellow Conservative MP Brigadier John Whiteley (1898–1943). Sikorski, Whiteley and everyone else on board (except first pilot Eduard Prchal) – sixteen in all – died in the crash.

Cazalet played Wimbledon Gentlemen's Doubles from 1922 to 1933, including with the academic and author Sir John Cecil Masterman OBE (1891–1977).

Kenneth Cecil Gandar-Dower (1908–1944) was born in Regent's Park and attended Harrow School before receiving a scholarship to Trinity College, Cambridge in 1927 to read History. He became a leading tennis player, competing in a number of tournaments throughout the 1930s, including Wimbledon and the French Championships. He was also a successful author, writing about his adventures.

At the outbreak of the Second World War, he was in the Belgian Congo photographing gorillas. Returning to England, he then worked on the Mass-Observation project with Major Tom Harrisson (1911–1961), a British polymath, before being hired by the Government of Kenya to improve its public relations with the native inhabitants. Later he acted as war correspondent, covering campaigns in Abyssinia and Madagascar, travelling vast distances by bicycle and canoe. On 6 February 1944, he boarded the *SS Khedive Ismail*, an ocean liner converted into a troop ship in 1940, at Kilindini Harbour at Mombasa, bound for Colombo. While approaching Addu Atoll in the Maldives, the vessel was attacked by Japanese submarine *I-27* on 12 February 1944. Struck by two torpedoes, the *Khedive Ismail* sank in two minutes, with a death toll of 1,297; Gandar-Dower among them. The sinking was the third largest loss of life from Allied shipping during the Second World War and the largest loss of servicewomen in the history of the Commonwealth of Nations. A wealthy man, he left more than £75,000 in his will.

All Saints' Parish Church, South Wimbledon

All Saints' Parish Church, a late Victorian building, in All Saints' Road, South

All Saints' Memorial Triptych.

Wimbledon has a wooden wall-mounted triptych painted blue and gold in memory of the ninety-six men of this parish who gave their lives in both World Wars. Sergeant <u>Percy Lenderyou</u>, Parachute Regiment, the son of Arthur Frederick and Sarah Lenderyou of Wimbledon, died on 28 March 1943. He was buried at Tabarka Ras Rajel War Cemetery, Tunisia.

Reverend Graham Clitheroe (1883–1968), who lived in Wimbledon, was curate at All Saints' from 1908 to 1911 and Vicar of Holy Trinity Church, Coventry from 1931 to 1964. Holy Trinity, Coventry was one of the few buildings of stature that escaped destruction during the bombing raids. He and a team of firefighters bravely averted the danger from the falling incendiaries during the heaviest raid on 14 November 1940 by extinguishing them and throwing them from the roof.

Christ Church West Wimbledon

A framed ROH at Christ Church West Wimbledon, Copse Hill, in memory of those from this church who died in the two World Wars.

The names listed are as follows:
Peter Michael Carpenter Bonn, RAFVR
Alexander Christopher Boswell, Royal Engineers
Edward Henry Cave-Browne, RAFVR
John Cringle, Royal Navy
Peter Cooley, RAFVR
Ernest Dann, The Queen's Own Royal West Kent Regiment
Edward Percy Aymer des Graz, The Rifle Brigade

All Saints' Church in the 1930s. (All Saints' Wimbledon)

Alan William Felton, RAF
Brian Firminger, RAFVR
William John Hamlin, 3rd King's Own Fusiliers
Edwin Morris Hill, Royal Inniskilling Fusiliers
Cecil George Hopton, RAF
Michael Isdell Blyth Job, Royal Artillery AOF
Charles Graham Lief
Maurice Cecil Charles Graham Lief
Vesey Newsome, 2nd KEO Gurkha Rifles
John Arthur Hampden Parker, RAFVR
Trevor Anthony Peeler, RAF
Dennis Arthur Pepperall, Grenadier Guards
Derrick David Ray, RAF
Charles Richards, Home Guard
Victor Charles Richards, 4th County of London Yeomanry
William Butterworth Ruth DFC, RAF
Norman Jagoe Smith, RAFVR
Anthony Peter Debroy-Somers, Royal Navy
Robert Everard Talbot, Grenadier Guards
Basil Tudor Williams, Merchant Navy

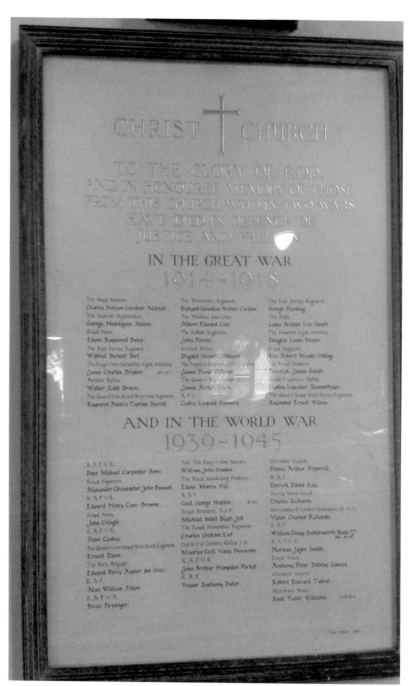

In memory of those who died in both World Wars. (Author)

Twenty-six names are listed. (Author)

When the standards were laid up. (Author)

Above the font in the baptistry of Christ Church West Wimbledon are two standards, or ceremonial flags. The inscription reads as follows:

> THE ROYAL NAVAL ASSOCIATION/ THESE STANDARDS OF THE WIMBLEDON AND MITCHAM BRANCHES/ WERE LAID-UP ON SUNDAY, 5TH MAY 1985/ ON THE FORMATION OF THE MITCHAM, MORDEN AND WIMBLEDON BRANCH/ OF THE ROYAL NAVAL ASSOCIATION/ 'WE WILL REMEMBER THEM'

Donhead Preparatory School, Wimbledon

An oval marble tablet with a figure of Christ crucified in relief is located at Donhead Preparatory School, Wimbledon, in memory of four men who died in the Second World War. It is above the fireplace in the hall and the names are John Anthony Hutchinson, Paul Victor Nolan, Michael Charles Jefferies and Anthony Peter Prosser. All four men are also on the Wimbledon College ROH.

Second Lieutenant Nolan (1925–1944), Royal Sussex Regiment, died of wounds on 19 November 1944 in Myanmar in the battle for Pinwe, Burma. He was buried in Yangon, Myanmar. Anthony Peter Prosser (1925–1945) died on 18 October 1945 in Ceylon, Maldive Islands and is buried at Trincomalee War Cemetery.

With thanks to Donhead Preparatory School.

Hazelhurst Road, Tooting

A green ceramic plaque honouring the thirty-five people, including fourteen children, who were killed when a *V2* rocket landed on the site of the Hazelhurst estate, on the border of Wimbledon and Tooting on 19 November 1944, was unveiled on Saturday, 6 June 2015. The plaque, installed by Wandsworth Council, is located on Sutton Courtney House, Hazelhurst Road. The names of the thirty-five people who were killed are listed on *summerstown182.wordpress. com*. They include the Farmer family; Benjamin (37), Thirza (34), Leonard (11), Dennis (7) and

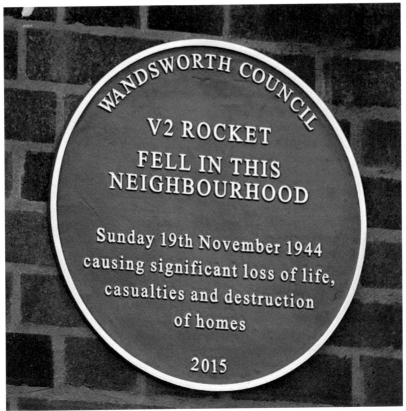

Two brothers from Tooting, Arthur and John Keeley, unveiled the plaque.

Kenneth (4). The youngest of the dead, Terence Bushaway, was 6 months old and the oldest, Harry Ogilvie, was 92. Some of the victims are buried in a cluster in the top north-west corner of Streatham Cemetery.

St Luke's Memorial Garden

A stone-walled octagonal garden at St Luke's Church, Ryfold Road, Wimbledon Park with inscribed stone is in memory of those who served in the Second World War.

Merton Bus Garage

At Merton Bus Garage, in Merton High Street is a tablet with an incised cross at the head, on a backboard. It is in memory of the men of Merton Garage who died in the Great War, the Second World War and the Korean War. No names are recorded.

The plaque on the gravestone of Minnie Matilda Ware and her daughter Eileen also remembers Minnie's first husband, William Pitts who was lost in action in the First World War. (summerstown182.wordpress.com)

Merton Civic Centre, Morden

The maker of the memorial, commissioned by the local council and completed in 2012, was a company called Stone Edge, which specialises in conservation and repair of structures.

Mitcham Common

On Saturday, 5 September 2015, the Friends of Mitcham Common unveiled a plaque that commemorates a 500kg Second World War German bomb that fell on the site in the early hours of 20 April 1941. While it caused no casualties, the bomb damaged houses some 200 yards away and left a crater 52 ft wide and 8 ft deep that exists to the present day. The crater is close to Commonside East and is easily reached from the footpath that starts at the roundabout linking Commonside East and Manor Road.

Morden Baptist Church

There are nine names on a Second World War memorial in the church hall at Morden Baptist Church in Crown Lane, Morden.

In memory of the men of Merton Garage. (Author)

The 93 bus, working from Merton garage on a summer Sunday in the late 1940s, pauses on its way to Dorking.

The Portland stone war memorial (no names) is located adjacent to the entrance of Merton Civic Centre. (Author)

The plaque at the site of the crater. (Author)

Morden Park

A plaque at South Thames College (Merton Campus), Morden Park, commemorating the death of Peter Walley (see chapter 10) was funded by voluntary subscription, principally by the residents of Green Lane, Morden over which he passed very low in his final efforts to keep his plane off houses. The plaque was originally located on a wall of the college adjacent to the entrance to the building. When the college was extended, it was relocated to a very prominent place, facing all who come into the college grounds.

The memorial plaque at South Thames College reads as follows:

> This plaque has been erected by
> Public subscription
> To honour the memory of
> No 819018. Sgt. P.K. Walley
> Who, when he was 20 years of age, was killed
> When his Hurricane crashed near this spot
> On the 18th August 1940. Having been shot down by enemy raiders.
> It is recalled with pride that
> Knowing he was about to crash
> Sgt. Walley bravely managed to guide
> His badly damaged aircraft over nearby houses
> Thereby safeguarding the lives of the residents.

The plaque in its second position at the entrance to the college. (With kind permission of Mike Squires)

Morden Park House of 1760, Morden Park was derelict and had been vandalised. Today, it is used as the borough's register office.

Queen's Road Baptist Church

Queen's Road Baptist Church, opened on 17 November 1897, is now Everyday Church, Wimbledon, (it changed its name as it undertook administration of some other Baptist sites). In 1941, Queen's Road Baptist Church services were held in Colliers Wood Underground shelter. On 15/16 July 1944, the church was damaged by bombs. For three months, the congregation met first with Worple Road Methodist Church, Wimbledon and then with Worple Road Congregational Church. Three members were killed in active service. But the only plaque the church holds relates to the First World War.

Raynes Park Methodist Church

A brass plaque that was located at Wesleyan Church, Worple Road, Wimbledon and unveiled on 11 November 1921 is now at Raynes Park Methodist Church. Its inscription reads that it is in memory of those who made the supreme sacrifice in the First and Second World Wars.

Rutlish School, originally located on Rutlish Road, Merton Park

A memorial screen comprising seven blue-painted panels bearing names and an inscription is at Rutlish School, Watery Lane, Merton. Eighty-four are listed in memoriam 1939–1945, and their names can be found on *cis. photoarchive.merton.gov.uk*

Flight-Lieutenant Ivor Philip Chester Goudge of Keswick Avenue, Merton Park, was the pilot of Lancaster ED996 which was operating with No 12 Squadron. The aircraft took off from RAF Wickenby, Lincolnshire on 29/30 May 1943, and was detailed to operations against Wuppertal, but failed to return from the mission. He was presumed lost over the target area due to enemy action. His wife was pregnant at the time.

VC's son Captain John Harrison, whose mother Lilian, lived at The Sanctuary on the Officers' estate of the Haig Trust, Morden, was killed in the defence of Dunkirk on 1 June 1940, and is buried in the Dunkirk town cemetery. Harrison, born in Hull, was in the Duke of Wellington West Riding Regiment. John Harrison's father was John 'Jack' Harrison VC (1890–1917), a professional rugby league player for Hull, East Yorkshire. He died on 3 May 1917 at Oppy, Pas-de-Calais and his body was never found; he became a posthumous recipient of the VC. The object of Haig Housing (established 1929) is to provide housing assistance to ex-Service people and/or their dependents. The Haig Housing Trust estate at Green Lane, Morden is one of its largest, with more than 270 homes in a mix of property types. A bas-relief portrait of Field Marshal Earl Haig of Bemersyde (1861–1928) can be found on most Haig Housing estates. At Morden, it is repeated several times around the estate.

Lieutenant <u>A.A. Macken</u>, at Rutlish from 1935 to 1941, died of wounds in 1943 while serving with the British 8th Army in North Africa (BNAF). BNAF was formed in September 1941 from the Western Desert Force, British 8th Army (comprising British, Commonwealth, Free French and Polish troops). It went on to wage a lengthy, hard-fought campaign against Axis forces across the deserts of North Africa.

There is a headstone to <u>Edward John Morgan</u> at Morden Cemetery. He was killed, in 1940, by shell splinters when on duty with the Home Guard. Sergeant-Pilot <u>James W. Parker</u>, whose father lived at Rosevine Road, was officially posted missing in April 1943. He was at Rutlish School from 1934 to 1939. Sub-Lieutenant <u>Murray Pennington</u>, Fleet Arm, died on active service. He was at Rutlish from 1933 to 1939. Lieutenant <u>H.J.L. Toms</u>, at Rutlish from 1931 to 1938, was killed in action on 16 April 1943. He joined the Rifle Brigade in February 1940, was gazetted in October of the same year and posted back to the Rifle Brigade. He went overseas to North Africa in November 1942.

St Saviour's, Grand Drive, Raynes Park

The St Saviour's Second World War memorial is a book of remembrance, together with the high altar being extended, with new candlesticks, altar cross and riddel posts and a set of new altar frontals, all dating from 1952. The main memorial is only dedicated to the First World War.

Southfields Methodist Church

A Second World War bronze plaque mounted on oak memorial is located at Southfields Methodist Church, Durnsford Road, Wimbledon Park. The church is to be demolished.

Streatham Park Cemetery

The cemetery, situated in Rowan Road, Streatham, is situated in Merton but not run by Merton. It contains Commonwealth war graves of both World Wars, and also a Screen Wall Memorial that commemorates service casualties of these wars buried in the cemetery's unmarked graves.

ON THIS WALL ARE RECORDED THE NAMES OF THOSE
SAILORS AND SOLDIERS OF THE GREAT WAR BURIED IN THIS
CEMETERY OF WHOM 64 HAVE NO SEPARATE HEADSTONES

1914–1918 1939–1945

THESE MEMBERS OF HIS MAJESTY'S FORCES DIED IN THE
SERVICE OF THEIR COUNTRY

Streatham Park Cemetery. (CWGC)

A wing has been added to this memorial upon which are carved the names of those who died during the Second World War who were cremated at the South London Crematorium, situated within the cemetery.

St Andrew's Church, Wimbledon

A font at St Andrew's Church, Herbert Road, Merton Park is a memorial to the Reverend <u>Herbert Peacock</u>, Curate of St Andrews', and his wife who were killed in an air raid on 23 February 1944.

St Luke's Church, Wimbledon Park

A stone-walled octagonal garden with inscribed stone at St Luke's Church, Farquhar Road, Wimbledon is in memory of the Second World War. It was dedicated in June 1949 by Reverend W.H. Parsons. Reverend Parsons, who served as an army chaplain, had previously been vicar of Bothenhampton near Bridgwater, Somerset. Mr Wright, St Luke's verger for many years, lost his home to bombing in September 1940. The church gave him £5.

St Mark's Church, Mitcham

The inscription on the Second World War bronze plaque at St Mark's Church, Mitcham is as follows:

IN SEPTEMBER 1940 THIS CHURCH WAS BADLY DAMAGED
BY A LAND MINE AND REMAINED DERELICT AND UNFIT
FOR PUBLIC WORSHIP.
IN MAY 1946, AFTER TEMPORARY REPAIRS, IT WAS
REDEDICATED BY BERTRAM, BISHOP OF SOUTHWARK.
ON DECEMBER 10TH 1950 A SERVICE OF THANKSGIVING
WAS HELD FOR THE COMPLETE RESTORATION OF THE
CHURCH AND THE STAINED GLASS WINDOWS IN THE CHANCEL
AND CHAPEL WERE DEDICATED
(NAMES)
LAUS DEO.

The Parish Hall became the parishioners' church. The church lay derelict for
eight years, only once being used for worship when the Reverend A.E. Smart
became vicar in 1944. It was re-opened on 17 May 1946 and a new organ
installed in 1947. It is the church's memorial to those of the parish who were
killed in the Second World War.

The War Damage Commission accepted a tender for the restoration of
the church and a design for the new east window was accepted from Laurence
Lee, who also designed the window of the Lady Chapel given in memory
of Reginald Hubbard, a member of the church. Lieutenant <u>Reginald John</u>

*In memory of Albert Reginald Charles Hubbard, who died in 1952, and
Lieutenant Reginald John Hubbard, at Mitcham Cemetery. (Author)*

Hubbard (1916–1939), 4th Battalion Royal Tank Regiment, of Caithness Road, Mitcham, died in active service in France on 27 December 1939, aged 23, of carbon monoxide poisoning due to a faulty stove. Hubbard, son of Albert Charles and Lily Hubbard of Mitcham, was found dead in bed. He is buried at Bienvillers Military Cemetery, Pas de Calais, France and commemorated at King's College Chapel, London. Also commemorated at King's College Chapel is Major Brian Dear Butler (1911–1944), East Surrey Regiment, husband of Hannah Butler of Wimbledon. He was killed in action in Normandy on 4 July 1944 and buried in Ranville War Cemetery, Calvados, France. It contains predominantly British soldiers killed during the early stages of the Battle of Normandy. A large proportion of those interred were members of the British 6th Airborne Division.

Trinity United Reformed Church, Wimbledon

There is a brass plaque at Trinity United Reform Church, Mansel Road, Wimbledon in memory of those who gave their lives in the First and Second World War.

United Apostolic Church, Wimbledon

There is a Second World War plaque on the south wall of the United Apostolic Church, Kohat Road, Wimbledon in memory of the men and women of this parish who died. Twenty-seven people are named.

A Book of Remembrance at St Olave's Church, Church Walk, Mitcham (in the Borough of Merton).

Wimbledon Cemetery (Gap Road)

Wimbledon Cemetery, situated on Gap Road, opened in 1876. The CWGC Cross of Sacrifice is the only memorial in the cemetery. However, this is not technically a war memorial (and therefore doesn't appear on the IWM system) because it is maintained by the CWGC. CWGC Crosses of Sacrifice represent all wars. As there are burials from the Second World War in the cemetery, it represents the Second World War even if not stated on it.

CWGC Cross of Sacrifice in Wimbledon Cemetery. The cemetery has two chapels. The one in the background is the one to the East. (Author)

Wimbledon College

Wimbledon College is a Roman Catholic comprehensive school founded in 1892, whose old boys include comedian Paul Merton. During the First World War, it lost 129 pupils. Wimbledon College is separate to Wimbledon College of Arts where exhibitions were open during the war. Father John Simmott arrived as Prefect of Studies in 1937. He made plans for further development of the site, but was frustrated by the outbreak of the Second World War, when tight restrictions were placed on the use of steel and timber.

A wall-mounted stone plaque at Wimbledon College in memory of the old boys of the college who died for their country from 1939 to 1945 was destroyed by fire in 1977; the current memorial is a replacement wooden board. Fifty-eight former members of Wimbledon College were killed in fighting in the Second World War; they are commemorated by a memorial above the door of the College Chapel.

The edition of the *Wimbledon College Magazine* in January 1940, the first since the outbreak of war, contains a list of thirty-five old boys known to have joined the forces. There is also reference to the death on active service on 16 October 1939 of Pilot-Officer Trevor Anthony Peeler (1914–1939) while training. The son of Philip Herbert and Ruby Peeler of West Wimbledon, he is remembered with honour at Huntingdon (Priory Road) Cemetery, Cambridgeshire.

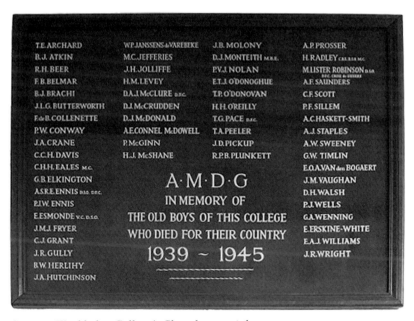

Caption: Wimbledon College's Chapel memorial.

Former Wimbledon College old boys include:

Flying Officer <u>Brian John Atkin</u>, who died in 1944, son of Frederick and Ethel Mary Atkin of Merton Park. He is remembered with honour on the Malta Memorial.

Rifleman <u>Basil Belmar</u>, 2nd Battalion, The London Irish Rifles, Royal Ulster Rifles, died in 1943 and is remembered with honour at Sangro River War Cemetery, Italy, where there are 1,768 United Kingdom burials.

<u>Basil John Brachi</u> (d1944), RAFVR,<u>Thomas Gilbert Pace</u> (d1941), RAF, <u>Reginald Patrick Blennerhassett Plunkett</u> (d1940), RAF and <u>John Michael Vaughan</u> (d1943), RAFVR are all remembered with honour at Runnymede Memorial near Egham, Surrey. The memorial is dedicated to 20,456 men and women from the air forces of the British Empire who were lost in air and other operations during the Second World War.

Squadron-Leader <u>Anthony Stewart Reginald Ennis</u> DSO DFC (1918– 1944) was on a Wellington XI shot down in Loktak Lake, India, and is buried at Imphal War Cemetery, India. His brother, Patrick, who died in 1941, was also killed whilst serving with the RAF.

<u>John Mario Joseph Fryer RAFVR</u>, died in 1943 and was the son of Hilary and Winifred Fryer of Wimbledon. He is remembered with honour at El Alamein War Cemetery.

<u>Colin Leslie Grant</u>, who died in 1943, was the son of Leslie Philip and Carmel Anne Grant of Wimbledon. He is remembered with honour at Catania War Cemetery, Sicily.

Lieutenant Commander <u>Douglas John McDonald</u>, HMS *Vulture*, Royal Navy, was the son of Allan John and Ellen Theresa McDonald of Wimbledon, and died on 30 May 1945. He is remembered with honour on the Lee-on-Solent Memorial, Hampshire. The memorial is dedicated to the 2,000 men of the Fleet Air Arm who died during the Second World War and have no known grave.

Leading Aircraftman <u>Peter McGinn</u> RAFVR, who died in 1945, was the son of Peter and Kathleen McGinn of Wimbledon. He is remembered with honour at Wimbledon (Gap Road) Cemetery.

Sergeant Pilot <u>John Bernard Molony</u>, RAF, was the youngest son of Sir Thomas Molony of Wimbledon, and was killed on 23 April 1941 (the CWG has his death listed as 23 March 1941, a mistake) on active service. He had been on a night navigation exercise when his plane, *No 18 OUT* Anson 1 *R3408*, strayed some twenty miles off course. The aircraft entered the Midlands barrage balloon protection area and struck a cable. It came down on Stole House in Walsgrave-on-Sowe, West Midlands. Five crew members, including Molony, died and one man, Sergeant Edmund Kosznik, survived. Molony, who won the Victor Ludorum at Wimbledon College in 1931 and who was married a year before he died, was buried at Wimbledon Cemetery (Gap Road).

Molony was the husband of Marjory.

Major <u>David John Monteith</u> OBE MC, died in 1944 and is remembered with honour at Taukkyan War Cemetery, Burma.

Squadron Leader <u>Michael Lister Robinson</u> DFC DSO, the son of Sir Roy (later Lord) Robinson of Kielder Forest, Northumberland, was posted to France on 16 March 1940 and joined 87 Squadron. On 9 May he injured a hand in a crash in a Master and was sent back to England. Fit again, he was posted to 601 Squadron at Tangmere on 16 August as Flight Commander. He was awarded the Croix de Guerre (Belgian) on 22 August 1941. He was appointed to lead the Tangmere Wing on 1 January 1942. He failed to return from a sweep on 10 April whilst leading the Wing at the head of 340 Squadron, and he and his aircraft were not seen again.

Corporal Frederick William Sargeant (1909-1944), lived in Cowdrey Road, Wimbledon (1911 England Census) and settled in Toronto, Canada. On 24 September 1944, the RAF Douglas C-47 Dakota transport plane he was flying in strayed far from its course in adverse weather as it travelled from Warwickshire to Italy. It was flying with 15 other aircraft as part of a mission to eventually arrive in India to aid the fight against the Imperial Japanese Army. Twenty-three soldiers and airmen were on board. When enemy gunfire struck one of its wings near the German village of Neuleiningen, Rhineland-Palatinate, the plane plummeted to the earth, killing all aboard. (Credit Erik Wieman, a former Dutch marine who now lives in Germany. He dedicates himself to locating the debris of downed warplanes in order to provide more information to crash victims' families and to erect memorials to the servicemen who lost their lives while flying over Germany).

All were initially buried at Neuleiningen, and, after the hostilities, were reinterred in the Rheinberg War Cemetery. The town of Rheinberg lies in the west of Germany to the north of Koln. The Felsenmuhle ("Crag Mill") in Neuleiningen was a prison camp in World War Two.

Major Charles Frederick Scott, HMS *Royal Albert*, Royal Marines, was the son of Joseph and Frances Scott, of Merton. He died in 1946 and is remembered with honour at Munster Heath War Cemetery in the west of Germany. Munster Heath was on the line of the Allied advance across northern Germany in 1945, but the majority of those buried in the cemetery died while serving with the Army of Occupation after the German surrender.

Wing-Commander Arthur Wellington Sweeney, son of Michael and Alice Sweeney of Wimbledon, was an English athlete who competed for Great Britain in the Olympic Games in Berlin, 1936. He was eliminated in the semi-finals of the 100 metres and in the first round of the 200 metres. Sweeney was killed in a flying accident in Takoradi, Gold Coast on 27 December 1940. He was buried in the Takoradi, European Public Cemetery, Ghana.

Captain Peter John Wells of the Royal Artillery died in 1943 while on action in North Africa. Wells, whose parents lived in Grosvenor Road, Wimbledon, later went to Ampleforth College in North Yorkshire and then to Oxford. The *Wimbledon Boro' News* of 1 January 1943 reported that his brother had been wounded in the fighting in the Middle East. He is remembered with honour at the Beja War Cemetery, Tunisia.

Wimbledon Methodist Church

There are two white marble plaques at Wimbledon Methodist Church, Griffiths Road in memory of those who gave their lives in both World Wars. No names are recorded for the Second World War.

Wimbledon & West Wimbledon Sorting Office

A Second World War ROH is at Wimbledon & West Wimbledon Sorting Office, Cranbrook Road, West Wimbledon. There are forty-three names on the memorial. Forty-one served and returned; two died:

K. J. Aktins
L. E. Avery
W. F. Batchelor
W. J. Beasley
F. F. Burren
J. Burrow
E. H. Cronin
C. R. Cock
H. E. Coombes
T. R. C. Dixon
R. Doherty
B. F. Edwards
F. W. Evan
F. C. Gray
W. C. Hentall
F. L. Hockins
R. J. Hoddinett
R. Holdstock
E. J. Hull
S. D. Jackson
W. J. Kendall
D. R. Kidd
S. W. Lessels
B. M. Mastoe
E. Mitchell
C. Moorcroft
M. Moxon
J. P. Ovenden
R. C. Owen
A. E. Parfitt
R. J. Richardson
J. A. Satchell

H. J. Savage
P. E. Skilton
A. F. Smith
C. Soul
C. Springall
A. E. Thomyson
L. E. White
F. E. Whittle

Wimbledon Village Club

An oak panel in the snooker room at the Wimbledon Village Club, Ridgeway is in memory of Wimbledon Village Club members serving in His Majesty's Forces during the Second World War. The club, which has strong links with the Wimbledon Society and Museum, was established in 1858 and now has a membership in excess of 800.

Further research

Please let me know of other Wimbledon memorials of note – the more unusual the better. I will then inform Ian Stuart Nicholson, a fieldworker for the IWM, who will add them to the IWM database.

Firemen Remembered

A memorial plaque at the Telegraph Public House, Telegraph Road, Putney, was installed by the charity Firemen Remembered in 2003. Firemen Remembered is dedicated to recording and remembering firemen and firewomen who served in the London region in the Second World War and commemorating those who died.

The memorial is in memory of three members of the Corps of Canadian Firefighters whose headquarters was located at 10-14 Inner Park Road, Wimbledon. Senior fireman John Stewart 'Jack' Coull (1907–1944) from Winnipeg, who was born and raised in Scotland, died as a result of enemy action when a *V1* flying bomb fell on part of Wildcroft Manor, a 1930s mansion block on Putney Heath, on 3 July 1944.

At St George's Circus, Elephant & Castle is a Firemen Remembered plaque in memory of eleven London Auxiliary Firemen, a Sub Officer of the London Fire Brigade and five Mitcham Auxiliary Firemen killed by enemy action on the night of 10/11 May 1941 while relaying water from the basement of the demolished Surrey Theatre (Surrey Theatre closed in 1924), which stood on this site and was then in use as an Emergency Water Supply (EWS), to fires at Elephant & Castle.

The five Mitcham firemen were Cecil Arthur Elliman (1909–1941), who lived at Longthornton Road, Mitcham (Merton); Harold Charles Parkes (1900–1941), who lived at Homefield Gardens, Mitcham (Merton); Edward George Pepper, who lived at Aberdeen Terrace, Church Road, Mitcham (Merton); Ernest Francis Robinson, who lived at Courtney Road, Collier's Wood (Merton); and Albert Henry Spiller (Leading Fireman), who lived at Heyford Road, Mitcham (Merton).

The inscription is as follows:

IN MEMORY OF ELEVEN LONDON AUXILIARY FIREMEN, A SUB
OFFICER OF THE LONDON FIRE BRIGADE AND FIVE MITCHAM
AUXILIARY FIREMEN, KILLED BY ENEMY ACTION WHILE
RELAYING WATER FROM THE BASEMENT OF THE DEMOLISHED
SURREY THEATRE, WHICH STOOD ON THIS SITE AND WAS THEN
IN USE AS AN EMERGENCY WATER SUPPLY, TO FIRES AT THE
ELEPHANT AND CASTLE ON THE NIGHT OF 10TH/11TH MAY 1941

Plaque at the site of the Surrey Theatre EWS.

Prisoners of War

Two hundred Merton and Morden men were PoWs in November 1943. Perched high on a rocky outcrop overlooking the River Mulde near Leipzig, eastern Germany, Colditz castle was considered by German authorities in the Second World War as the ideal site for a high-security prison for Allied officers with a history of escape. Thirty-two men escaped from Colditz. One of those was Pat Reid MBE, MC (1910–1990), who had attended Wimbledon College. Along with Major Ronald Littledale, Lieutenant Commander William Stephens and Flight Lieutenant Howard Wardle, he escaped on the night of 14/15 October 1942 by cutting through the bars on a window in the prisoners' kitchen. They entered a storage cellar under the Commandant's HQ, crawled out through a narrow air shaft leading to the dry moat, and exited through the park. They split into two pairs, with Reid and Wardle disguised as Flemish workmen, travelling by train to Tuttlingen, near the Swiss border, via Zwickau and Munich. They crossed the border near Ramsen on the evening of 18 October. Reid remained in Switzerland until after the end of the war. He was discreet about his duties there, and was working for the Secret Intelligence Service (MI6) gathering intelligence from arriving escapees. *The Colditz Story* (Hodder & Stoughton, 1952) was Reid's memoir of his time in Colditz, which later became the basis for the 1955 film *The Colditz Story*.

Ernest Colman (1878–1964) was Senior Vice President of Wimbledon Chess Club. He was captured by the Japanese during the Second World War and spent a short period as a PoW (*Surviving Changi, EE Colman: a Chess Biography*). He taught chess to his fellow inmates as a way to keep their mind off their hardships, and with them analysed his variation of the Two Knights Defence. He returned to Wimbledon after the Second World War, and wanted to call his discovery the 'Wimbledon Variation' (as he wrote in a letter to the *British Chess Magazine* in 1952). He was buried at Gap Road Cemetery.

On the outbreak of war, Douglas Young, younger brother of Kenneth Young (see pages 14 and 223), was commissioned in the Seaforth Highlanders and sent to France. He was taken prisoner at St Valerie in 1940 and spent the remainder of the war in German PoW camps. After the war, he was appointed a master at Wellington College in Berkshire.

Private OD Spackman, East Surrey Regiment, son of Mr and Mrs R.J. Spackman of Newton Road, Wimbledon, had been a PoW in Stalag VIII-B, a notorious German PoW camp later renumbered Stalag-344, since 1940. His parents received letters from him fairly regularly. His brother, L. Spackman, served with the Royal Corps of Signals in the Far East. (Source *Merton and Morden News*, 15 January 1943).

Major Christopher Coppinger Mahony of Vineyard Hill, Wimbledon Park was stated to be a PoW in the hands of the Germans, the *Wimbledon Boro'*

News reported on 26 July 1940. It was glad news because he had previously been reported by the War Office as 'missing presumed killed'.

Acting Flight-Lieutenant <u>Thurston Meiggs Wetherall Smith</u> DFC (1916–1984) of Wimbledon was one of the crew of a flying boat shot down by Italian fighters while carrying out reconnaissance work in the Tobruk (Libya) area on 6 August 1940. Smith was taken prisoner by the Italians, according to the *Wimbledon Boro' News* of 16 August 1940. He received the DFC in November 1939 for his part in rescuing the crew (thirty-four men) of the cargo ship *Kensington Court* torpedoed in the Atlantic on 18 September 1939 between the Fastnet and Bishops Rock. She was en route from Argentina for Liverpool carrying cereals when she was sunk by gunfire from *U-32*. There were no casualties. An article about the sinking appeared in *The War Illustrated* of 14 October 1939:

> The ship was stopped by fire from a U-boat. An SOS had been sent out before the *Kensington Court* sunk, and soon after the overloaded boat carrying thirty-four had pushed off, a flying-boat appeared and alighted near by, followed soon after by a second. Eventually all thirty-four men were transferred to a collapsible rubber boat launched by one of the planes and carried to the aircraft. A few hours later they were safe in England.

Smith was the pilot of the first flying boat on the spot. He explained:

> We at once set our course for the spot indicated and eventually found the Kensington Court sinking. We alighted and, after signalling the men in the boat, blew up our rubber dinghy and pushed it out with a line to each end, and by this means we were able to ferry the men across two or three at a time.

U-32 was herself sunk on 30 October 1940 northwest of Ireland by depth charges from British destroyers, *Harvester* and *Highlander*.

Reverend <u>David Smith</u>, son of Canon L.P. Smith of Sydenham, south-east London and chaplain with the British Expeditionary Force, was a PoW in Germany in September 1940. The *Manchester Evening News* of 4 November 1940 reported: 'Birth of daughter is announced today at Wimbledon to Maud, wife of the Rev David G Smith.'

A report in the *Wimbledon Boro' News* of 27 December 1940 entitled *Last Look Through the Files of a Memorable Year* refers to Senior Apprentice Officer <u>Peter Filcek</u>, born in 1921, one of the 299 British prisoners rescued on 16 February 1940 (by HMS *Cossack*) from the Nazi slave ship *Altmark* after a daring feat off the coast of Norway. Filcek, of Lucian Road, Tooting, was the guest of honour at a 'Keep Fit' dance at the Town Hall. He told of his experiences after his ship, British cargo steamer *Trevanion*, was sunk by the German battleship *Graf Spee* on 22 October 1939 in the South

Atlantic. Thirty-two survivors were transferred to the *Altmark* (disguised as a Norwegian vessel). On board the *Altmark* was also the crew of the cargo ships *Newton Beech* and the *Ashlea*, both of which had been sunk earlier by the *Graf Spee*. (The *Graf Spee* was scuttled off the coast of Montevideo, Uruguay on 17 December 1939).

Private <u>Albert Charles Asklof</u>, East Surrey Regiment, of Wolsey Crescent, Morden died in a PoW camp in Germany on 17 Sepember 1941, and was buried in Berlin War Cemetery. He was taken prisoner in the fighting around Dunkirk. His death was attributed to tuberculosis. His father, Able Seaman Karl August Emil Asklof, died in Dover Hospital on 27 July 1940 from injuries sustained when his shop was blown up. He was buried in Morden Cemetery. The site of Berlin 1939–45 War Cemetery was selected by the British Occupation Authorities and Commission officials jointly in 1945, soon after hostilities ceased. The great majority of those buried here, around 80 per cent of the total, were airmen who were lost in the air raids over Berlin and the towns in eastern Germany. The remainder were men who died as PoWs, some of them in the forced march into Germany from camps in Poland, in front of the advancing Russians.

Information that <u>Charles William Leslie Frederick Clarke</u> (1916–1976), of the Royal Marines from 3 June 1940 to 22 December 1945, was a PoW was received at his home in South Wimbledon in October 1941. He had been posted as missing in July 1941.

Lieutenant <u>David W.E. Chubb</u> (1914–1993), Royal Navy, of Lethbridge, Wimbledon and missing in March 1942 from HMS *Exeter*, was reported PoW in Japan, according to the *Wimbledon Boro' News* of 19 February 1943. He died in Romsey, Hampshire in March 1993.

Private <u>A.R. Dennis Varney</u> of the Parachute Regiment, previously reported missing, was a PoW in Italy, the *Merton and Morden News* reported on 5 Feburary 1943. Varney, whose mother lived in Buckfast Road, Morden, was a member of the No 7 Group Morden Scouts.

The *Wimbledon and Merton Boro' News* of 21 May 1943 reported that Sergeant <u>John Webb</u>, whose last known location was Java, 'is a PoW interned at Fukuoka Camp, Japan.' He was of Mostlyn Road, Wimbledon and his father was Frank Webb of Linkway, West Wimbledon. News was also received that F.J. Hossack, missing for some time, was now a PoW. He was an old Rutlish boy of Hillside, Ridgway, Wimbledon. The *Wimbledon Boro' News* of 30 July 1943 reported that Frank Webb had received a letter from his son at Fukuoka Camp that he was in excellent health.

Sorrow turned to joy when parents Mr and Mrs Collcutt received news that their son, Second Radio Officer <u>R.F. Collcutt</u>, was a PoW in Japan, as the *Wimbledon Boro' News* reported on 7 May 1943. They lived in Belmont at the time but used to live in Poplar Road, Wimbledon. In April 1942, his ship was reported lost and the crew missing. In November 1942, Mr and Mrs Collcutt

Visit of the delegate ICRC M Friedrich to Stalag 18A, Wolfsberg in July 1942.
Copyright ICRC.

English prisoners working in a quarry at Stalag 18A on 22 October 1941.
Copyright International Committee of the Red Cross (ICRC)

were officially notified that all hope of survival had been abandoned, and a death certificate was issued. His parents never gave up hope.

'Flags out to welcome repatriated,' read a headline in the *Wimbledon Boro' News* of 3 September 1943. More than six homes in Wimbledon and Merton were ready to welcome back into their families long absent PoWs in Germany who had arrived safely in British ports. The *Wimbledon Boro' News* of 29 October 1943 reported that two repatriated men from Florence Road were Private <u>Robert Harper</u> and Private <u>Leonard Cook</u>. Harper was one of the party of British PoWs who embarked on board ship to come to England in 1942, when the arrangements for the exchange of PoWs with the Germans broke down. Also back were Sergeant Pilot <u>R. T. Kindred</u>, who had had his leg amputated, Company Sergeant Major <u>J. P. D. Daly</u> of Hillside Close, Merton, Sergeant <u>A. S. Turnham</u> of Worple Road, Wimbledon, <u>Charles Victor Seaby</u> of Link Way, Raynes Park, and Private <u>Archie Payne</u> of Tennyson Avenue, New Malden.

Corporal <u>George Hawkins</u> of Oxford Avenue, Wimbledon Chase, escaped from Stalag 18A, Wolfsberg, one of the biggest PoW camps in Austria, and was home in January 1945, according to the *Merton and Morden News* of 5 January 1945. He was a PoW in Austria for four years. During the time he was in a prison camp, he learned four languages.

Lieutenant <u>J. W. Tidy</u>, a PoW in Italy, discovered two more old Rutlishians in the same camp. One was David Briggs; he did not mention the name of the other. J.W. Tidy is listed on the Rutlish School 1939–1945 war memorial to those old boys of Rutlish who gave their lives.

The wedding took place at St Mary's of <u>Peter Haigh Whitbread</u>, a repatriated PoW, and Margaret J. Cain, the *Merton and Morden News* reported on 12 January 1945. He was in the Tank Regiment, but then discharged.

About 61,000 Allied PoWs were subjected to forced labour during the construction of the 415-kilometre (251 mile) Burma Railway, also known as the Death Railway, the Burma-Siam Railway, and other names. About 90,000 civilian labourers and more than 12,000 Allied prisoners died.

Most of the casualties of the railway are buried or commemorated in the cemeteries at Thanbyuzayat, Burma, Kanchanaburi in the west of Thailand, and Chungkai, Thailand, with those who have no known grave remembered on the Rangoon or Singapore memorials. Lieutenant <u>Archibald Victor Gerrish</u> (d1943), Royal Corps of Signals, son of Archie Ernest and Beatrice Gerrish, and husband of Ethel May Gerrish of Morden, is buried at Thanbyuzayat. Driver <u>Horace John Markin</u> (d1943), Royal Army Service Corps, son of Horace and Ethel Florence Markin of Wimbledon Park, is buried at Thanbyuzayat. Also buried at Thanbyuzayat is Sergeant <u>Ronald William Charles Nicholson</u> (d1943), Royal Army Service Corps, son of William Nicholson and Eliza Nicholson of Morden.

Camp 1026 Raynes Park

Each Second World War prisoner of war camp in Britain was allocated an official number. Some sites have different numbers at different dates and not all sites listed within the numbering sequence are true PoW camps. Many are hostels situated some distance away from the parent site, or base camp. *Churchill's Unexpected Guests* by Sophie Jackson lists the UK's PoW camps. There was a PoW camp at Raynes Park. However, there may have been more.

Camp 1026 Raynes Park was on Prince George's Playing Fields, south of Bushey Road, and was demolished around 1957. Kenneth Young joined the Territorial Army in 1938. In an interview for the Museum of Wimbledon, he said the Italian PoW camp on the Common was gone by the time he returned to Wimbledon. In his diary entry of 16 October 1945 Fred French noted that he had seen Italian PoWs lifting potatoes on Wimbledon Common and putting them into clamps.

A report about life at Raynes Park Camp in February 1947 is at the *National Archives*:

> During the last month, growing inactivity was noticed amongst the PoWs of our camp caused by the receipt of the bad news from Germany, and also due to the numerous cases of illness in this unit. Another reason being the very small allotment of PoWs for repatriation to Germany, which was only two for the month from this unit.

The report was broken up into the following sections: political, religion, welfare, education, entertainment, sport, medical care, miscellaneous, sport.

> The New Year has brought a great increase in the amount of interest shown towards football, mainly due to the better weather conditions. Both of our teams have played their first matches with civilian teams on our ground in the Camp, and everybody who has been present has remarked on the cordial spirit which has been shown during these games.

One match, on 5 January 1947, was against 125 Camp Hostel, Wimbledon.

Beltane School

A secret feature of Wimbledon at the end of the Second World War was an internment camp at Beltane School in Queensmere Road. It held 250 German scientists and technologists abducted from Germany in 1945 and 1946. The idea was to obtain information and expertise by interrogating them about techniques such as cameras where Germany was ahead of Britain. A large number of reports were published to provide the information to British industry. In addition to the prisoners, the camp had forty-four staff. It was moved to Hampstead in 1947 because the house was needed for an extension to Southlands teacher training college.

Tennis Players and the Second World War

Fred Perry (1909–1995)

Frederick John Perry became an American citizen in 1938. He signed up with the air force, which at that time was part of the US Army. Official documents list him as having joined the army on 15 December 1942 and as having been discharged on 10 October 1945. He received two decorations, the Second World War Victory Medal and Service Lapel Button, both of which were awarded in recognition of service rather than for any specific action.

During these years, he rose no higher than staff sergeant and remained mainly in California, at Santa Ana, which was used for basic training and had no planes, hangars or runways. According to the *Last Champion: The Life of Fred Perry* by Jon Henderson, his stalling at such a lowly rank was partly the result of his showing the same antipathy towards the US military hierarchy as he had towards the English establishment.

Henry Wilfred 'Bunny' Austin (1906–2006)

'Bunny' Austin was brought up in South Norwood, London. In 1938, he played Don Budge in the final, but only won four games. The next year, he was seeded first, but lost in an early round. It was the last time he played at Wimbledon. According to Austin's friend, the actor Peter Ustinov, Austin was 'disgracefully ostracised by the All England Tennis Club because he was a conscientious objector'.

Austin and his wife Phyllis had been drawn towards American minister Frank Buchman's Oxford Group (not to be confused with Oxford Movement), and worked for the movement from the early 1930s. It combined social activities with religion. In 1938, its name was changed to Moral Rearmament (MRA). Buchman hoped that the world would avoid war if individuals experienced a moral and spiritual awakening. Also in 1938, Austin edited the book *Moral Rearmament (The Battle for Peace)*, which sold half a million copies.

When war broke out, MRA workers joined the Allied forces in large numbers. Others worked to heighten morale and overcome bottlenecks, particularly in war-related industries. In Britain, around thirty MRA workers were exempted from military service to continue this work. When Ernest Bevin became Minister of Labour in 1940, he decided to conscript them.

During the war, Henry and Phyllis Austin went to America to promote the MRA. Despite rumours, however, Austin was not a conscientious objector. Indeed from 1943 to 1945, he served with the US Army Air Corps.

On his return to Britain in 1961, he was told his All England Tennis Club membership had 'been lapsed'. Although no one at the Club ever commented on the issue, Austin was convinced that his ties with the MRA led to his being blackballed. The All England Tennis Club restored his membership when he was 77 years old. Austin noted: 'In 1984, forty years after getting rid of me, they suddenly let me back in and [were] all very nice to me.' A few months before his death in 2006, he had joined other past Wimbledon champions and finalists on Wimbledon's Centre Court for a millennium-year parade of champions.

Jaroslav Drobny (1921–2001)

One of the more popular players to grace Wimbledon either side of the Second World War was Jaroslav Drobny, a left-hander born in Prague who reached the semis in 1946 and quarters in 1947. He competed at Wimbledon under four different nationalities. The war meant he became something of a wandering nomad, forsaking his Czech citizenship for that of Bohemia-Moravia in 1939 (the rump of Czech territory which had not yet been taken over by the Germans), before later (1950) accepting the offer of an Egyptian passport. He spent the war working in a munitions factory in Prague. He chose to defect from the communist regime in 1949 and left Czechoslovakia for good on 11 July 1949. Becoming stateless, he attempted to gain Swiss, US and Australian papers until finally accepting Egyptian citizenship.

It was as an Egyptian that he won Wimbledon, in his third final, in 1954, though by that time his victory was greeted more like a British triumph. He married an English woman, Rita Anderson, in 1958 and settled in London. He later (1959) became a British citizen and competed as such in the Veterans' Doubles competitions at the All England Tennis Club. He remained a London resident for the rest of his life.

Alice Marble (1913–1990)

'Meet the Women's Wimbledon Champion Who Was Also a Spy', read a headline in *Time* on 29 June 2015. Born in California, Alice Marble was the No 1 female player in America between 1936 and 1940. Days after she suffered a miscarriage, her husband Joe Crowley, a fighter pilot, was shot down and killed over Germany. Marble reported in her memoir that she accepted without hesitation when the US government approached her about operating as a spy in 1945.

According to *Stories from History's Dust Bin* by Wayne Winterton, 'The mission called for her to travel to Switzerland and to meet a man with whom she had once been intimate, a Swiss banker suspected of harbouring Nazi wealth during the war. Her task was to see if she could obtain some specific Nazi financial information. The mission ended when a Nazi agent, suspicious of her intentions, shot her in the back.' After recovering and re-establishing herself in the US, she set her sights on a new cause: the racial integration of tennis.

Ted Schroeder (1921–2006)

The 1949 Wimbledon Championships, which ran from 20 June until 1 July, was the 63rd staging of the Wimbledon Championships. The Men's Singles were won by American Ted Schroeder. Schroeder had enlisted in the Navy (1942), serving on destroyers and as a fighter pilot until his discharge in 1945.

Dr Daniel Prenn (1904–1991)

One of Germany's leading lawn tennis players, he defeated British players Henry Wilson Austin and Fred Perry in the Davis Cup Competition in 1932. He arrived in London on 5 June 1933 to play at Wimbledon and in other tournaments as a 'free lance'. Due to his Jewish origin, he was banned from playing in any tournaments in Germany and moved to Britain in 1933. He died in Dorking, Surrey in 1991.

'Enemy tennis players'

The idea of an International Lawn Tennis Club, whose members would be players who had represented their country in international team competition, arose out of a conversation at the 1923 Wimbledon Championships between Lord Balfour, then British Prime Minister, and Arthur Wallis Myers, a tennis correspondent, editor, author and player. Myers, who lived in Epsom and who was attached to the Department of Information in the Great War, founded the International Lawn Tennis Club of Great Britain (IC of GB) in November 1924. It is based in Wimbledon.

A motion to remove names of 'enemy subjects' from the list of honorary members of the IC of GB was considered on 16 November 1939. The nine individuals included Otto Froitzheim (1884–1962), who in 1914 had been ranked World No 4, and who had been a PoW at Donington Hall, near Derby, for the duration of the First World War.

Bibliography

Anon, *55ᵗʰ Surrey (Sutton and Cheam) Home Guard, A Historical Survey*

Anon, *Kelly's Directory of Wimbledon* (1939)

Anon, *River and Cloth* (London Borough of Merton, 2010)

Anon, *Wartime Memories, Fifty Years On, members of Holy Cross remember World War II* (Holy Cross, Motspur Park, 1995)

Bannister, Kirk, *New Wimbledon: A Story of Suburban Growth and Metropolitan Expansion* (Wimbledon Society, 2014)

Barnes, James, J., and Patience P., *Nazis in Pre-War London 1930–1939, the Fate and Role of German Party Members and British Sympathizers* (Sussex Academic Press)

Beckett, Francis, *Fascist in the Family: The Tragedy of John Beckett MP* (2016)

Brock, Colin, *Rutlish School, The First 100 Years* (1995)

Brooksbank, B. W. L., *London Main Line War Damage* (Capital Transport, 2007)

Bruley, Sue and Edwards, Nick, *Factory Life and Labour in Merton and Beddington 1920–1960* (Merton Print and Design, 1997)

Bruley, Sue, *'A Very Happy Crowd': Women in Industry in South London in World War Two* (Oxford University Press, 1997)

Carroll, Tim, *The Dodger: The Extraordinary Story of Churchill's Cousin and the Great Escape* (Mainstream Publishing, 2012)

Cockett, Olivia, *Love and War in London: A Women's Diary 1939–1942* (2005)

Connelly, Mark, *We Can Take It!* (Routledge, 2004)

Creaton, Heather, *Sources for the History of London 1939–45, A Guide and Bibliography* (British Records Association, 1998)

Crook, Paul, *Surrey Home Guard* (Middleton Press, 2000)

Crossley, James, *Bismarck: The Epic Chase* (2010)

Essex-Lopresti, Tim, *A Brief History of Civil Defence* (Civil Defence Association, 2005)

Field, Geoffrey G., *Blood, Sweat, and Toil: Remaking the British Working Class, 1939–1945* (2011)

Gardiner, Juliet, *War on the Home Front* (2012)

Gardiner, Juliet, *Wartime Britain 1939–1945* (Headline Publishing Group, 2016)

Gilmour, John, *Sweden, the Swastika and Stalin: The Swedish experience in the Second World War* (Edinburgh University Press, 2011)

Gordon Cleather, Nora, *The Wimbledon Story* (Sporting Handbooks Ltd, 1947)

Grieg, Geordie, *The King Maker The Man Who Saved George VI* (2011)

Hartley, John, *In the War Decided* (1985)

Hawtin, Gillian, *A New View of Old Wimbledon, Wimbledon during the XXth century, c 1905–1965* (Merton Public Libraries, 1993)

Hawtin, Gillian, *Wimbledon* (1994)

Hayward, Kate, *Who Was Atkinson Morley* (Historical Research Centre)

Henderson, John, *The Last Champion: The Life of Fred Perry* (2009)

Heynick, Frank, *Jews and Medicine: An Epic Saga* (Ktav Publishing House, 2002)

Higgs, Tom, *300 Years of Mitcham Cricket, 1685–1985* (Kenafest)

Hume, Ivor Noël, *A Passion for the Past: The Odyssey of a Transatlantic Archaeologist* (University of Virginia Press, 2010)

Jackson, Alan A., *Semi-Detached London* (George Allen & Unwin, 1973)

Jackson, Sophie, *Churchill's Unexpected Guests: Prisoners of War in Britain in World War Two* (The History Press, 2010)

James, Donald, *World's End* (Cornerstone Digital, 2011)

Kramer, Ann, *Conscientious Objectors of the Second World War* (Pen & Sword, 2013)

Leyden, Kevin, *A Historical Guide to Merton Abbey Mills* (The Wandle Industrial Museum, 2000)

Luff, David, *Trouble at Mill* (Merton Historical Society, 2002)

Mackay, Robert, *Half the Battle: Civilian Morale in Britain During the Second World War* (Manchester University Press, 2002)

Malies, J., *Oxford Dictionary of National Biography* (Oxford University Press, 2004)

Marillier, Henry Currie, *History of the Merton Abbey Tapestry Works* (Constable and Company, 1927)

McMurray, Matthew, *Women's Voluntary Services Roll of Honour 1939-1945*, (Royal Voluntary Service Archive and Heritage Collection, 2016)

Mearns, David and White, Rob, *Hood and Bismarck* (2001)

Merton Historical Society, *The Bridges and Roads of Mitcham* (2000)

Merton Historical Society, *The Elms Mitcham* (1969)

Miles, Frank and Cranch, Graeme, *King's College School, The First 150 Years* (1979)

Milward, Richard, *Portrait of a Church, the Sacred Heart Wimbledon 1887–1987* (Roebuck, 1987)

Milward, Richard, *Wimbledon, 200 Years Ago* (Milward Press, 1996)

Milward, Richard, *Wimbledon Past* (Historical Publications, 1998)

Minney, R. J., *Carve Her Name with Pride* (Pen & Sword, 2006)

Minney, R. J., *The Private Papers of Hore-Belisha* (Collins, 1960)

Nye, James, *A Long Time in Making: The History of Smiths* (Oxford University Press, 2012)

Ogley, Bob, *Surrey at War 1939–1945* (Froglets, 1995)

Plastow, Norman, *Safe as Houses, Wimbledon at War* (AAPPL, 2007)

Read, Ronald, *Memories of a Morden Lad 1932–1957* (Merton Historical Society, 2010)

Reid, D. A. B., *The Development of the Borough of Wimbledon* (Selwyn College, 1950)

Rohl, John C. G., *Wilheim II: The Kaiser's Personal Monarchy, 1888–1900* (Cambridge, 2014)

Scheer, Jonathan, *Ministers at War: Winston Churchill and his War Cabinet* (Oneworld, 2015)

Spencer, Adam, *The Twentieth Century Merton* (Sutton Publishing, 1999)

Swift, Ralph, *Boyhood Memories of the Blitz* (2002)

Thompson, C. R. (ed), *The Biography of William Schermuly* (Victoria House Printing, 1946)

Topman, Heidi, *Book Eighty Year of Wimbledon Labour Hall 1921 to 2001* (on behalf of Wimbledon Labour Hall Co-operative Society)

Urcan, Olimpiu G., *Surviving Changi: E. E. Colman – a Chess Biography* (Talisman, 2007)

Vasser Tall, Christine, *London War Letters of a Separated Family: 1940–1945* (2008)

Vignes, Spencer and Lynam, Des, *The Wimbledon Miscellany* (The History Press, July 2013)

Wallace, John, *Spring House in Merton* (1996)

Williams, Michael, *Steaming to Victory: How Britain's Railways Won the War* (Preface Digital, 2013)

Winterton, Wayne, *Stories from History's Dust Bin, Volume 3* (Xlibris, 2015)

Wodehouse, P. G., *PG Wodehouse: a Life in Letters* (Cornerstone Digital, 2012)

Zetterlling, Niklas and Tamelander, Michael, *Bismarck: The Final Days of Germany's Greatest Battleship* (2009)

Online sources

The Gordon Highlanders Museum, *Gordonhighlanders.com*

www.bbc.co.uk/ww2peopleswar

Childhood Memories of Colliers Wood and Somerset, Albert Dunning, *bbc.co.uk*

Naval-history.net

Yorkshire-aircraft.co.uk

Uboat.net

Museums

IWM
London Bus Museum
Wandle Industrial Museum
Wimbledon Lawn Tennis Museum
Wimbledon Museum, Wimbledon Hill

Newspapers

Mitcham and Colliers Wood Gazette
Surrey Mirror
Sutton Times & Cheam Mail
Wimbledon Boro' News
Wimbledon Guardian

Please note that every attempt has been made, where possible, to obtain permission for use of images.

Index